W9-BKQ-024

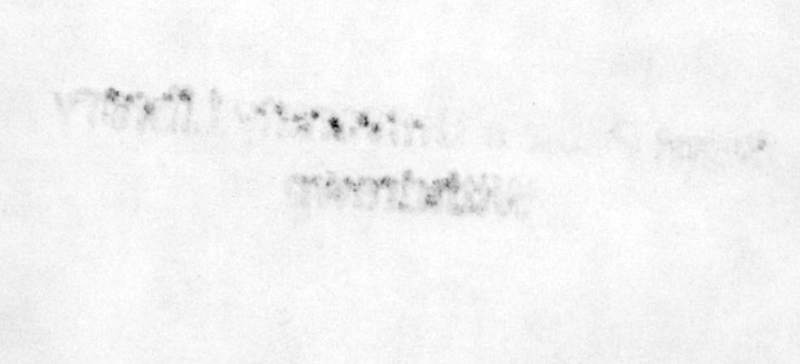

Edition de Luxe

THE WORKS

OF

MATTHEW ARNOLD

IN

FIFTEEN VOLUMES

VOLUME VI

CULTURE & ANARCHY

AN ESSAY IN
POLITICAL AND SOCIAL CRITICISM

AND

FRIENDSHIP'S GARLAND

BEING THE CONVERSATIONS, LETTERS, AND OPINIONS
OF THE LATE
ARMINIUS, BARON VON THUNDER-TEN-TRONCKH

COLLECTED AND EDITED
WITH A DEDICATORY LETTER TO ADOLESCENS LEO, Esq.
OF 'THE DAILY TELEGRAPH'

BY

MATTHEW ARNOLD

London
MACMILLAN AND CO., Limited
SMITH, ELDER AND COMPANY
1903

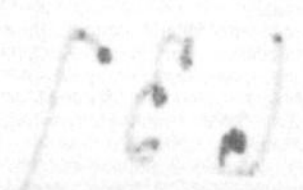

This Edition consists of Seven Hundred and Seventy-five Copies

637

CULTURE AND ANARCHY

Estote ergo vos perfecti !

PREFACE

(1869)

My foremost design in writing this Preface is to address a word of exhortation to the Society for Promoting Christian Knowledge. In the essay which follows, the reader will often find Bishop Wilson quoted. To me and to the members of the Society for Promoting Christian Knowledge his name and writings are still, no doubt, familiar. But the world is fast going away from old-fashioned people of his sort, and I learnt with consternation lately from a brilliant and distinguished votary of the natural sciences, that he had never so much as heard of Bishop Wilson, and that he imagined me to have invented him. At a moment when the Courts of Law have just taken off the embargo from the recreative religion furnished on Sundays by my gifted acquaintance and others, and when St. Martin's Hall and the Alhambra will soon be beginning again to resound with their pulpit-eloquence, it distresses one to think that the new lights should not only have, in general, a very low opinion of the preachers of the old religion, but that they should have it without knowing the best that these preachers can do. And that they are in this case is owing in part, certainly, to the negligence of the Christian Knowledge Society. In the old times they used to print and spread abroad Bishop Wilson's *Maxims of Piety and Christianity*. The copy of this work which I use is one of their publications, bearing their imprint, and bound in the well-known brown calf which they made familiar to our childhood; but the date of my copy is 1812. I know of no copy besides, and I believe the work is no longer one of those printed and circulated by the Society.[1] Hence the error, flattering, I own, to me personally, yet in itself to be regretted, of the distinguished physicist already mentioned.

But Bishop Wilson's *Maxims* deserve to be circulated as a religious book, not only by comparison with the cartloads of rubbish circulated at present under this designation, but for their own sake, and even by comparison with the other works of the same author. Over the far better known *Sacra Privata* they have this advantage, that they were prepared by him for his own private use, while the *Sacra Privata* were prepared by him for the use of the

[1] The Christian Knowledge Society has, since 1869, republished the *Maxims* of Bishop Wilson.

public. The *Maxims* were never meant to be printed, and have on that account, like a work of, doubtless, far deeper emotion and power, the *Meditations* of Marcus Aurelius, something peculiarly sincere and first-hand about them. Some of the best things from the *Maxims* have passed into the *Sacra Privata*. Still, in the *Maxims*, we have them as they first arose; and whereas, too, in the *Sacra Privata* the writer speaks very often as one of the clergy, and as addressing the clergy, in the *Maxims* he almost always speaks solely as a man. I am not saying a word against the *Sacra Privata*, for which I have the highest respect; only the *Maxims* seem to me a better and more edifying book still. They should be read, as Joubert says Nicole should be read, with a direct aim at practice. The reader will leave on one side things which, from the change of time and from the changed point of view which the change of time inevitably brings with it, no longer suit him; enough will remain to serve as a sample of the very best, perhaps, which our nation and race can do in the way of religious writing. M. Michelet makes it a reproach to us that, in all the doubt as to the real author of the *Imitation*, no one has ever dreamed of ascribing that work to an Englishman. It is true, the *Imitation* could not well have been written by an Englishman; the religious delicacy and the profound asceticism of that admirable book are hardly in our nature. This would be more of a reproach to us if in poetry, which requires, no less than religion, a true delicacy of spiritual perception, our race had not done great things; and if the *Imitation*, exquisite as it is, did not, as I have elsewhere remarked, belong to a class of works in which the perfect balance of human nature is lost, and which have therefore, as spiritual productions, in their contents something excessive and morbid, in their form something not thoroughly sound. On a lower range than the *Imitation*, and awakening in our nature chords less poetical and delicate, the *Maxims* of Bishop Wilson are, as a religious work, far more solid. To the most sincere ardour and unction, Bishop Wilson unites, in these *Maxims*, that downright honesty and plain good sense which our English race has so powerfully applied to the divine impossibilities of religion; by which it has brought religion so much into practical life, and has done its allotted part in promoting upon earth the kingdom of God.

With ardour and unction religion, as we all know, may still be fanatical; with honesty and good sense, it may still be prosaic; and the fruit of honesty and good sense united with ardour and unction is often only a prosaic religion held fanatically. Bishop Wilson's excellence lies in a balance of the four qualities, and in a fulness and perfection of them, which makes this untoward result impossible. His unction is so perfect, and in such happy alliance with his good sense, that it becomes tenderness and fervent charity. His good sense is so perfect, and in such happy alliance with his unction, that it becomes moderation and insight. While, therefore, the type of religion exhibited in his *Maxims* is English, it is yet a type of a far higher kind than is in general reached by Bishop Wilson's countrymen; and yet, being English, it is possible and attainable for them. And so I conclude as I began, by saying that a work of this sort is one which the Society for Promoting Christian Knowledge should not suffer to remain out of print and out of currency.

And now to pass to the matters canvassed in the following essay. The whole scope of the essay is to recommend culture as the great help out of our present difficulties; culture being a pursuit of our total perfection by means of getting to know, on all the matters which most concern us, the best which has been thought and said in the world; and through this knowledge, turning a stream of fresh and free thought upon our stock notions and habits, which we now follow staunchly but mechanically, vainly imagining that there is a virtue in following them staunchly which makes up for the mischief of following them mechanically. This, and this alone, is the scope of the following essay. And the culture we recommend is, above all, an inward operation.

But we are often supposed, when we criticise by the help of culture some imperfect doing or other, to have in our eye some well-known rival plan of doing, which we want to serve and recommend. Thus, for instance, because we have freely pointed out the dangers and inconveniences to which our literature is exposed in the absence of any centre of taste and authority like the French Academy, it is constantly said that we want to introduce here in England an institution like the French Academy. We have, indeed, expressly declared that we wanted no such thing; but let us notice how it is just our worship of machinery, and of external doing, which leads to this charge being brought; and how the inwardness of culture makes us seize, for watching and cure, the faults to which our want of an Academy inclines us, and yet prevents us from trusting to an arm of flesh, as the Puritans say,—from blindly flying to this outward machinery of an Academy, in order to help ourselves. For the very same culture and free inward play of thought which shows how the Corinthian style, or the whimsies about the One Primeval Language, are generated and strengthened in the absence of an Academy, shows us, too, how little any Academy, such as we should be likely to get, would cure them. Every one who knows the characteristics of our national life, and the tendencies so fully discussed in the following pages, knows exactly what an English Academy would be like. One can see the happy family in one's mind's eye as distinctly as if it were already constituted. Lord Stanhope, the Dean of St. Paul's,[1] the Bishop of Oxford,[2] Mr. Gladstone, the Dean of Westminster, Mr. Froude, Mr. Henry Reeve,—everything which is influential, accomplished, and distinguished; and then, some fine morning, a dissatisfaction of the public mind with this brilliant and select coterie, a flight of Corinthian leading articles, and an irruption of Mr. G. A. Sala. Clearly, this is not what will do us good. The very same faults,—the want of sensitiveness of intellectual conscience, the disbelief in right reason, the dislike of authority,—which have hindered our having an Academy and have worked injuriously in our literature, would also hinder us from making our Academy, if we established it, one which would really correct them. And culture, which shows us truly the faults to be corrected, shows us this also just as truly.

Natural, as we have said, the sort of misunderstanding just noticed is; yet our usefulness depends upon our being able to clear it away, and to convince those who mechanically serve some stock notion or operation, and thereby go astray, that it is not culture's work or aim to give the victory to some rival fetish, but simply

[1] The late Dean Milman. [2] The late Bishop Wilberforce.

to turn a free and fresh stream of thought upon the whole matter in question. In a thing of more immediate interest, just now, than any question of an Academy, the like misunderstanding prevails; and until it is dissipated, culture can do no good work in the matter. When we criticise the present operation of disestablishing the Irish Church, not by the power of reason and justice, but by the power of the antipathy of the Protestant Nonconformists, English and Scotch, to establishments, we are called enemies of the Nonconformists, blind partisans of the Anglican Establishment, possessed with the one desire to help the clergy and to harm the Dissenters. More than a few words we must give to showing how erroneous are these charges; because if they were true, we should be actually subverting our own design, and playing false to that culture which it is our very purpose to recommend.

Certainly we are no enemies of the Nonconformists; for, on the contrary, what we aim at is their perfection. But culture, which is the study of perfection, leads us, as we in the following pages have shown, to conceive of true human perfection as a *harmonious* perfection, developing all sides of our humanity; and as a *general* perfection, developing all parts of our society. For if one member suffer, the other members must suffer with it; and the fewer there are that follow the true way of salvation, the harder that way is to find. And while the Nonconformists, the successors and representatives of the Puritans, and like them staunchly walking by the best light they have, make a large part of what is strongest and most serious in this nation, and therefore attract our respect and interest, yet all which, in what follows, is said about Hebraism and Hellenism, has for its main result to show how our Puritans, ancient and modern, have not enough added to their care for walking staunchly by the best light they have, a care that that light be not darkness; how they have developed one side of their humanity at the expense of all others, and have become incomplete and mutilated men in consequence. Thus falling short of harmonious perfection, they fail to follow the true way of salvation. Therefore that way is made the harder for others to find, general perfection is put further off out of our reach, and the confusion and perplexity, in which our society now labours, is increased by the Nonconformists rather than diminished by them. So, while we praise and esteem the zeal of the Nonconformists in walking staunchly by the best light they have, and desire to take no whit from it, we seek to add to this what we call sweetness and light, and to develop their full humanity more perfectly. To seek this is certainly not to be the enemy of the Nonconformists.

But now, with these ideas in our head, we

come upon the operation for disestablishing the Irish Church by the power of the Nonconformists' antipathy to religious establishments and endowments. And we see Liberal statesmen, for whose purpose this antipathy happens to be convenient, flattering it all they can; saying that though they have no intention of laying hands on an Establishment which is efficient and popular, like the Anglican Establishment here in England, yet it is in the abstract a fine and good thing that religion should be left to the voluntary support of its promoters, and should thus gain in energy and independence; and Mr. Gladstone has no words strong enough to express his admiration of the refusal of State-aid by the Irish Roman Catholics, who have never yet been seriously asked to accept it, but who would a good deal embarrass him if they demanded it. And we see philosophical politicians with a turn for swimming with the stream, and philosophical divines with the same turn, seeking to give a sort of grand stamp of generality and solemnity to this antipathy of the Nonconformists, and to dress it out as a law of human progress in the future. Now, nothing can be pleasanter than swimming with the stream; and we might gladly, if we could, try in our unsystematic way to take part in labours at once so philosophical and so popular. But we have got fixed in our minds that a more full and harmonious development of their humanity is what the Nonconformists most want, that narrowness, one-sidedness, and incompleteness is what they most suffer from ; in a word, that in what we call *provinciality* they abound, but in what we may call *totality* they fall short.

And they fall short more than the members of Establishments. The great works by which, not only in literature, art, and science generally, but in religion itself, the human spirit has manifested its approaches to totality and to a full, harmonious perfection, and by which it stimulates and helps forward the world's general perfection, come, not from Nonconformists, but from men who either belong to Establishments or have been trained in them. A Nonconformist minister, the Rev. Edward White, who has written a temperate and well-reasoned pamplet against Church Establishments, says that 'the unendowed and unestablished communities of England exert full as much moral and ennobling influence upon the conduct of statesmen as that Church which is both established and endowed.' That depends upon what one means by moral and ennobling influence. The believer in machinery may think that to get a Government to abolish Church-rates or to legalise marriage with a deceased wife's sister is to exert a moral and ennobling influence upon Government. But a lover of perfection, who looks to inward ripeness for the true springs of conduct, will surely think that as Shakspeare has done more for the inward ripeness of our statesmen than Dr. Watts, and has, therefore, done more to moralise and ennoble them, so an Establishment which has produced Hooker, Barrow, Butler, has done more to moralise and ennoble English statesmen and their conduct than communities which have produced the Nonconformist divines. The fruitful men of English Puritanism and Nonconformity are men who were trained within the pale of the Establishment, — Milton, Baxter, Wesley. A generation or two outside the Establishment, and Puritanism produces men of national mark no more. With the same doctrine and discipline, men of national mark are produced in Scotland; but in an Establishment. With the same doctrine and discipline, men of national and even European mark are produced in Germany, Switzerland, France; but in Establishments. Only two religious disciplines seem exempted, or comparatively exempted, from the operation of the law which appears to forbid the rearing, outside of national Churches, of men of the highest spiritual significance. These two are the Roman Catholic and the Jewish. And these, both of them, rest on Establishments, which, though not indeed national, are cosmopolitan; and perhaps here, what the individual man does not lose by these conditions of his rearing, the citizen, and the State of which he is a citizen, loses.

PREFACE

What, now, can be the reason of this undeniable provincialism of the English Puritans and Protestant Nonconformists? Men of genius and character are born and reared in this medium as in any other. From the faults of the mass such men will always be comparatively free, and they will always excite our interest; yet in this medium they seem to have a special difficulty in breaking through what bounds them, and in developing their totality. Surely the reason is, that the Nonconformist is not in contact with the main current of national life, like the member of an Establishment. In a matter of such deep and vital concern as religion, this separation from the main current of the national life has peculiar importance. In the following essay we have discussed at length the tendency in us to *Hebraise*, as we call it; that is, to sacrifice all other sides of our being to the religious side. This tendency has its cause in the divine beauty and grandeur of religion, and bears affecting testimony to them. But we have seen that it has dangers for us, we have seen that it leads to a narrow and twisted growth of our religious side itself, and to a failure in perfection. But if we tend to Hebraise even in an Establishment, with the main current of national life flowing round us, and reminding us in all ways of the variety and fulness of human existence,—by a Church which is historical as the State itself is historical, and whose order, ceremonies, and monuments reach, like those of the State, far beyond any fancies and devisings of ours; and by institutions such as the Universities, formed to defend and advance that very culture and many-sided development which it is the danger of Hebraising to make us neglect,—how much more must we tend to Hebraise when we lack these preventives. One may say that to be reared a member of a national Church is in itself a lesson of religious moderation, and a help towards culture and harmonious perfection. Instead of battling for his own private forms for expressing the inexpressible and defining the undefinable, a man takes those which have commended themselves most to the religious life of his nation; and while he may be sure that within those forms the religious side of his own nature may find its satisfaction, he has leisure and composure to satisfy other sides of his nature as well.

But with the member of a Nonconforming or self-made religious community, how different! The sectary's *eigene grosse Erfindungen*, as Goethe calls them,—the precious discoveries of himself and his friends for expressing the inexpressible and defining the undefinable in peculiar forms of their own, cannot but, as he has voluntarily chosen them, and is personally responsible for them, fill his whole mind. He is zealous to do battle for them and affirm them; for in affirming them he affirms himself, and that is what we all like. Other sides of his being are thus neglected, because the religious side, always tending in every serious man to predominance over our other spiritual sides, is in him made quite absorbing and tyrannous by the condition of self-assertion and challenge which he has chosen for himself. And just what is not essential in religion he comes to mistake for essential, and a thousand times the more readily because he has chosen it of himself; and religious activity he fancies to consist in battling for it. All this leaves him little leisure or inclination for culture; to which, besides, he has no great institutions not of his own making, like the Universities connected with the National Church, to invite him; but only such institutions, as, like the order and discipline of his religion, he may have invented for himself, and invented under the sway of the narrow and tyrannous notions of religion fostered in him as we have seen. Thus, while a national establishment of religion favours totality, *hole-and-corner* forms of religion (to use an expressive popular word) inevitably favour provincialism.

But the Nonconformists, and many of our Liberal friends along with them, have a plausible plan for getting rid of this provincialism, if, as they can hardly quite deny, it exists. 'Let us all be in the same boat,' they cry; 'open the Universities to everybody, and let there be no establishment of religion at all!' Open the

Universities by all means ; but, as to the second point about establishment, let us sift the proposal a little. It does seem at first a little like that proposal of the fox, who had lost his own tail, to put all the other foxes in the same case by a general cutting off of tails ; and we know that moralists have decided that the right course here was, not to adopt this plausible suggestion, and cut off tails all round, but rather that the other foxes should keep their tails, and that the fox without a tail should get one. And so we might be inclined to urge, that, to cure the evil of the Nonconformists' provincialism, the right way can hardly be to provincialise us all round.

However, perhaps we shall not be provincialised. For Mr. White says that probably, 'when all good men alike are placed in a condition of religious equality, and the whole complicated iniquity of Government Church patronage is swept away, more of moral and ennobling influence than ever will be brought to bear upon the action of statesmen.'

We already have an example of religious equality in our colonies. 'In the colonies,' says the *Times*, 'we see religious communities unfettered by State-control, and the State relieved from one of the most troublesome and irritating responsibilities.' But America is the great example alleged by those who are against establishments for religion. Our topic at this moment is the influence of religious establishments on culture ; and it is remarkable that Mr. Bright, who has taken lately to representing himself as, above all, a promoter of reason and of the simple natural truth of things, and his policy as a fostering of the growth of intelligence,—just the aims, as is well known, of culture also,—Mr. Bright, in a speech at Birmingham about education, seized on the very point which seems to concern our topic, when he said : 'I believe the people of the United States have offered to the world more valuable information during the last forty years, than all Europe put together.' So America, without religious establishments, seems to get ahead of us all, even in light and the things of the mind.

On the other hand, another friend of reason and the simple natural truth of things, M. Renan, says of America, in a book he has recently published, what seems to conflict violently with what Mr. Bright says. Mr. Bright avers that not only have the United States thus informed Europe, but they have done it without a great apparatus of higher and scientific instruction, and by dint of all classes in America being 'sufficiently educated to be able to read, and to comprehend, and to think ; and that, I maintain, is the foundation of all subsequent progress.' And then comes M. Renan, and says : 'The sound instruction of the people is an effect of the high culture of certain classes. *The countries which, like the United States, have created a considerable popular instruction without any serious higher instruction, will long have to expiate this fault by their intellectual mediocrity, their vulgarity of manners, their superficial spirit, their lack of general intelligence.'*[1]

Now, which of these two friends of light are we to believe? M. Renan seems more to have in view what we ourselves mean by culture; because Mr. Bright always has in his eye what he calls 'a commendable interest' in politics and in political agitations. As he said only the other day at Birmingham: 'At this moment,—in fact, I may say at every moment in the history of a free country,—there is nothing that is so much worth discussing as politics.' And he keeps repeating, with all the powers of his noble oratory, the old story, how to the thoughtfulness and intelligence of the people of great towns we owe all our improvements in the last thirty years, and how these improvements have hitherto consisted in Parliamentary reform, and free trade, and abolition of Church-rates, and so on; and how they are now about to consist in getting rid of minority-members, and in introducing a free breakfast-table, and in abolishing the Irish Church by the power of the Nonconformists' antipathy to establishments,

[1] 'Les pays qui, comme les Etats-Unis, ont créé un enseignement populaire considérable sans instruction supérieure sérieuse, expieront longtemps encore leur faute par leur médiocrité intellectuelle, leur grossièreté de mœurs, leur esprit superficiel, leur manque d'intelligence générale.'

and much more of the same kind. And though our pauperism and ignorance, and all the questions which are called social, seem now to be forcing themselves upon his mind, yet he still goes on with his glorifying of the great towns, and the Liberals, and their operations for the last thirty years. It never seems to occur to him that the present troubled state of our social life has anything to do with the thirty years' blind worship of their nostrums by himself and our Liberal friends, or that it throws any doubts upon the sufficiency of this worship. But he thinks that what is still amiss is due to the stupidity of the Tories, and will be cured by the thoughtfulness and intelligence of the great towns, and by the Liberals going on gloriously with their political operations as before; or that it will cure itself. So we see what Mr. Bright means by thoughtfulness and intelligence, and in what matter, according to him, we are to grow in them. And, no doubt, in America all classes read their newspaper, and take a commendable interest in politics, more than here or anywhere else in Europe.

But in the following essay we have been led to doubt the sufficiency of all this political operating, pursued mechanically as our race pursues it; and we found that *general intelligence*, as M. Renan calls it, or, as we say, attention to the reason of things, was just what we were without, and that we were without it because we worshipped our machinery so devoutly. Therefore, we conclude that M. Renan, more than Mr. Bright, means by reason and intelligence the same thing as we do. And when M. Renan says that America, that chosen home of newspapers and politics, is without general intelligence, we think it likely, from the circumstances of the case, that this is so; and that in the things of the mind, and in culture and totality, America, instead of surpassing us all, falls short.

And,—to keep to our point of the influence of religious establishments upon culture and a high development of our humanity,—we can surely see reasons why, with all her energy and fine gifts, America does not show more of this development, or more promise of this. In the following essay it will be seen how our society distributes itself into Barbarians, Philistines, and Populace; and America is just ourselves, with the Barbarians quite left out, and the Populace nearly. This leaves the Philistines for the great bulk of the nation;—a livelier sort of Philistine than ours, and with the pressure and false ideal of our Barbarians taken away, but left all the more to himself and to have his full swing. And as we have found that the strongest and most vital part of English Philistinism was the Puritan and Hebraising middle class, and that its Hebraising keeps it from culture and totality, so it is notorious that the people of the United

States issues from this class, and reproduces its tendencies,—its narrow conception of man's spiritual range and of his one thing needful. From Maine to Florida, and back again, all America Hebraises. Difficult as it is to speak of a people merely from what one reads, yet that, I think, one may without much fear of contradiction say. I mean, when in the United States any spiritual side in man is wakened to activity, it is generally the religious side, and the religious side in a narrow way. Social reformers go to Moses or St. Paul for their doctrines, and have no notion there is anywhere else to go to; earnest young men at schools and universities, instead of conceiving salvation as a harmonious perfection only to be won by unreservedly cultivating many sides in us, conceive of it in thc old Puritan fashion, and fling themselves ardently upon it in the old, false ways of this fashion, which we know so well, and such as Mr. Hammond, the American revivalist, has lately at Mr. Spurgeon's Tabernacle been refreshing our memory with.

Now, if America thus Hebraises more than either England or Germany, will any one deny that the absence of religious establishments has much to do with it? We have seen how establishments tend to give us a sense of a historical life of the human spirit, outside and beyond our own fancies and feelings; how they thus tend to suggest new sides and sympathies in us to cultivate; how, further, by saving us from having to invent and fight for our own forms of religion, they give us leisure and calm to steady our view of religion itself,—the most overpowering of objects, as it is the grandest,—and to enlarge our first crude notions of the one thing needful. But, in a serious people, where every one has to choose and strive for his own order and discipline of religion, the contention about these non-essentials occupies his mind. His first crude notions about the one thing needful do not get purged, and they invade the whole spiritual man in him, and then, making a solitude, they call it heavenly peace.

I remember a Nonconformist manufacturer, in a town of the Midland counties, telling me that when he first came there, some years ago, the place had no Dissenters; but he had opened an Independent chapel in it, and now Church and Dissent were pretty equally divided, with sharp contests between them. I said that this seemed a pity. 'A pity?' cried he; 'not at all! Only think of all the zeal and activity which the collision calls forth!' 'Ah, but, my dear friend,' I answered, 'only think of all the nonsense which you now hold quite firmly, which you would never have held if you had not been contradicting your adversary in it all these years!' The more serious the people, and the more prominent the religious side in it, the greater is the danger of this side, if set to choose out forms for itself and fight for existence, swelling and spreading till it swallows all other spiritual sides up, intercepts and absorbs all nutriment which should have gone to them, and leaves Hebraism rampant in us and Hellenism stamped out.

Culture, and the harmonious perfection of our whole being, and what we call totality, then become quite secondary matters. And even the institutions, which should develop these, take the same narrow and partial view of humanity and its wants as the free religious communities take. Just as the free churches of Mr. Beecher or Brother Noyes, with their provincialism and want of centrality, make mere Hebraisers in religion, and not perfect men, so the university of Mr. Ezra Cornell, a really noble monument of his munificence, yet seems to rest on a misconception of what culture truly is, and to be calculated to produce miners, or engineers, or architects, not sweetness and light.

And, therefore, when Mr. White asks the same kind of question about America that he has asked about England, and wants to know whether, without religious establishments, as much is not done in America for the higher national life as is done for that life here, we answer in the same way as we did before, that as much is not done. Because to enable and stir up people to read their Bible and the newspapers, and to get a practical knowledge of their business, does not serve to the higher spiritual life of a nation so much as culture, truly conceived, serves; and a true conception of culture is, as M. Renan's words show, just what America fails in.

To the many who think that spirituality, and sweetness, and light, are all moonshine, this will not appear to matter much; but with us, who value them, and who think that we have traced much of our present discomfort to the want of them, it weighs a great deal. So not only do we say that the Nonconformists have got provincialism and lost totality by the want of a religious establishment, but we say that the very example which they bring forward to help their case makes against them; and that when they triumphantly show us America without religious establishments, they only show us a whole nation touched, amidst all its greatness and promise, with that provincialism which it is our aim to extirpate in the English Nonconformists.

But now to evince the disinterestedness which culture teaches us. We have seen the narrowness generated in Puritanism by its hole-and-corner organisation, and we propose to cure it by bringing Puritanism more into contact with the main current of national life. Here we are fully at one with the Dean of Westminster; and, indeed, he and we were trained in the same school to mark the narrowness of Puritanism, and to wish to cure it. But he and others seem disposed simply to give to the present Anglican Establishment a character the most latitudinarian, as it is called, possible; availing themselves for this purpose of the diversity of tendencies and doctrines which does undoubtedly exist already in the Anglican formularies; and then they would say to the Puritans: 'Come all of you into this liberally conceived Anglican Establishment.' But to say this is hardly, perhaps, to take sufficient account of the course of history, or of the strength of men's feelings in what concerns religion, or of the gravity which may have come to attach to points of religious order and discipline merely. When Mr. White talks of 'sweeping away the whole complicated iniquity of Government Church patronage,' he uses language which has been forced upon him by his position, but which is devoid of all real solidity. But when he talks of the religious communities 'which have for three hundred years contended for the power of the congregation in the management of their own affairs,' then he talks history; and his language has behind it, in my opinion, facts which make the latitudinarianism of our Broad Churchmen quite illusory.

Certainly, culture will never make us think it an essential of religion whether we have in our Church discipline 'a popular authority of elders,' as Hooker calls it, or whether we have Episcopal jurisdiction. Certainly, Hooker himself did not think it an essential ; for in the dedication of his *Ecclesiastical Polity*, speaking of these questions of church-discipline which gave occasion to his great work, he says they are 'in truth, for the greatest part, such silly things, that very easiness doth make them hard to be disputed of in serious manner.' Hooker's great work against the impugners of the order and discipline of the Church of England was written (and this is too indistinctly seized by many who read it), not because Episcopalianism is essential, but because its impugners maintained that Presbyterianism is essential, and that Episcopalianism is sinful. Neither the one nor the other is either essential or sinful, and much may be said on behalf of both. But what is important to be remarked is, *that both were in the Church of England at the Reformation*, and that Presbyterianism was only extruded gradually. We have mentioned Hooker, and nothing better illustrates what has just been asserted than the following incident in Hooker's own career, which every one has read, for it is related in Isaac Walton's *Life of Hooker*, but of which, probably, the significance has been fully grasped by very few of those who have read it.

Hooker was through the influence of Archbishop Whitgift appointed, in 1585, Master of the Temple ; but a great effort had first been made to obtain the place for a Mr. Walter Travers, well known in that day, though now it is Hooker's name which alone preserves his. This Travers was then afternoon-lecturer at the Temple. The Master whose death made the vacancy, Alvey, recommended on his death-bed Travers for his successor. The Society was favourable to Travers, and he had the support of the Lord Treasurer Burghley. Although Hooker was appointed to the Mastership, Travers remained afternoon-lecturer, and combated in the afternoons the doctrine which Hooker preached in the mornings. Now, this Travers, originally a Fellow of Trinity College, Cambridge, afterwards afternoon-lecturer at the Temple, recommended for the Mastership by the foregoing Master whose opinions, it is said, agreed with his, favoured by the Society of the Temple and supported by the Prime Minister,—this Travers was not an Episcopally ordained clergyman at all. He was a Presbyterian, a partisan of the Geneva church-discipline, as it was then called, and 'had taken orders,' says Walton, 'by the Presbyters in Antwerp.' In another place Walton speaks of his orders yet more fully:— 'He had disowned,' he says, 'the English Established Church and Episcopacy, and went to Geneva, and afterwards to Antwerp, to be ordained minister, as he was by Villers and Cartwright and others the heads of a congregation there; and so came back again more confirmed for the discipline.' Villers and Cartwright are in like manner examples of

Presbyterianism within the Church of England, which was common enough at that time. But perhaps nothing can better give us a lively sense of its presence there than this history of Travers, which is as if Mr. Binney were now[1] afternoon-reader at Lincoln's Inn or the Temple; were to be a candidate, favoured by the Benchers and by the Prime Minister, for the Mastership; and were only kept out of the post by the accident of the Archbishop of Canterbury's influence with the Queen carrying a rival candidate.

Presbyterianism, with its popular principle of the power of the congregation in the management of their own affairs, was extruded from the Church of England, and men like Travers can no longer appear in her pulpits. Perhaps if a government like that of Elizabeth, with secular statesmen like the Cecils, and ecclesiastical statesmen like Whitgift, could have been prolonged, Presbyterianism might, by a wise mixture of concession and firmness, have been absorbed in the Establishment. Lord Bolingbroke, on a matter of this kind a very clear-judging and impartial witness, says, in a work far too little read, his *Remarks on English History*:—'The measures pursued and the temper observed in Queen Elizabeth's time tended to diminish the religious opposition by a slow, a gentle, and for that very reason an effectual progression. There was even room to hope that when the first fire

[1] 1869.

of the Dissenters' zeal was passed, reasonable terms of union with the Established Church might be accepted by such of them as were not intoxicated with fanaticism. These were friends to order, though they disputed about it. If these friends of Calvin's discipline had been once incorporated with the Established Church, the remaining sectaries would have been of little moment, either for numbers or reputation; and the very means which were proper to gain these friends were likewise the most effectual to hinder the increase of them, and of the other sectaries in the meantime.' The temper and ill judgment of the Stuarts made shipwreck of all policy of this kind. Yet speaking even of the time of the Stuarts, but their early time, Clarendon says that if Bishop Andrewes had succeeded Bancroft at Canterbury, the disaffection of separatists might have been stayed and healed. This, however, was not to be; and Presbyterianism, after exercising for some years the law of the strongest, itself in Charles the Second's reign suffered under this law, and was finally cast out from the Church of England.

Now the points of church-discipline at issue between Presbyterianism and Episcopalianism are, as has been said, not essential. They might probably once have been settled in a sense altogether favourable to Episcopalianism. Hooker may have been right in thinking that there were in his time circumstances which made it essential that they should be settled in this sense, though the points in themselves were not essential. But by the very fact of the settlement not having then been effected, of the breach having gone on and widened, of the Nonconformists not having been amicably incorporated with the Establishment but violently cast out from it, the circumstances are now altogether altered. Isaac Walton, a fervent Churchman, complains that 'the principles of the Nonconformists grew at last to such a height and were vented so daringly, that, beside the loss of life and limbs, the Church and State were both forced to use such other severities as will not admit of an excuse, if it had not been to prevent confusion and the perilous consequences of it.' But those very severities have of themselves made union on an Episcopalian footing impossible. Besides, Presbyterianism, the popular authority of elders, the power of the congregation in the management of their own affairs, has that warrant given to it by Scripture and by the proceedings of the early Christian Churches, it is so consonant with the spirit of Protestantism which made the Reformation and which has great strength in this country, it is so predominant in the practice of other Reformed Churches, it was so strong in the original Reformed Church of England, that one cannot help doubting whether any settlement which suppressed it could have been really permanent, and whether it would not have kept appearing again and again, and causing dissension.

Well, then, if culture is the disinterested endeavour after man's perfection, will it not make us wish to cure the provincialism of the Nonconformists, not by rendering Churchmen provincial along with them, but by letting their popular church-discipline, formerly present in the national Church and still present in the affections and practice of a good part of the nation, appear in the national Church once more; and thus to bring Nonconformists into contact again, as their greater fathers were, with the main stream of national life? Why should not a Presbyterian Church, based on this considerable and important, though not essential principle, of the congregation's share in the church-management, be established,—with equal rank for its chiefs with the chiefs of Episcopacy, and with admissibility of its ministers, under a revised system of patronage and preferment to benefices,—side by side with the Episcopal Church, as the Calvinist and Lutheran Churches are established side by side in France and Germany? Such a Presbyterian Church would unite the main bodies of Protestants who are now separatists; and separation would cease to be the law of their religious order. And thus,—through this concession on a really considerable point of difference,—that endless splitting into hole-and-corner churches on quite inconsiderable points of difference, which must prevail so long as separatism is the first law of a Nonconformist's religious existence, would be checked. Culture would then find a place among English followers of the popular authority of Elders, as it has long found it among the followers of Episcopal jurisdiction. And this we should gain by merely recognising, regularising, and restoring an element which appeared once in the reformed national Church, and which is considerable and national enough to have a sound claim to appear there still.

So far, then, is culture from making us unjust to the Nonconformists because it forbids us to worship their fetishes, that it even leads us to propose to do more for them than they themselves venture to claim. It leads us, also, to respect what is solid and respectable in their convictions. Not that the forms in which the human spirit tries to express the inexpressible, or the forms by which man tries to worship, have or can have, as has been said, for the follower of perfection, anything necessary or eternal. If the New Testament and the practice of the primitive Christians sanctioned the popular form of church-government a thousand times more expressly than they do, if the Church since Constantine were a thousand times more of a departure from the scheme of primitive Christianity than it can be shown to be, that does not at all make, as is supposed by men in bondage to the letter, the popular form of church-government alone and always sacred and binding, or the work of Constantine a thing to be regretted.

What is alone and always sacred and binding for man is the making progress towards his total perfection; and the machinery by which he does this varies in value according as it helps him to do it. The planters of Christianity had their roots in deep and rich grounds of human life and achievement, both Jewish and also Greek; and had thus a comparatively firm and wide basis amidst all the vehement inspiration of their mighty movement and change. By their strong inspiration they carried men off the old basis of life and culture, whether Jewish or Greek, and generations arose who had their roots in neither world, and were in contact therefore with no full and great stream of human life. If it had not been for some such change as that of the fourth century, Christianity might have lost itself in a multitude of hole-and-corner churches like the churches of English Nonconformity after its founders departed; churches without great men, and without furtherance for the higher life of humanity. At a critical moment came Constantine, and placed Christianity,—or let us rather say, placed the human spirit, whose totality was endangered,—in contact with the main current of human life. And his work was justified by its fruits, in men like Augustine and Dante, and indeed in all the great men of Christianity, Catholics or Protestants, ever since.

And one may go beyond this. M. Albert Réville, whose religious writings are always interesting, says that the conception which cultivated and philosophical Jews now entertain of Christianity and its Founder, is probably destined to become the conception which Christians themselves will entertain. Socinians are fond of saying the same thing about the Socinian conception of Christianity. Now, even if this were true, it would still have been better for a man, during the last eighteen hundred years, to have been a Christian and a member of one of the great Christian communions, than to have been a Jew or a Socinian ; because the being in contact with the main stream of human life is of more moment for a man's total spiritual growth, and for his bringing to perfection the gifts committed to him, which is his business on earth, than any speculative opinion which he may hold or think he holds. Luther,—whom we have called a Philistine of genius, and who, because he was a Philistine, had a coarseness and lack of spiritual delicacy which have harmed his disciples, but who, because he was a genius, had splendid flashes of spiritual insight,—Luther says admirably in his Commentary on the Book of Daniel : 'A God is simply *that* whereon the human heart rests with trust, faith, hope, and love. If the resting is right, then the God too is right ; if the resting is wrong, then the God too is illusory.' In other words, the worth of what a man thinks about God and the objects of religion depends on what the man *is*; and what the man *is*, depends upon his having more or less reached the measure of a perfect and total man.

Culture, disinterestedly seeking in its aim at perfection to see things as they really are, shows us how worthy and divine a thing is the religious side in man, though it is not the whole of man. But while recognising the grandeur of the religious side in man, culture yet makes us also eschew an inadequate conception of man's totality. Therefore to the worth and grandeur of the religious side in man, culture is rejoiced and willing to pay any tribute, except the tribute of man's totality. Unless it is proved that contact with the main current of national life is of no value (and we have shown that it is of the greatest value), we cannot safely, even to please the Nonconformists in a matter where we would please them as much as possible, admit their doctrines of disestablishment and separation.

Culture, again, can be disinterested enough to perceive and avow, that for Ireland the ends of human perfection might be best served by establishing,—that is, by bringing into contact with the main current of the national life,—the Roman Catholic and the Presbyterian Churches along with the Anglican Church. It can perceive and avow that we should really, in this way, be working to make reason and the will of God prevail ; because we should be making Roman Catholics better citizens, and both Protestants and Roman Catholics larger-minded and more complete men. Undoubtedly there are great difficulties in such a plan as this ; and the plan is not one which looks very likely to be adopted. The Churchman must rise above his ordinary self in order to favour it. And the Nonconformist has worshipped his fetish of separatism so long that he is likely to wish to remain, like Ephraim, 'a wild ass alone by himself.' It is a plan more for a time of creative statesmen, like the time of Elizabeth, than for a time of instrumental statesmen like the present. The centre of power being where it is, our statesmen have every temptation, when they must act, to go along as they do with the ordinary self of those on whose favour they depend, to adopt as their own its desires, and to serve them with fidelity, and even, if possible, with ardour. This is the more easy for them, because there are not wanting,—and there never will be wanting,—thinkers to call the desires of the ordinary self of any great section of the community edicts of the national mind and laws of human progress, and to give them a general, a philosophic, and imposing expression. Therefore a plan such as that which we have indicated does not seem a plan so likely to find favour as a plan for abolishing the Irish Church by the power of the Nonconformists' antipathy to establishments.

But although culture makes us fond stickers to no machinery, not even our own, and therefore we are willing to grant that perfection can be reached without it,—with free churches as with established churches, and with instrumental statesmen as with creative statesmen,—yet perfection can never be reached without seeing things as they really are; and it is to this, therefore, and to no machinery in the world, that we stick. We insist that men should not mistake, as they are prone to mistake, their natural taste for the bathos for a relish for the sublime. And if statesmen, either with their tongue in their cheek or with a fine impulsiveness, tell people that their natural taste for the bathos is a relish for the sublime, there is the more need to tell them the contrary.

It is delusion on this point which is fatal, and against delusion on this point culture works. It is not fatal to our Liberal friends to labour for free trade, extension of the suffrage, and abolition of church-rates, instead of graver social ends; but it is fatal to them to be told by their flatterers, and to believe, with our social condition what it is, that they have performed a great, a heroic work, by occupying themselves exclusively, for the last thirty years, with these Liberal nostrums, and that the right and good course for them now is to go on occupying themselves with the like for the future. It is not fatal to Americans to have no religious establishments and no effective centres of high culture ; but it is fatal to them to be told by their flatterers, and to believe, that they are the most intelligent people in the whole world, when of intelligence, in the true and fruitful sense of the word, they even singularly, as we have seen, come short. It is not fatal to the Nonconformists to remain with their separated churches ; but it is fatal to them to be told by their flatterers, and to believe, that theirs is the one true way of worshipping God, that provincialism and loss of totality have not come to them from following it, or that provincialism and loss of totality are not evils. It is not fatal to the English nation to abolish the Irish Church by the power of the Nonconformists' antipathy to establishments ; but it is fatal to it to be told by its flatterers, and to believe, that it is abolishing it through reason and justice, when it is really abolishing it through this power : or to expect the fruits of reason and justice from anything but the spirit of reason and justice themselves.

Now culture, because of its keen sense of what is really fatal, is all the more disposed to be rather indifferent about what is not fatal. And because machinery is the one concern of our actual politics, and an inward working, and not machinery, is what we most want, we keep advising our ardent young Liberal friends to think less of machinery, to stand more aloof from the arena of politics at present, and rather to try and promote, with us, an inward working. They do not listen to us, and they rush into the arena of politics, where their merits, indeed, seem to be little appreciated as yet; and then they complain of the reformed constituencies, and call the new Parliament a Philistine Parliament. As if a nation, nourished and reared as ours has been, could give us, just yet, anything but a Philistine Parliament!—and would a Barbarian Parliament be even so good, or a Populace Parliament? For our part, we rejoice to see our dear old friends, the Hebraising Philistines, gathered in force in the Valley of Jehoshaphat previous to their final conversion, which will certainly come. But, to attain this conversion, we must not try to oust them from their places and to contend for machinery with them, but we must work on them inwardly and cure their spirit. Ousted they will not be, but transformed. Ousted they do not deserve to be, and will not be.

For *the days of Israel are innumerable*; and in its blame of Hebraising too, and in its praise of Hellenising, culture must not fail to keep its flexibility, and to give to its judgments that passing and provisional character which we have seen it impose on its preferences and rejections of machinery. Now, and for us, it is a time to Hellenise, and to praise knowing; for we have Hebraised too much, and have over-valued doing. But the habits and discipline received from Hebraism remain for our race an eternal possession ; and, as humanity is constituted, one must never assign to them the second rank to-day, without being prepared to restore to them the first rank to-morrow. Let us conclude by marking this distinctly.

To walk staunchly by the best light one has, to be strict and sincere with oneself, not to be of the number of those who say and do not, to be in earnest,—this is the discipline by which alone man is enabled to rescue his life from thraldom to the passing moment and to his bodily senses, to ennoble it, and to make it eternal. And this discipline has been nowhere so effectively taught as in the school of Hebraism. The intense and convinced energy with which the Hebrew, both of the Old and of the New Testament, threw himself upon his ideal of righteousness, and which inspired the incomparable definition of the great Christian virtue, faith,—*the substance of things hoped for, the evidence of things not seen*,—this energy of devotion to its ideal has belonged to Hebraism alone. As our idea of perfection widens beyond the narrow limits to which the over-rigour of Hebraising has tended to confine it, we shall yet come again to Hebraism for that devout energy in embracing our ideal, which alone can give to man the happiness of doing what he knows. 'If ye know these things, happy are ye if ye do them!'—the last word for infirm humanity will always be that. For this word, reiterated with a power now sublime, now affecting, but always admirable, our race will, as long as the world lasts, return to Hebraism; and the Bible, which preaches this word, will for ever remain, as Goethe called it, not only a national book, but the Book of the Nations. Again and again, after what seemed breaches and separations, the prophetic promise to Jerusalem will still be true:—*Lo, thy sons come, whom thou sentest away; they come gathered from the west unto the east by the word of the Holy One, rejoicing in the remembrance of God.*

CONTENTS

CULTURE AND ANARCHY

INTRODUCTION

In one of his speeches a short time ago, that fine speaker and famous Liberal, Mr. Bright, took occasion to have a fling at the friends and preachers of culture. 'People who talk about what they call *culture!*' said he, contemptuously; 'by which they mean a smattering of the two dead languages of Greek and Latin.' And he went on to remark, in a strain with which modern speakers and writers have made us very familiar, how poor a thing this culture is, how little good it can do to the world, and how absurd it is for its possessors to set much store by it. And the other day a younger Liberal than Mr. Bright, one of a school whose mission it is to bring into order and system that body of truth with which the earlier Liberals merely fumbled, a member of the University of Oxford, and a very clever writer, Mr. Frederic Harrison, developed, in the systematic and stringent manner of his school, the thesis which Mr. Bright had propounded in only general terms. 'Perhaps the very silliest cant of the day,' said Mr. Frederic Harrison, 'is the cant about culture. Culture is a desirable quality in a critic of new books, and sits well on a possessor of *belles-lettres;* but as applied to politics, it means simply a turn for small fault-finding, love of selfish ease, and indecision in action. The man of culture is in politics one of the poorest mortals alive. For simple pedantry and want of good sense no man is his equal. No assumption is too unreal, no end is too unpractical for him. But the active exercise of politics requires common sense, sympathy, trust, resolution, and enthusiasm, qualities which your man of culture has carefully rooted up, lest they damage the delicacy of his critical olfactories. Perhaps they are the only class of responsible beings in the community who cannot with safety be entrusted with power.'

Now for my part I do not wish to see men of culture asking to be entrusted with power; and, indeed, I have freely said, that in my opinion the speech most proper, at present, for a man of culture to make to a body of his fellow-countrymen who get him into a committee-room, is Socrates's: *Know thyself!* and this is not a speech to be made by men wanting to be entrusted with power. For this very indifference to direct political action I have been taken to task by the *Daily Telegraph*, coupled, by a strange perversity of fate, with just that very one of the Hebrew prophets whose style I admire the least, and called 'an elegant Jeremiah.' It is because I say (to use the words which the *Daily Telegraph* puts in my mouth):—'You mustn't make a fuss because you have no vote,—that is vulgarity; you mustn't hold big meetings to agitate for reform bills and to repeal corn laws,—that is the very height of vulgarity,'—it is for this reason that I am called sometimes an elegant Jeremiah, sometimes a spurious Jeremiah, a Jeremiah about the reality of whose mission the writer in the *Daily Telegraph* has his doubts. It is evident, therefore, that I have so taken my line as not to be exposed to the whole brunt of Mr. Frederic Harrison's censure. Still, I have often spoken in praise of culture, I have striven to make all my works and ways serve the interests of culture. I take culture to be something a great deal more than what Mr. Frederic Harrison and others call it: 'a desirable quality in a critic of new books.' Nay, even though to a certain extent I am disposed to agree with Mr. Frederic Harrison, that men of culture are just the class of responsible beings in this community of ours who cannot properly, at present, be entrusted with power, I am not sure that I do not think this the fault of our community rather than of the men of culture. In short, although, like Mr. Bright and Mr. Frederic Harrison, and the editor of the *Daily Telegraph*, and a large body of valued ds of mine, I am a Liberal, yet I am a eral tempered by experience, reflection, and renouncement, and I am, above all, a believer in culture. Therefore I propose now to try and inquire, in the simple unsystematic way which best suits both my taste and my powers, what culture really is, what good it can do, what is our own special need of it ; and I shall seek to find some plain grounds on which a faith in culture,—both my own faith in it and the faith of others,—may rest securely.

CHAPTER I

SWEETNESS AND LIGHT

THE disparagers of culture make its motive curiosity; sometimes, indeed, they make its motive mere exclusiveness and vanity. The culture which is supposed to plume itself on a smattering of Greek and Latin is a culture which is begotten by nothing so intellectual as curiosity; it is valued either out of sheer vanity and ignorance or else as an engine of social and class distinction, separating its holder, like a badge or title, from other people who have not got it. No serious man would call this *culture*, or attach any value to it, as culture, at all. To find the real ground for the very different estimate which serious people will set upon culture, we must find some motive for culture in the terms of which may lie a real ambiguity; and such a motive the word *curiosity* gives us.

I have before now pointed out that we English do not, like the foreigners, use this word in a good sense as well as in a bad sense. With us the word is always used in a somewhat disapproving sense. A liberal and intelligent eagerness about the things of the mind may be meant by a foreigner when he speaks of curiosity, but with us the word always conveys a certain notion of frivolous and unedifying activity. In the *Quarterly Review*, some little time ago, was an estimate of the celebrated French critic, M. Sainte-Beuve, and a very inadequate estimate it in my judgment was. And its inadequacy consisted chiefly in this: that in our English way it left out of sight the double sense really involved in the word *curiosity*, thinking enough was said to stamp M. Sainte-Beuve with blame if it was said that he was impelled in his operations as a critic by curiosity, and omitting either to perceive that M. Sainte-Beuve himself, and many other people with him, would consider that this was praiseworthy and not blameworthy, or to point out why it ought really to be accounted worthy of blame and not of praise. For as there is a curiosity about intellectual matters which is futile, and merely a disease, so there is certainly a curiosity,—a desire after the things of the mind simply for their own sakes and for the pleasure of seeing them as they are,—which is, in an intelligent being, natural and laudable. Nay, and the very desire to see things as they are implies a balance and regulation of mind which is not often attained without fruitful effort, and which is the very opposite of the blind and diseased impulse of mind which is what we mean to blame when we blame curiosity. Montesquieu says: 'The first motive which ought to impel us to study is the desire to augment the excellence of our nature, and to render an intelligent being yet more intelligent.' This is the true ground to assign for the genuine scientific passion, however manifested, and for culture, viewed simply as a fruit of this passion; and it is a worthy ground, even though we let the term *curiosity* stand to describe it.

But there is of culture another view, in which not solely the scientific passion, the sheer desire to see things as they are, natural and proper in an intelligent being, appears as the ground of it. There is a view in which all the love of our neighbour, the impulses towards action, help, and beneficence, the desire for removing human error, clearing human confusion, and diminishing human misery, the noble aspiration to leave the world better and happier than we found it,—motives eminently such as are called social,—come in as part of the grounds of culture, and the main and pre-eminent part. Culture is then properly described not as having its origin in curiosity, but as having its origin in the love of perfection; it is *a study of perfection*. It moves by the force, not merely or primarily of the scientific passion for pure knowledge, but also of the moral and social passion for doing good. As, in the first view of it, we took for its worthy motto Montesquieu's words: 'To render an intelligent being yet more intelligent!' so, in the second view of it, there is no better motto which it can have than these words of Bishop Wilson: 'To make reason and the will of God prevail!'

Only, whereas the passion for doing good is apt to be overhasty in determining what reason and the will of God say, because its turn is for acting rather than thinking and it wants to be beginning to act; and whereas it is apt to take its own conceptions, which proceed from its own state of development and share in all the imperfections and immaturities of this, for a basis of action; what distinguishes culture is, that it is possessed by the scientific passion as well as by the passion of doing good; that it demands worthy notions of reason and the will of God, and does not readily suffer its own crude conceptions to substitute themselves for them. And knowing that no action or institution can be salutary and stable which is not based on reason and the will of God, it is not so bent on acting and instituting, even with the great aim of diminishing human error and misery ever before its thoughts, but that it can remember that acting and instituting are of little use, unless we know how and what we ought to act and to institute.

This culture is more interesting and more far-reaching than that other, which is founded solely on the scientific passion for knowing. But it needs times of faith and ardour, times when the intellectual horizon is opening and widening all round us, to flourish in. And is not the close and bounded intellectual horizon within which we have long lived and moved now lifting up, and are not new lights finding free passage to shine in upon us? For a long time there was no passage for them to make their way in upon us, and then it was of no use to think of adapting the world's action to them. Where was the hope of making reason and the will of God prevail among people who had a routine which they had christened reason and the will of God, in which they were inextricably bound, and beyond which they had no power of looking? But now the iron force of adhesion to the old routine,—social, political, religious,—has wonderfully yielded; the iron force of exclusion of all which is new has wonderfully yielded. The danger now is, not that people should obstinately refuse to allow anything but their old routine to pass for reason and the will of God, but either that they should allow some novelty or other to pass for these too easily, or else that they should underrate the importance of them altogether, and think it enough to follow action for its own sake, without troubling themselves to make reason and the will of God prevail therein. Now, then, is the moment for culture to be of service, culture which believes in making reason and the will of God prevail, believes in perfection, is the study and pursuit of perfection, and is no longer debarred, by a rigid invincible exclusion of whatever is new, from getting acceptance for its ideas, simply because they are new.

The moment this view of culture is seized, the moment it is regarded not solely as the endeavour to see things as they are, to draw towards a knowledge of the universal order which seems to be intended and aimed at in the world, and which it is a man's happiness to go along with or his misery to go counter to,—to learn, in short, the will of God,—the moment, I say, culture is considered not merely as the endeavour to *see* and *learn* this, but as the endeavour, also, to make it *prevail*, the moral, social, and beneficent character of culture becomes manifest. The mere endeavour to see and learn the truth for our own personal satisfaction is indeed a commencement for making it prevail, a preparing the way for this, which always serves this, and is wrongly, therefore, stamped with blame absolutely in itself and not only in its caricature and degeneration. But perhaps it has got stamped with blame, and disparaged with the dubious title of curiosity, because in comparison with this wider endeavour of such great and plain utility it looks selfish, petty, and unprofitable.

And religion, the greatest and most important of the efforts by which the human race has manifested its impulse to perfect itself,—religion, that voice of the deepest human experience,—

does not only enjoin and sanction the aim which is the great aim of culture, the aim of setting ourselves to ascertain what perfection is and to make it prevail; but also, in determining generally in what human perfection consists, religion comes to a conclusion identical with that which culture,—culture seeking the determination of this question through *all* the voices of human experience which have been heard upon it, of art, science, poetry, philosophy, history, as well as of religion, in order to give a greater fulness and certainty to its solution,—likewise reaches. Religion says: *The kingdom of God is within you;* and culture, in like manner, places human perfection in an *internal* condition, in the growth and predominance of our humanity proper, as distinguished from our animality. It places it in the ever-increasing efficacy and in the general harmonious expansion of those gifts of thought and feeling, which make the peculiar dignity, wealth, and happiness of human nature. As I have said on a former occasion: 'It is in making endless additions to itself, in the endless expansion of its powers, in endless growth in wisdom and beauty, that the spirit of the human race finds its ideal. To reach this ideal, culture is an indispensable aid, and that is the true value of culture.' Not a having and a resting, but a growing and a becoming, is the character of perfection as culture conceives it; and here, too, it coincides with religion.

And because men are all members of one great whole, and the sympathy which is in human nature will not allow one member to be indifferent to the rest or to have a perfect welfare independent of the rest, the expansion of our humanity, to suit the idea of perfection which culture forms, must be a *general* expansion. Perfection, as culture conceives it, is not possible while the individual remains isolated. The individual is required, under pain of being stunted and enfeebled in his own development if he disobeys, to carry others along with him in his march towards perfection, to be continually doing all he can to enlarge and increase the volume of the human stream sweeping thitherward. And here, once more, culture lays on us the same obligation as religion, which says, as Bishop Wilson has admirably put it, that 'to promote the kingdom of God is to increase and hasten one's own happiness.'

But, finally, perfection,—as culture from a thorough disinterested study of human nature and human experience learns to conceive it,—is a harmonious expansion of *all* the powers which make the beauty and worth of human nature, and is not consistent with the over-development of any one power at the expense of the rest. Here culture goes beyond religion, as religion is generally conceived by us.

If culture, then, is a study of perfection, and of harmonious perfection, general perfection, and perfection which consists in becoming something rather than in having something, in an inward condition of the mind and spirit, not in an outward set of circumstances,—it is clear that culture, instead of being the frivolous and useless thing which Mr. Bright, and Mr. Frederic Harrison, and many other Liberals are apt to call it, has a very important function to fulfil for mankind. And this function is particularly important in our modern world, of which the whole civilisation is, to a much greater degree than the civilisation of Greece and Rome, mechanical and external, and tends constantly to become more so. But above all in our own country has culture a weighty part to perform, because here that mechanical character, which civilisation tends to take everywhere, is shown in the most eminent degree. Indeed nearly all the characters of perfection, as culture teaches us to fix them, meet in this country with some powerful tendency which thwarts them and sets them at defiance. The idea of perfection as an *inward* condition of the mind and spirit is at variance with the mechanical and material civilisation in esteem with us, and nowhere, as I have said, so much in esteem as with us. The idea of perfection as a *general* expansion of the human family is at variance with our strong individualism, our hatred of all limits to the unrestrained swing of the individual's personality, our maxim of 'every man for himself.' Above all, the idea of perfection as a *harmonious* expansion of human nature is at variance with our want of flexibility, with our inaptitude for seeing more than one side of a thing, with our intense energetic absorption in the particular pursuit we happen to be following. So culture has a rough task to achieve in this country. Its preachers have, and are likely long to have, a hard time of it, and they will much oftener be regarded, for a great while to come, as elegant or spurious Jeremiahs than as friends and benefactors. That, however, will not prevent their doing in the end good service if they persevere. And, meanwhile, the mode of action they have to pursue, and the sort of habits they must fight against, ought to be made quite clear for every one to see, who may be willing to look at the matter attentively and dispassionately.

Faith in machinery is, I said, our besetting danger; often in machinery most absurdly disproportioned to the end which this machinery, if it is to do any good at all, is to serve; but always in machinery, as if it had a value in and for itself. What is freedom but machinery? what is population but machinery? what is coal but machinery? what are railroads but machinery? what is wealth but machinery? what are, even, religious organisations but machinery? Now almost every voice in England is accustomed to speak of these things as if they were precious ends in themselves, and therefore had some of the characters of perfection indisputably joined to them. I have before now noticed Mr. Roebuck's stock argument for proving the greatness and happiness of England as she is, and for quite stopping the mouths of all gainsayers. Mr. Roebuck is never weary of reiterating this argument of his, so I do not know why I should be weary of noticing it. 'May not every man in England say what he likes?'—Mr. Roebuck perpetually asks; and that, he thinks, is quite sufficient, and when every man may say what he likes, our aspirations ought to be satisfied. But the aspirations of culture, which is the study of perfection, are not satisfied, unless what men say, when they may say what they like, is worth saying,—has good in it, and more good than bad. In the same way the *Times*, replying to some foreign strictures on the dress, looks, and behaviour of the English abroad, urges that the English ideal is that every one should be free to do and to look just as he likes. But culture indefatigably tries, not to make what each raw person may like the rule by which he fashions himself; but to draw ever nearer to a sense of what is indeed beautiful, graceful, and becoming, and to get the raw person to like that.

And in the same way with respect to railroads and coal. Every one must have observed the strange language current during the late discussions as to the possible failure of our supplies of coal. Our coal, thousands of people were saying, is the real basis of our national greatness; if our coal runs short, there is an end of the greatness of England. But what *is* greatness?—culture makes us ask. Greatness is a spiritual condition worthy to excite love, interest, and admiration; and the outward proof of possessing greatness is that we excite love, interest, and admiration. If England were swallowed up by the sea to-morrow, which of the two, a hundred years hence, would most excite the love, interest, and admiration of mankind, —would most, therefore, show the evidences of having possessed greatness,—the England of the last twenty years, or the England of Elizabeth, of a time of splendid spiritual effort, but when our coal, and our industrial operations depending on coal, were very little developed? Well, then, what an unsound habit of mind it must be which makes us talk of things like coal or iron as constituting the greatness of England, and how salutary a friend is culture, bent on seeing things as they are, and thus dissipating delusions of this kind and fixing standards of perfection that are real!

Wealth, again, that end to which our prodigious works for material advantage are directed, —the commonest of commonplaces tells us how men are always apt to regard wealth as a precious end in itself; and certainly they have never been so apt thus to regard it as they are in England at the present time. Never did people believe anything more firmly than nine Englishmen out of ten at the present day believe that our greatness and welfare are proved by our being so very rich. Now, the use of culture is that it helps us, by means of its spiritual standard of perfection, to regard wealth as but machinery, and not only to say as a matter of words that we regard wealth as but machinery, but really to perceive and feel that it is so. If it were not for this purging effect wrought upon our minds by culture, the whole world, the future as well as the present, would inevitably belong to the Philistines. The people who believe most that our greatness and welfare are proved by our being very rich, and who most give their lives and thoughts to becoming rich, are just the very people whom we call Philistines. Culture says: 'Consider these people, then, their way of life, their habits, their manners, the very tones of their voice; look at them attentively; observe the literature they read, the things which give them pleasure, the words which come forth out of their mouths, the thoughts which make the furniture of their minds: would any amount of wealth be worth having with the condition that one was to become just like these people by having it?' And thus culture begets a dissatisfaction which is of the highest possible value in stemming the common tide of men's thoughts in a wealthy and industrial community, and which saves the future, as one may hope, from being vulgarised, even if it cannot save the present.

Population, again, and bodily health and vigour, are things which are nowhere treated in such an unintelligent, misleading, exaggerated way as in England. Both are really machinery; yet how many people all around us do we see rest in them and fail to look beyond them! Why, one has heard people, fresh from reading certain articles of the *Times* on the Registrar-General's returns of marriages and births in this country, who would talk of our large English families in quite a solemn strain, as if they had something in itself beautiful, elevating, and meritorious in them; as if the British Philistine would have only to present himself before the Great Judge with his twelve children, in order to be received among the sheep as a matter of right!

But bodily health and vigour, it may be said, are not to be classed with wealth and population as mere machinery; they have a more real and essential value. True; but only as they are more intimately connected with a perfect spiritual condition than wealth or population are. The moment we disjoin them from the idea of a perfect spiritual condition, and pursue them, as we do pursue them, for their own sake and as ends in themselves, our worship of them becomes as mere worship of machinery, as our worship of wealth or population, and as unintelligent and vulgarising a worship as that is. Every one with anything like an adequate idea of human perfection has distinctly marked this subordination to higher and spiritual ends of the cultivation of bodily vigour and activity. 'Bodily exercise profiteth little; but godliness is profitable unto all things,' says the author of the Epistle to Timothy. And the utilitarian Franklin says just as explicitly:—'Eat and drink such an exact quantity as suits the constitution of thy body, *in reference to the services of the mind.*' But the point of view of culture, keeping the mark of human perfection simply and broadly in view, and not assigning to this perfection, as religion or utilitarianism assigns to it, a special and limited character, this point of view, I say, of culture is best given by these words of Epictetus:—'It is a sign of ἀφυΐα,' says he,—that is, of a nature not finely tempered,—'to give yourselves up to things which relate to the body; to make, for instance, a great fuss about exercise, a great fuss about eating, a great fuss about drinking, a great fuss about walking, a great fuss about riding. All these things ought to be done merely by the way: the formation of the spirit and character must be our real concern.' This is admirable; and, indeed, the Greek word εὐφυΐα, a finely tempered nature, gives exactly the notion of perfection as culture brings us to conceive it: a harmonious perfection, a perfection in which the characters of beauty and intelligence are both present, which unites 'the two noblest of things,'—as Swift, who of one of the two, at any rate, had himself all too little, most happily calls them in his *Battle of the Books*,—'the two noblest of things, *sweetness and light*.' The εὐφυής is the man who tends towards sweetness and light; the ἀφυής, on the other hand, is our Philistine. The immense spiritual significance of the Greeks is due to their having been inspired with this central and happy idea of the essential character of human perfection; and Mr. Bright's misconception of culture, as a smattering of Greek and Latin, comes itself, after all, from this wonderful significance of the Greeks having affected the very machinery of our education, and is in itself a kind of homage to it.

In thus making sweetness and light to be characters of perfection, culture is of like spirit with poetry, follows one law with poetry. Far more than on our freedom, our population, and our industrialism, many amongst us rely upon our religious organisations to save us. I have called religion a yet more important manifestation of human nature than poetry, because it has worked on a broader scale for perfection, and with greater masses of men. But the idea of beauty and of a human nature perfect on all its sides, which is the dominant idea of poetry, is a true and invaluable idea, though it has not yet had the success that the idea of conquering the obvious faults of our animality, and of a human nature perfect on the moral side,—which is the dominant idea of religion,—has been enabled to have ; and it is destined, adding to itself the religious idea of a devout energy, to transform and govern the other.

The best art and poetry of the Greeks, in which religion and poetry are one, in which the idea of beauty and of a human nature perfect on all sides adds to itself a religious and devout energy, and works in the strength of that, is on this account of such surpassing interest and instructiveness for us, though it was,—as, having regard to the human race in general, and, indeed, having regard to the Greeks themselves, we must own,—a premature attempt, an attempt which for success needed the moral and religious fibre in humanity to be more braced and developed than it had yet been. But Greece did not err in having the idea of beauty, harmony, and complete human perfection, so present and paramount. It is impossible to have this idea too present and paramount ; only, the moral fibre must be braced too. And we, because we have braced the moral fibre, are not on that account in the right way, if at the same time the idea of beauty, harmony, and complete human perfection, is wanting or misapprehended amongst us ; and evidently it *is* wanting or misapprehended at present. And when we rely as we do on our religious organisations, which in themselves do not and cannot give us this idea, and think we have done enough if we make them spread and prevail, then, I say, we fall into our common fault of overvaluing machinery.

Nothing is more common than for people to confound the inward peace and satisfaction which follows the subduing of the obvious faults of our animality with what I may call absolute inward peace and satisfaction,—the peace and satisfaction which are reached as we draw near to complete spiritual perfection, and not merely to moral perfection, or rather to relative moral perfection. No people in the world have done more and struggled more to attain this relative moral perfection than our English race has. For no people in the world has the command to *resist the devil*, to *overcome the wicked one*, in the nearest and most obvious sense of those words, had such a pressing force and reality. And we have had our reward, not only in the great worldly prosperity which our obedience to this command has brought us, but also, and far more, in great inward peace and satisfaction. But to me few things are more pathetic than to see people, on the strength of the inward peace and satisfaction which their rudimentary efforts towards perfection have brought them, employ, concerning their incomplete perfection and the religious organisations within which they have found it, language which properly applies only to complete perfection, and is a far-off echo of the human soul's prophecy of it. Religion itself, I need hardly say, supplies them in abundance with this grand language. And very freely do they use it; yet it is really the severest possible criticism of such an incomplete perfection as alone we have yet reached through our religious organisations.

The impulse of the English race towards moral development and self-conquest has nowhere so powerfully manifested itself as in Puritanism. Nowhere has Puritanism found so adequate an expression as in the religious organisation of the Independents. The modern Independents have a newspaper, the *Nonconformist*, written with great sincerity and ability. The motto, the standard, the profession of faith which this organ of theirs carries aloft, is: 'The Dissidence of Dissent and the Protestantism of the Protestant religion.' There is sweetness and light, and an ideal of complete harmonious human perfection! One need not go to culture and poetry to find language to judge it. Religion, with its instinct for perfection, supplies language to judge it, language, too, which is in our mouths every day. 'Finally, be of one mind, united in feeling,' says St. Peter. There is an ideal which judges the Puritan ideal: 'The Dissidence of Dissent and the Protestantism of the Protestant religion!' And religious organisations like this are what people believe in, rest in, would give their lives for! Such, I say, is the wonderful virtue of even the beginnings of perfection, of having conquered even the plain faults of our animality, that the religious organisation which has helped us to do it can seem to us something precious, salutary, and to be propagated, even when it wears such a brand of imperfection on its forehead as this. And men have got such a habit of giving to the language of religion a special application, of making it a mere jargon, that for the condemnation which religion itself passes on the shortcomings of their religious organisations they have no ear; they are sure to cheat themselves and to explain this condemnation away. They can only be reached by the criticism which culture, like poetry, speaking a language not to be sophisticated, and resolutely testing these organisations by the ideal of a human perfection complete on all sides, applies to them.

But men of culture and poetry, it will be said, are again and again failing, and failing conspicuously, in the necessary first stage to a harmonious perfection, in the subduing of the great obvious faults of our animality, which it is the glory of these religious organisations to have helped us to subdue. True, they do often so fail. They have often been without the virtues as well as the faults of the Puritan; it has been one of their dangers that they so felt the Puritan's faults that they too much neglected the practice of his virtues. I will not, however, exculpate them at the Puritan's expense. They have often failed in morality, and morality is indispensable. And they have been punished for their failure, as the Puritan has been rewarded for his performance. They have been punished wherein they erred; but their ideal of beauty, of sweetness and light, and a human nature complete on all its sides, remains the true ideal of perfection still; just as the Puritan's ideal of perfection remains narrow and inadequate, although for what he did well he has been richly rewarded. Notwithstanding the mighty results of the Pilgrim Fathers' voyage, they and their standard of perfection are rightly judged when we figure to ourselves Shakspeare or Virgil,—souls in whom sweetness and light, and all that in human nature is most humane, were eminent,—accompanying them on their voyage, and think what intolerable company Shakspeare and Virgil would have found them! In the same way let us judge the religious organisations which we see all around us. Do not let us deny the good and the happiness which they have accomplished; but do not let us fail to see clearly that their idea of human perfection is narrow and inadequate, and that the Dissidence of Dissent and the Protestantism of the Protestant religion will never bring humanity to its true goal. As I said with regard to wealth: Let us look at the life of those who live in and for it,—so I say with regard to the religious organisations. Look at the life imaged in such a newspaper as the

Nonconformist,—a life of jealousy of the Establishment, disputes, tea-meetings, openings of chapels, sermons; and then think of it as an ideal of a human life completing itself on all sides, and aspiring with all its organs after sweetness, light, and perfection!

Another newspaper, representing, like the *Nonconformist*, one of the religious organisations of this country, was a short time ago giving an account of the crowd at Epsom on the Derby day, and of all the vice and hideousness which was to be seen in that crowd; and then the writer turned suddenly round upon Professor Huxley, and asked him how he proposed to cure all this vice and hideousness without religion. I confess I felt disposed to ask the asker this question: and how do you propose to cure it with such a religion as yours? How is the ideal of a life so unlovely, so unattractive, so incomplete, so narrow, so far removed from a true and satisfying ideal of human perfection, as is the life of your religious organisation as you yourself reflect it, to conquer and transform all this vice and hideousness? Indeed, the strongest plea for the study of perfection as pursued by culture, the clearest proof of the actual inadequacy of the idea of perfection held by the religious organisations,—expressing, as I have said, the most widespread effort which the human race has yet made after perfection,—is to be found in the state of our life and society with these in possession of it, and having been in possession of it I know not how many hundred years. We are all of us included in some religious organisation or other; we all call ourselves, in the sublime and aspiring language of religion which I have before noticed, *children of God*. Children of God;—it is an immense pretension!—and how are we to justify it? By the works which we do, and the words which we speak. And the work which we collective children of God do, our grand centre of life, our *city* which we have builded for us to dwell in, is London! London, with its unutterable external hideousness, and with its internal canker of *publice egestas*, *privatim opulentia*,—to use the words which Sallust puts into Cato's mouth about Rome,—unequalled in the world! The word, again, which we children of God speak, the voice which most hits our collective thought, the newspaper with the largest circulation in England, nay, with the largest circulation in the whole world, is the *Daily Telegraph!* I say that when our religious organisations,—which I admit to express the most considerable effort after perfection that our race has yet made,—land us in no better result than this, it is high time to examine carefully their idea of perfection, to see whether it does not leave out of account sides and forces of human nature which we might turn to great use; whether it would not be more operative if it were more complete.

And I say that the English reliance on our religious organisations and on their ideas of human perfection just as they stand, is like our reliance on freedom, on muscular Christianity, on population, on coal, on wealth,—mere belief in machinery, and unfruitful; and that it is wholesomely counteracted by culture, bent on seeing things as they are, and on drawing the human race onwards to a more complete, a harmonious perfection.

Culture, however, shows its single-minded love of perfection, its desire simply to make reason and the will of God prevail, its freedom from fanaticism, by its attitude towards all this machinery, even while it insists that it *is* machinery. Fanatics, seeing the mischief men do themselves by their blind belief in some machinery or other,—whether it is wealth and industrialism, or whether it is the cultivation of bodily strength and activity, or whether it is a political organisation,—or whether it is a religious organisation,—oppose with might and main the tendency to this or that political and religious organisation, or to games and athletic exercises, or to wealth and industrialism, and try violently to stop it. But the flexibility which sweetness and light give, and which is one of the rewards of culture pursued in good faith, enables a man to see that a tendency may be necessary, and even, as a preparation for something in the future, salutary, and yet that the generations or individuals who obey this tendency are sacrificed to it, that they fall short of the hope of perfection by following it ; and that its mischiefs are to be criticised, lest it should take too firm a hold and last after it has served its purpose.

Mr. Gladstone well pointed out, in a speech at Paris,—and others have pointed out the same thing,—how necessary is the present great movement towards wealth and industrialism, in order to lay broad foundations of material well-being for the society of the future. The worst of these justifications is, that they are generally addressed to the very people engaged, body and soul, in the movement in question ; at all events, that they are always seized with the greatest avidity by these people, and taken by them as quite justifying their life ; and that thus they tend to harden them in their sins. Now, culture admits the necessity of the movement towards fortune-making and exaggerated industrialism, readily allows that the future may derive benefit from it ; but insists, at the same time, that the passing generations of industrialists,—forming, for the most part, the stout main body of Philistinism,—are sacrificed to it. In the same way, the result of all the games and sports which occupy the passing generation of boys and young men may be the establishment of a better and sounder physical type for the future to work with. Culture does not set itself against the games and sports ; it congratulates the future, and hopes it will make a good use of its improved physical basis; but it points out that our passing generation of boys and young men is, meantime, sacrificed. Puritanism was perhaps necessary to develop the moral fibre of the English race, Nonconformity to break the yoke of ecclesiastical domination over men's minds and to prepare the way for freedom of thought in the distant future; still, culture points out that the harmonious perfection of generations of Puritans and Nonconformists have been, in consequence, sacrificed. Freedom of speech may be necessary for the society of the future, but the young lions of the *Daily Telegraph* in the meanwhile are sacrificed. A voice for every man in his country's government may be necessary for the society of the future, but meanwhile Mr. Beales and Mr. Bradlaugh are sacrificed.

Oxford, the Oxford of the past, has many faults; and she has heavily paid for them in defeat, in isolation, in want of hold upon the modern world. Yet we in Oxford, brought up amidst the beauty and sweetness of that beautiful place, have not failed to seize one truth,—the truth that beauty and sweetness are essential characters of a complete human perfection. When I insist on this, I am all in the faith and tradition of Oxford. I say boldly that this our sentiment for beauty and sweetness, our sentiment against hideousness and rawness, has been at the bottom of our attachment to so many beaten causes, of our opposition to so many triumphant movements. And the sentiment is true, and has never been wholly defeated, and has shown its power even in its defeat. We have not won our political battles, we have not carried our main points, we have not stopped our adversaries' advance, we have not marched victoriously with the modern world; but we have told silently upon the mind of the country, we have prepared currents of feeling which sap our adversaries' position when it seems gained, we have kept up our own communications with the future. Look at the course of the great movement which shook Oxford to its centre some thirty years ago! It was directed, as any one who reads Dr. Newman's *Apology* may see, against what in one word may be called 'Liberalism.' Liberalism prevailed; it was the appointed force to do the work of the hour; it was necessary, it was inevitable that it should prevail. The Oxford movement was broken, it failed; our wrecks are scattered on every shore:—

Quae regio in terris nostri non plena laboris?

But what was it, this liberalism, as Dr. Newman saw it, and as it really broke the Oxford movement? It was the great middle-class liberalism, which had for the cardinal points of its belief the Reform Bill of 1832, and local self-government, in politics; in the social sphere, free-trade, unrestricted competition, and the making of large industrial fortunes ; in the religious sphere, the Dissidence of Dissent and the Protestantism of the Protestant religion. I do not say that other and more intelligent forces than this were not opposed to the Oxford movement : but this was the force which really beat it ; this was the force which Dr. Newman felt himself fighting with ; this was the force which till only the other day seemed to be the paramount force in this country, and to be in possession of the future ; this was the force whose achievements fill Mr. Lowe with such inexpressible admiration, and whose rule he was so horror-struck to see threatened. And where is this great force of Philistinism now? It is thrust into the second rank, it is become a power of yesterday, it has lost the future. A new power has suddenly appeared, a power which it is impossible yet to judge fully, but which is certainly a wholly different force from middle-class liberalism ; different in its cardinal points of belief, different in its tendencies in every sphere. It loves and admires neither the legislation of middle-class Parliaments, nor the local self-government of middle-class vestries, nor the unrestricted competition of middle-class industrialists, nor the dissidence of middle-class Dissent and the Protestantism of middle-class Protestant religion. I am not now praising this new force, or saying that its own ideals are better ; all I say is, that they are wholly different. And who will estimate how much the currents of feeling created by Dr. Newman's movements, the keen desire for beauty and sweetness which it nourished, the deep aversion it manifested to the hardness and vulgarity of middle-class liberalism, the strong light it turned on the hideous and grotesque illusions of middle-class Protestantism,—who will estimate how much all these contributed to swell the tide of secret dissatisfaction which has mined the ground under self-confident liberalism of the last thirty years, and has prepared the way for its sudden collapse and supersession? It is in this manner that the sentiment of Oxford for beauty and sweetness conquers, and in this manner long may it continue to conquer!

In this manner it works to the same end as culture, and there is plenty of work for it yet to do. I have said that the new and more democratic force which is now superseding our old middle-class liberalism cannot yet be rightly judged. It has its main tendencies still to form. We hear promises of its giving us administrative reform, law reform, reform of education, and I know not what; but those promises come rather from its advocates, wishing to make a good plea for it and to justify it for superseding middle-class liberalism, than from clear tendencies which it has itself yet developed. But meanwhile it has plenty of well-intentioned friends against whom culture may with advantage continue to uphold steadily its ideal of human perfection;

that this is *an inward spiritual activity, having for its characters increased sweetness, increased light, increased life, increased sympathy*. Mr. Bright, who has a foot in both worlds, the world of middle-class liberalism and the world of democracy, but who brings most of his ideas from the world of middle-class liberalism in which he was bred, always inclines to inculcate that faith in machinery to which, as we have seen, Englishmen are so prone, and which has been the bane of middle-class liberalism. He complains with a sorrowful indignation of people who 'appear to have no proper estimate of the value of the franchise'; he leads his disciples to believe,—what the Englishman is always too ready to believe,—that the having a vote, like the having a large family, or a large business, or large muscles, has in itself some edifying and perfecting effect upon human nature. Or else he cries out to the democracy,—'the men,' as he calls them, 'upon whose shoulders the greatness of England rests,'—he cries out to them: 'See what you have done! I look over this country and see the cities you have built, the railroads you have made, the manufactures you have produced, the cargoes which freight the ships of the greatest mercantile navy the world has ever seen! I see that you have converted by your labours what was once a wilderness, these islands, into a fruitful garden; I know that you have created this wealth, and are a nation whose name is a word of power throughout all the world.' Why, this is just the very style of laudation with which Mr. Roebuck or Mr. Lowe debauches the minds of the middle classes, and makes such Philistines of them. It is the same fashion of teaching a man to value himself not on what he *is*, not on his progress in sweetness and light, but on the number of the railroads he has constructed, or the bigness of the tabernacle he has built. Only the middle classes are told they have done it all with their energy, self-reliance, and capital, and the democracy are told they have done it all with their hands and sinews. But teaching the democracy to put its trust in achievements of this kind is merely training them to be Philistines to take the place of the Philistines whom they are superseding ; and they too, like the middle class, will be encouraged to sit down at the banquet of the future without having on a wedding garment, and nothing excellent can then come from them. Those who know their besetting faults, those who have watched them and listened to them, or those who will read the instructive account recently given of them by one of themselves, the *Journeyman Engineer*, will agree that the idea which culture sets before us of perfection,—an increased spiritual activity, having for its characters increased sweetness, increased light, increased life, increased sympathy,—is an idea which the new democracy needs far more than the idea of the blessedness of the franchise, or the wonderfulness of its own industrial performances.

Other well-meaning friends of this new power are for leading it, not in the old ruts of middle-class Philistinism, but in ways which are naturally alluring to the feet of democracy, though in this country they are novel and untried ways. I may call them the ways of Jacobinism. Violent indignation with the past, abstract systems of renovation applied wholesale, a new doctrine drawn up in black and white for elaborating down to the very smallest details a rational society for the future,—these are the ways of Jacobinism. Mr. Frederic Harrison and other disciples of Comte,—one of them, Mr. Congreve, is an old friend of mine, and I am glad to have an opportunity of publicly expressing my respect for his talents and character,—are among the friends of democracy who are for leading it in paths of this kind. Mr. Frederic Harrison is very hostile to culture, and from a natural enough motive; for culture is the eternal opponent of the two things which are the signal marks of Jacobinism,—its fierceness, and its addiction to an abstract system. Culture is always assigning to system-makers and systems a smaller share in the bent of human destiny than their friends like. A current in people's minds sets towards new ideas; people are dissatisfied with their old narrow stock of Philistine ideas, Anglo-Saxon ideas, or any other; and some man, some

Bentham or Comte, who has the real merit of having early and strongly felt and helped the new current, but who brings plenty of narrowness and mistakes of his own into his feeling and help of it, is credited with being the author of the whole current, the fit person to be entrusted with its regulation and to guide the human race.

The excellent German historian of the mythology of Rome, Preller, relating the introduction at Rome under the Tarquins of the worship of Apollo, the god of light, healing, and reconciliation, will have us observe that it was not so much the Tarquins who brought to Rome the new worship of Apollo, as a current in the mind of the Roman people which set powerfully at that time towards a new worship of this kind, and away from the old run of Latin and Sabine religious ideas. In a similar way, culture directs our attention to the natural current there is in human affairs, and to its continual working, and will not let us rivet our faith upon any one man and his doings. It makes us see not only his good side, but also how much in him was of necessity limited and transient; nay, it even feels a pleasure, a sense of an increased freedom and of an ampler future, in so doing.

I remember, when I was under the influence of a mind to which I feel the greatest obligations, the mind of a man who was the very incarnation of sanity and clear sense, a man the most considerable, it seems to me, whom America has yet produced,—Benjamin Franklin,—I remember the relief with which, after long feeling the sway of Franklin's imperturbable common-sense, I came upon a project of his for a new version of the Book of Job, to replace the old version, the style of which, says Franklin, has become obsolete, and thence less agreeable. 'I give,' he continues, 'a few verses, which may serve as a sample of the kind of version I would recommend.' We all recollect the famous verse in our translation: 'Then Satan answered the Lord and said: "Doth Job fear God for nought?"' Franklin makes this: 'Does your Majesty imagine that Job's good conduct is the effect of mere personal attachment and affection?' I well remember how, when first I read that, I drew a deep breath of relief, and said to myself: 'After all, there is a stretch of humanity beyond Franklin's victorious good sense!' So, after hearing Bentham cried loudly up as the renovator of modern society, and Bentham's mind and ideas proposed as the rulers of our future, I open the *Deontology*. There I read: 'While Xenophon was writing his history and Euclid teaching geometry, Socrates and Plato were talking nonsense under pretence of talking wisdom and morality. This morality of theirs consisted in words; this wisdom of theirs was the denial of matters known to every man's experience.' From the moment of reading that, I am delivered from the bondage of Bentham! the fanaticism of his adherents can touch me no longer. I feel the inadequacy of his mind and ideas for supplying the rule of human society, for perfection.

Culture tends always thus to deal with the men of a system, of disciples, of a school; with men like Comte, or the late Mr. Buckle, or Mr. Mill. However much it may find to admire in these personages, or in some of them, it nevertheless remembers the text: 'Be not ye called Rabbi!' and it soon passes on from any Rabbi. But Jacobinism loves a Rabbi; it does not want to pass on from its Rabbi in pursuit of a future and still unreached perfection; it wants its Rabbi and his ideas to stand for perfection, that they may with the more authority recast the world; and for Jacobinism, therefore, culture,—eternally passing onwards and seeking,—is an impertinence and an offence. But culture, just because it resists this tendency of Jacobinism to impose on us a man with limitations and errors of his own along with the true ideas of which he is the organ, really does the world and Jacobinism itself a service.

So, too, Jacobinism, in its fierce hatred of the past and of those whom it makes liable for the sins of the past, cannot away with the inexhaustible indulgence proper to culture, the consideration of circumstances, the severe judgment of actions joined to the merciful judgment of persons. 'The man of culture is in politics,' cries Mr. Frederic Harrison, 'one of the poorest mortals alive!' Mr. Frederic Harrison wants to be doing business, and he complains that the man of culture stops him with a 'turn for small fault-finding, love of selfish ease, and indecision in action.' Of what use is culture, he asks, except for 'a critic of new books or a professor of *belles-lettres?'* Why, it is of use because, in presence of the fierce exasperation which breathes, or rather, I may say, hisses through the whole production in which Mr. Frederic Harrison asks that question, it reminds us that the perfection of human nature is sweetness and light. It is of use because, like religion,—that other effort after perfection,—it testifies that, where bitter envying and strife are, there is confusion and every evil work.

The pursuit of perfection, then, is the pursuit of sweetness and light. He who works for sweetness and light, works to make reason and the will of God prevail. He who works for machinery, he who works for hatred, works only for confusion. Culture looks beyond machinery, culture hates hatred; culture has one great passion, the passion for sweetness and light. It has one even yet greater!—the passion for making them *prevail.* It is not satisfied till we *all* come to a perfect man; it knows that the sweetness and light of the few must be imperfect until the raw and unkindled masses of humanity are touched with sweetness and light. If I have not shrunk from saying that we must work for sweetness and light, so neither have I shrunk from saying that we must have a broad basis, must have sweetness and light for as many as possible. Again and again I have insisted how those are the happy moments of humanity, how those are the marking epochs of a people's life, how those are the flowering times for literature and art and all the creative power of genius, when there is a *national* glow of life and thought, when the whole of society is in the fullest measure permeated by thought, sensible to beauty, intelligent and alive. Only it must be *real* thought and *real* beauty ; *real* sweetness and *real* light. Plenty of people will try to give the masses, as they call them, an intellectual food prepared and adapted in the way they think proper for the actual condition of the masses. The ordinary popular literature is an example of this way of working on the masses. Plenty of people will try to indoctrinate the masses with the set of ideas and judgments constituting the creed of their own profession or party. Our religious and political organisations give an example of this way of working on the masses. I condemn neither way ; but culture works differently. It does not try to teach down to the level of inferior classes ; it does not try to win them for this or that sect of its own, with ready-made judgments and watchwords. It seeks to do away with classes ; to make the best that has been thought and known in the world current everywhere; to make all men live in an atmosphere of sweetness and light, where they may use ideas, as it uses them itself, freely,—nourished, and not bound by them.

This is the *social idea;* and the men of culture are the true apostles of equality. The great men of culture are those who have had a passion for diffusing, for making prevail, for carrying from one end of society to the other, the best knowledge, the best ideas of their time; who have laboured to divest knowledge of all that was harsh, uncouth, difficult, abstract, professional, exclusive; to humanise it, to make it efficient outside the clique of the cultivated and learned, yet still remaining the *best* knowledge and thought of the time, and a true source, therefore, of sweetness and light. Such a man was Abelard in the Middle Ages, in spite of all his imperfections; and thence the boundless emotion and enthusiasm which Abelard excited. Such were Lessing and Herder in Germany, at the end of the last century; and their services to Germany were in this way inestimably precious. Generations will pass, and literary monuments will accumulate, and works far more perfect than the works of Lessing and Herder will be produced in Germany; and yet the names of these two men will fill a German with a reverence and enthusiasm such as the names of the most gifted masters will hardly awaken. And why? Because they *humanised* knowledge; because they broadened the basis of life and intelligence; because they worked powerfully to diffuse sweetness and light, to make reason and the will of God prevail. With Saint Augustine they said: 'Let us not leave thee alone to make in the secret of thy knowledge, as thou didst before the creation of the firmament, the division of light from darkness; let the children of thy spirit, placed in their firmament, make their light shine upon the earth, mark the division of night and day, and announce the revolution of the times; for the old order is passed, and the new arises; the night is spent, the day is come forth; and thou shalt crown the year with thy blessing, when thou shalt send forth labourers into thy harvest sown by other hands than theirs; when thou shalt send forth new labourers to new seed-times, whereof the harvest shall be not yet.'

CHAPTER II

DOING AS ONE LIKES

I HAVE been trying to show that culture is, or ought to be, the study and pursuit of perfection; and that of perfection as pursued by culture, beauty and intelligence, or, in other words, sweetness and light, are the main characters. But hitherto I have been insisting chiefly on beauty, or sweetness, as a character of perfection. To complete rightly my design, it evidently remains to speak also of intelligence, or light, as a character of perfection.

First, however, I ought perhaps to notice that, both here and on the other side of the Atlantic, all sorts of objections are raised against the 'religion of culture,' as the objectors mockingly call it, which I am supposed to be promulgating. It is said to be a religion proposing parmaceti, or some scented salve or other, as a cure for human miseries; a religion breathing a spirit of cultivated inaction, making its believer refuse to lend a hand at uprooting the definite evils on all sides of us, and filling him with antipathy against the reforms and reformers which try to extirpate them. In general, it is summed up as being not practical, or,—as some critics familiarly put it,—all moonshine. That Alcibiades, the editor of the *Morning Star*, taunts me, as its promulgator, with living out of the world and knowing nothing of life and men. That great austere toiler, the editor of the *Daily Telegraph*, upbraids me,—but kindly, and more in sorrow than in anger,—for trifling with æsthetics and poetical fancies, while he himself, in that arsenal of his in Fleet Street, is bearing the burden and heat of the day. An intelligent American newspaper, the *Nation*, says that it is very easy to sit in one's study and find fault with the course of modern society, but the thing is to propose practical improvements for it. While, finally, Mr. Frederic Harrison, in a very good-tempered and witty satire, which makes me quite understand his having apparently achieved such a conquest of my young Prussian friend, Arminius, at last gets moved to an almost stern moral impatience, to behold, as he says, 'Death, sin, cruelty stalk among us, filling their maws with innocence and youth,' and me, in the midst of the general tribulation, handing out my pouncet-box.

It is impossible that all these remonstrances and reproofs should not affect me, and I shall try my very best, in completing my design and in speaking of light as one of the characters of perfection, and of culture as giving us light, to profit by the objections I have heard and read, and to drive at practice as much as I can, by showing the communications and passages into practical life from the doctrine which I am inculcating.

It is said that a man with my theories of sweetness and light is full of antipathy against the rougher or coarser movements going on around him, that he will not lend a hand to the humble operation of uprooting evil by their means, and that therefore the believers in action grow impatient with him. But what if rough and coarse action, ill-calculated action, action with insufficient light, is, and has for a long time been, our bane? What if our urgent want now is, not to act at any price, but rather to lay in a stock of light for our difficulties? In that case, to refuse to lend a hand to the rougher and coarser movements going on round us, to make the primary need, both for oneself and others, to consist in enlightening ourselves and qualifying ourselves to act less at random, is surely the best and in real truth the most practical line our endeavours can take. So that if I can show what my opponents call rough or coarse action, but what I would rather call random and ill-regulated action,—action with insufficient light, action pursued because we like to be doing something and doing it as we please, and do not like the trouble of thinking and the severe constraint of any kind of rule,—if I can show this to be, at the present moment, a practical mischief and dangerous to us, then I have found a practical use for light in correcting this state of things, and have only to exemplify how, in cases which fall under everybody's observation, it may deal with it.

When I began to speak of culture, I insisted on our bondage to machinery, on our proneness to value machinery as an end in itself, without looking beyond it to the end for which alone, in truth, it is valuable. Freedom, I said, was one of those things which we thus worshipped in itself, without enough regarding the ends for which freedom is to be desired. In our common notions and talk about freedom, we eminently show our idolatry of machinery. Our prevalent notion is,—and I quoted a number of instances to prove it,—that it is a most happy and important thing for a man merely to be able to do as he likes. On what he is to do when he is thus free to do as he likes, we do not lay so much stress. Our familiar praise of the British Constitution under which we live, is that it is a system of checks,—a system which stops and paralyses any power in interfering with the free action of individuals. To this effect Mr. Bright, who loves to walk in the old ways of the Constitution, said forcibly in one of his great speeches, what many other people are every day saying less forcibly, that the central idea of English life and politics is *the assertion of personal liberty*. Evidently this is so; but evidently, also, as feudalism, which with its ideas and habits of subordination was for many centuries silently behind the British Constitution, dies out, and we are left with nothing but our system of checks, and our notion of its being the great right and happiness of an Englishman to do as far as possible what he likes, we are in danger of drifting towards anarchy. We have not the notion, so familiar on the Continent and to antiquity, of *the State*, — the nation in its collective and corporate character, entrusted with stringent powers for the general advantage, and controlling individual wills in the name of an interest wider than that of individuals. We say, what is very true, that this notion is often made instrumental to tyranny; we say that a State is in reality made up of the individuals who compose it, and that every individual is the best judge of his own interests. Our leading class is an aristocracy, and no aristocracy likes the notion of a State-authority greater than itself, with a stringent administrative machinery superseding the decorative inutilities of lord-lieutenancy, deputy-lieutenancy, and the *posse comitatus*, which are all in its own hands. Our middle class, the great representative of trade and Dissent, with its maxims of every man for himself in business, every man for himself in religion, dreads a powerful administration which might somehow interfere with it; and besides, it has its own decorative inutilities of vestrymanship and guardianship, which are to this class what lord-lieutenancy and the county magistracy are to the aristocratic class, and a stringent administration might either take these functions out of its hands, or prevent its exercising them in its own comfortable, independent manner, as at present.

Then as to our working class. This class, pressed constantly by the hard daily compulsion of material wants, is naturally the very centre and stronghold of our national idea, that it is man's ideal right and felicity to do as he likes. I think I have somewhere related how M. Michelet said to me of the people of France, that it was 'a nation of barbarians civilised by the conscription.' He meant that through their military service the idea of public duty and of discipline was brought to the mind of these masses, in other respects so raw and uncultivated. Our masses are quite as raw and uncultivated as the French; and so far from their having the idea of public duty and of discipline, superior to the individual's self-will, brought to their mind by a universal obligation of military service, such as that of the conscription,—so far from their having this, the very idea of a conscription is so at variance with our English notion of the prime right and blessedness of doing as one likes, that I remember the manager of the Clay Cross works in Derbyshire told me during the Crimean war, when our want of soldiers was much felt and some people were talking of a conscription, that sooner than submit to a conscription the population of that district would flee to the mines, and lead a sort of Robin Hood life under ground.

For a long time, as I have said, the strong feudal habits of subordination and deference continued to tell upon the working class. The modern spirit has now almost entirely dissolved those habits, and the anarchical tendency of our worship of freedom in and for itself, of our superstitious faith, as I say, in machinery, is becoming very manifest. More and more, because of this our blind faith in machinery, because of our want of light to enable us to look beyond machinery to the end for which machinery is valuable, this and that man, and this and that body of men, all over the country, are beginning to assert and put in practice an Englishman's right to do what he likes; his right to march where he likes, meet where he likes, enter where he likes, hoot as he likes, threaten as he likes, smash as he likes. All this, I say, tends to anarchy; and though a number of excellent people, and particularly my friends of the Liberal or progressive party, as they call themselves, are kind enough to reassure us by saying that these are trifles, that a few transient outbreaks of rowdyism signify nothing, that our system of liberty is one which itself cures all the evils which it works, that the educated and intelligent classes stand in overwhelming strength and majestic repose, ready, like our military force in riots, to act at a moment's notice,—yet one finds that one's Liberal friends generally say this because they have such faith in themselves and their nostrums, when they shall return, as the public welfare requires, to place and power. But this faith of theirs one cannot exactly share, when one has so long had them and their nostrums at work, and sees that they have not prevented our coming to our present embarrassed condition. And one finds, also, that the outbreaks of rowdyism tend to become less and less of trifles, to become more frequent rather than less frequent; and that meanwhile our educated and intelligent classes remain in their majestic repose, and somehow or other, whatever happens, their overwhelming strength, like our military force in riots, never does act.

How, indeed, *should* their overwhelming strength act, when the man who gives an inflammatory lecture, or breaks down the park railings, or invades a Secretary of State's office, is only following an Englishman's impulse to do as he likes; and our own conscience tells us that we ourselves have always regarded this impulse as something primary and sacred? Mr. Murphy lectures at Birmingham, and showers on the Catholic population of that town 'words,' says the Home Secretary, 'only fit to be addressed to thieves or murderers.' What then?

Mr. Murphy has his own reasons of several kinds. He suspects the Roman Catholic Church of designs upon Mrs. Murphy; and he says if mayors and magistrates do not care for their wives and daughters, he does. But, above all, he is doing as he likes; or, in worthier language, asserting his personal liberty. 'I will carry out my lectures if they walk over my body as a dead corpse; and I say to the Mayor of Birmingham that he is my servant while I am in Birmingham, and as my servant he must do his duty and protect me.' Touching and beautiful words, which find a sympathetic chord in every British bosom! The moment it is plainly put before us that a man is asserting his personal liberty, we are half disarmed; because we are believers in freedom, and not in some dream of a right reason to which the assertion of our freedom is to be subordinated. Accordingly, the Secretary of State had to say that although the lecturer's language was 'only fit to be addressed to thieves or murderers,' yet 'I do not think he is to be deprived, I do not think that anything I have said could justify the inference that he is to be deprived, of the right of protection in a place built by him for the purpose of these lectures; because the language was not language which afforded grounds for a criminal prosecution.' No, nor to be silenced by Mayor, or Home Secretary, or any administrative authority on earth, simply on their notion of what is discreet and reasonable! This is in perfect consonance with our public opinion, and with our national love for the assertion of personal liberty.

In quite another department of affairs, an experienced and distinguished Chancery Judge relates an incident which is just to the same effect as this of Mr. Murphy. A testator bequeathed £300 a year, to be for ever applied as a pension to some person who had been unsuccessful in literature, and whose duty should be to support and diffuse, by his writings, the testator's own views, as enforced in the testator's publications. The views were not worth a straw, and the bequest was appealed against in the Court of Chancery on the ground of its absurdity; but, being only absurd, it was upheld, and the so-called charity was established. Having, I say, at the bottom of our English hearts a very strong belief in freedom, and a very weak belief in right reason, we are soon silenced when a man pleads the prime right to do as he likes, because this is the prime right for ourselves too; and even if we attempt now and then to mumble something about reason, yet we have ourselves thought so little about this and so much about liberty, that we are in conscience forced, when our brother Philistine with whom we are meddling turns boldly round upon us and asks: *Have you any light?*—to shake our heads ruefully, and to let him go his own way after all.

There are many things to be said on behalf of this exclusive attention of ours to liberty, and of the relaxed habits of government which it has engendered. It is very easy to mistake or to exaggerate the sort of anarchy from which we are in danger through them. We are not in danger from Fenianism, fierce and turbulent as it may show itself; for against this our conscience is free enough to let us act resolutely and put forth our overwhelming strength the moment there is any real need for it. In the first place, it never was any part of our creed that the great right and blessedness of an Irishman, or, indeed, of anybody on earth except an Englishman, is to do as he likes; and we can have no scruple at all about abridging, if necessary, a non-Englishman's assertion of personal liberty. The British Constitution, its checks, and its prime virtues, are for Englishmen. We may extend them to others out of love and kindness; but we find no real divine law written on our hearts constraining us so to extend them. And then the difference between an Irish Fenian and an English rough is so immense, and the case, in dealing with the Fenian, so much more clear! He is so evidently desperate and dangerous, a man of a conquered race, a Papist, with centuries of ill-usage to inflame him against us, with an alien religion established in his country by us at his expense, with no admiration of our institutions, no love of our virtues, no talents for our business, no turn for our comfort! Show him our symbolical Truss Manufactory on the finest site in Europe, and tell him that British industrialism and individualism can bring a man to that, and he remains cold! Evidently, if we deal tenderly with a sentimentalist like this, it is out of pure philanthropy.

But with the Hyde Park rioter how different! He is our own flesh and blood; he is a Protestant; he is framed by nature to do as we do, hate what we hate, love what we love; he is capable of feeling the symbolical force of the Truss Manufactory; the question of questions, for him, is a wages question. That beautiful sentence Sir Daniel Gooch quoted to the Swindon workmen, and which I treasure as Mrs. Gooch's Golden Rule, or the Divine Injunction 'Be ye Perfect' done into British,—the sentence Sir Daniel Gooch's mother repeated to him every morning when he was a boy going to work:—'*Ever remember, my dear Dan, that you should look forward to being some day manager of that concern!*'—this truthful maxim is perfectly fitted to shine forth in the heart of the Hyde Park rough also, and to be his guiding-star through life. He has no visionary schemes of revolution and transformation, though of course he would like his class to rule, as the aristocratic class like their class to rule, and the middle class theirs. But meanwhile our social machine is a little out of order; there are a good many people in our paradisiacal centres of industrialism and individualism taking the bread out of one another's mouths. The rough has not yet quite found his groove and settled down to his work, and so he is just asserting his personal liberty a little, going where he likes, assembling where he likes, bawling as he likes, hustling as he likes. Just as the rest of us,—as the country squires in the aristocratic class, as the political dissenters in the middle class,—he has no idea of a *State*, of the nation in its collective and corporate character controlling, as government, the free swing of this or that one of its members in the name of the higher reason of all of them, his own as well as that of others. He sees the rich, the aristocratic class, in occupation of the executive government, and so if he is stopped from making Hyde Park a bear-garden or the streets impassable, he says he is being butchered by the aristocracy.

His apparition is somewhat embarrassing, because too many cooks spoil the broth; because, while the aristocratic and middle classes have long been doing as they like with great vigour, he has been too undeveloped and submissive hitherto to join in the game; and now, when he does come, he comes in immense numbers, and is rather raw and rough. But he does not break many laws, or not many at one time; and, as our laws were made for very different circumstances from our present (but always with an eye to Englishmen doing as they like), and as the clear letter of the law must be against our Englishman who does as he likes and not only the spirit of the law and public policy, and as Government must neither have any discretionary power nor act resolutely on its own interpretation of the law if any one disputes it, it is evident our laws give our playful giant, in doing as he likes, considerable advantage. Besides, even if he can be clearly proved to commit an illegality in doing as he likes, there is always the resource of not putting the law in force, or of abolishing it. So he has his way, and if he has his way he is soon satisfied for the time. However, he falls into the habit of taking it oftener and oftener, and at last begins to create by his operations a confusion of which mischievous people can take advantage, and which, at any rate, by troubling the common course of business throughout the country, tends to cause distress, and so to increase the sort of anarchy and social disintegration which had previously commenced. And thus that profound sense of settled order and security, without which a society like ours cannot live and grow at all, sometimes seems to be beginning to threaten us with taking its departure.

Now, if culture, which simply means trying to perfect oneself, and one's mind as part of oneself, brings us light, and if light shows us that there is nothing so very blessed in merely doing as one likes, that the worship of the mere freedom to do as one likes is worship of machinery, that the really blessed thing is to like what right reason ordains, and to follow her authority, then we have got a practical benefit out of culture. We have got a much wanted principle, a principle of authority, to counteract the tendency to anarchy which seems to be threatening us.

But how to organise this authority, or to what hands to entrust the wielding of it? How to get your *State*, summing up the right reason of the community, and giving effect to it, as circumstances may require, with vigour? And here I think I see my enemies waiting for me with a hungry joy in their eyes. But I shall elude them.

The *State*, the power most representing the right reason of the nation, and most worthy, therefore, of ruling,—of exercising, when circumstances require it, authority over us all,—is for Mr. Carlyle the aristocracy. For Mr. Lowe, it is the middle class with its incomparable Parliament. For the Reform League, it is the working class, the class with 'the brightest powers of sympathy and readiest powers of action.' Now culture, with its disinterested pursuit of perfection, culture, simply trying to see things as they are in order to seize on the best and to make it prevail, is surely well fitted to help us to judge rightly, by all the aids of observing, reading, and thinking, the qualifications and titles to our confidence of these three candidates for authority, and can thus render us a practical service of no mean value.

So when Mr. Carlyle, a man of genius to whom we have all at one time or other been indebted for refreshment and stimulus, says we should give rule to the aristocracy, mainly because of its dignity and politeness, surely culture is useful in reminding us, that in our idea of perfection the characters of beauty and intelligence are both of them present, and sweetness and light, the two noblest of things, are united. Allowing, therefore, with Mr. Carlyle, the aristocratic class to possess sweetness, culture insists on the necessity of light also, and shows us that aristocracies, being by the very nature of things inaccessible to ideas, unapt to see how the world is going, must be somewhat wanting in light, and must therefore be, at a moment when light is our great requisite, inadequate to our needs. Aristocracies, those children of the established fact, are for epochs of concentration. In epochs of expansion, epochs such as that in which we now live, epochs when always the warning voice is again heard : *Now is the judgment of this world*,—in such epochs aristocracies with their natural clinging to the established fact, their want of sense for the flux of things, for the inevitable transitoriness of all human institutions, are bewildered and helpless. Their serenity, their high spirit, their power of haughty resistance,—the great qualities of an aristocracy, and the secret of its distinguished manners and dignity,—these very qualities, in an epoch of expansion, turn against their possessors. Again and again I have said how the refinement of an aristocracy may be precious and educative to a raw nation as a kind of shadow of true refinement; how its serenity and dignified freedom from petty cares may serve as a useful foil to set off the vulgarity and hideousness of that type of life which a hard middle class tends to establish, and to help people to see this vulgarity and hideousness in their true colours. But the true grace and serenity is that of which Greece and Greek art suggest the admirable ideals of perfection,—a serenity which comes from having made order among ideas and harmonised them; whereas the serenity of aristocracies, at least the peculiar serenity of aristocracies of Teutonic origin, appears to come from their never having had any ideas to trouble them. And so, in a time of expansion like the present, a time for ideas, one gets perhaps, in regarding an aristocracy, even more than the idea of serenity, the idea of futility and sterility.

One has often wondered whether upon the whole earth there is anything so unintelligent, so unapt to perceive how the world is really going, as an ordinary young Englishman of our upper class. Ideas he has not, and neither has he that seriousness of our middle class which is, as I have often said, the great strength of this class, and may become its salvation. Why, a man may hear a young Dives of the aristocratic class, when the whim takes him to sing the praises of wealth and material comfort, sing them with a cynicism from which the conscience of the veriest Philistine of our industrial middle class would recoil in affright. And when, with the natural sympathy of aristocracies for firm dealing with the multitude, and his uneasiness at our feeble dealing with it at home, an unvarnished young Englishman of our aristocratic class applauds the absolute rulers on the Continent, he in general manages completely to miss the grounds of reason and intelligence which alone can give any colour of justification, any possibility of existence, to those rulers, and applauds them on grounds which it would make their own hair stand on end to listen to.

And all this time we are in an epoch of expansion; and the essence of an epoch of expansion is a movement of ideas, and the one salvation of an epoch of expansion is a harmony of ideas. The very principle of the authority which we are seeking as a defence against anarchy is right reason, ideas, light. The more, therefore, an aristocracy calls to its aid its innate forces,—its impenetrability, its high spirit, its power of haughty resistance,—to deal with an epoch of expansion, the graver is the danger, the greater the certainty of explosion, the surer the aristocracy's defeat; for it is trying to do violence to nature instead of working along with it. The best powers shown by the best men of an aristocracy at such an epoch are, it will be observed, non-aristocratical powers, powers of industry, powers of intelligence; and these powers thus exhibited, tend really not to strengthen the aristocracy, but to take their owners out of it, to expose them to the dissolving agencies of thought and change, to make them men of the modern spirit and of the future. If, as sometimes happens, they add to their non-aristocratical qualities of labour and thought, a strong dose of aristocratical qualities also,—of pride, defiance, turn for resistance,—this truly aristocratical side of them, so far from adding any strength to them, really neutralises their force and makes them impracticable and ineffective.

Knowing myself to be indeed sadly to seek, as one of my many critics says, in 'a philosophy with coherent, interdependent, subordinate, and derivative principles,' I continually have recourse to a plain man's expedient of trying to make what few simple notions I have, clearer and more intelligible to myself by means of example and illustration. And having been brought up at Oxford in the bad old times, when we were stuffed with Greek and Aristotle, and thought nothing of preparing ourselves by the study of modern languages,—as after Mr. Lowe's great speech at Edinburgh we shall do,—to fight the battle of life with the waiters in foreign hotels, my head is still full of a lumber of phrases we learnt at Oxford from Aristotle, about virtue being in a mean, and about excess and defect, and so on. Once when I had had the advantage of listening to the Reform debates in the House of Commons, having heard a number of interesting speakers, and among them a well-known lord and a well-known baronet, I remember it struck me, applying Aristotle's machinery of the mean to my ideas about our aristocracy, that the lord was exactly the perfection, or happy mean, or virtue, of aristocracy, and the baronet the excess. And I fancied that by observing these two we might see both the inadequacy of aristocracy to supply the principle of authority needful for our present wants, and the danger of its trying to supply it when it was not really competent for the business. On the one hand, in the brilliant lord, showing plenty of high spirit, but remarkable, far above and beyond his gift of high spirit, for the fine tempering of his high spirit, for ease, serenity, politeness,—the great virtues, as Mr. Carlyle says, of aristocracy,—in this beautiful and virtuous mean, there seemed evidently some insufficiency of light; while, on the other hand, the worthy baronet, in whom the high spirit of aristocracy, its impenetrability, defiant courage, and pride of resistance, were developed even in excess, was manifestly capable, if he had his way given him, of causing us great danger, and, indeed, of throwing the whole commonwealth into confusion. Then I reverted to that old fundamental notion of mine about the grand merit of our race being really our honesty. And the very helplessness of our aristocratic or governing class in dealing with our perturbed social condition, their jealousy of entrusting too much power to the State as it now actually exists—that is to themselves—gave me a sort of pride and satisfaction; because I saw they were, as a whole, too honest to try and manage a business for which they did not feel themselves capable.

Surely, now, it is no inconsiderable boon which culture confers upon us, if in embarrassed times like the present it enables us to look at the ins and the outs of things in this way, without hatred and without partiality, and with a disposition to see the good in everybody all round. And I try to follow just the same course with our middle class as with our aristocracy. Mr. Lowe talks to us of this strong middle part of the nation, of the unrivalled deeds of our Liberal middle-class Parliament, of the noble, the heroic work it has performed in the last thirty years; and I begin to ask myself if we shall not, then, find in our middle class the principle of authority we want, and if we had not better take administration as well as legislation away from the weak extreme which now administers for us, and commit both to the strong middle part. I observe, too, that the heroes of middle-class liberalism, such as we have hitherto known it, speak with a kind of prophetic anticipation of the great destiny which awaits them, and as if the future was clearly theirs. The advanced party, the progressive party, the party in alliance with the future, are the names they like to give themselves. 'The principles which will obtain recognition in the future,' says Mr. Miall, a personage of deserved eminence among the political Dissenters, as they are called, who have been the backbone of middle-class liberalism,—'the principles which will obtain recognition in the future are the principles for which I have long and zealously laboured. I qualified myself for joining in the work of harvest by doing to the best of my ability the duties of seedtime.' These duties, if one is to gather them from the works of the great Liberal party in the last thirty years, are, as I have elsewhere summed them up, the advocacy of free trade, of Parliamentary reform, of abolition of church-rates, of voluntaryism in religion and education, of non-interference of the State between employers and employed, and of marriage with one's deceased wife's sister.

Now I know, when I object that all this is machinery, the great Liberal middle class has by this time grown cunning enough to answer that it always meant more by these things than meets the eye ; that it has had that within which passes show, and that we are soon going to see, in a Free Church and all manner of good things, what it was. But I have learned from Bishop Wilson (if Mr. Frederic Harrison will forgive my again quoting that poor old hierophant of a decayed superstition) : 'If we would really know our heart let us impartially view our actions'; and I cannot help thinking that if our Liberals had had so much sweetness and light in their inner minds as they allege, more of it must have come out in their sayings and doings.

An American friend of the English Liberals says, indeed, that their Dissidence of Dissent has been a mere instrument of the political Dissenters for making reason and the will of God prevail (and no doubt he would say the same of marriage with one's deceased wife's sister) ; and that the abolition of a State Church is merely the Dissenter's means to this end, just as culture is mine. Another American defender of theirs says just the same of their industrialism and free trade ; indeed, this gentleman, taking the bull by the horns, proposes that we should for the future call industrialism culture, and the industrialists the men of culture, and then of course there can be no longer any misapprehension about their true character ; and besides the pleasure of being wealthy and comfortable, they will have authentic recognition as vessels of sweetness and light.

All this is undoubtedly specious ; but I must remark that the culture of which I talked was an endeavour to come at reason and the will of God by means of reading, observing, and thinking ; and that whoever calls anything else culture, may, indeed, call it so if he likes, but then he talks of something quite different from what I talked of. And, again, as culture's way of working for reason and the will of God is by directly trying to know more about them, while the Dissidence of Dissent is evidently in itself no effort of this kind, nor is its Free Church, in fact, a church with worthier conceptions of God and the ordering of the world than the State Church professes, but with mainly the same conceptions of these as the State Church has, only that every man is to comport himself as he likes in professing them,—this being so, I cannot at once accept the Nonconformity any more than the industrialism and the other great works of our Liberal middle class as proof positive that this class is in possession of light, and that here is the true seat of authority for which we are in search ; but I must try a little further, and seek for other indications which may enable me to make up my mind.

Why should we not do with the middle class as we have done with the aristocratic class,—find in it some representative men who may stand for the virtuous mean of this class, for the perfection of its present qualities and mode of being, and also for the excess of them. Such men must clearly not be men of genius like Mr. Bright; for, as I have formerly said, so far as a man has genius he tends to take himself out of the category of class altogether, and to become simply a man. Some more ordinary man would be more to the purpose,—would sum up better in himself, without disturbing influences, the general liberal force of the middle class, the force by which it has done its great works of free trade, Parliamentary reform, voluntaryism, and so on, and the spirit in which it has done them. Now it happens that a typical middle-class man, the member for one of our chief industrial cities, has given us a famous sentence which bears directly on the resolution of our present question: whether there is light enough in our middle class to make it the proper seat of the authority we wish to establish. When there was a talk some little while ago about the state of middle-class education, our friend, as the representative of that class, spoke some memorable words:—'There had been a cry that middle-class education ought to receive more attention. He confessed himself very much surprised by the clamour that was raised. He did not think that class need excite the sympathy either of the legislature or the public.' Now this satisfaction of our middle-class member of Parliament with the mental state of the middle class was truly representative, and makes good his claim to stand as the beautiful and virtuous mean of that class. But it is obviously at variance with our definition of culture, or the pursuit of light and perfection, which made light and perfection consist, not in resting and being, but in growing and becoming, in a perpetual advance in beauty and wisdom. So the middle class is by its essence, as one may say, by its incomparable self-satisfaction decisively expressed through its beautiful and virtuous mean, self-excluded from wielding an authority of which light is to be the very soul.

Clear as this is, it will be made clearer still if we take some representative man as the excess of the middle class, and remember that the middle class, in general, is to be conceived as a body swaying between the qualities of its mean and of its excess, and on the whole, of course, as human nature is constituted, inclining rather towards the excess than the mean. Of its excess no better representative can possibly be imagined than a Dissenting minister from Walsall, who came before the public in connection with the proceedings at Birmingham of Mr. Murphy, already mentioned. Speaking in the midst of an irritated population of Catholics, this Walsall gentleman exclaimed: 'I say, then, away with the Mass! It is from the bottomless pit; and in the bottomless pit shall all liars have their part, in the lake that burneth with fire and brimstone.' And again: 'When all the praties were black in Ireland, why didn't the priests say the hocus-pocus over them, and make them all good again?' He shared, too, Mr. Murphy's fears of some invasion of his domestic happiness: 'What I wish to say to you as Protestant husbands is, *Take care of your wives!*' And finally, in the true vein of an Englishman doing as he likes, a vein of which I have at some length pointed out the present dangers, he recommended for imitation the example of some churchwardens at Dublin, among whom, said he, 'there was a Luther and also a Melanchthon,' who had made very short work with some ritualist or other, hauled him down from his pulpit, and kicked him out of church. Now it is manifest, as I said in the case of our aristocratical baronet, that if we let this excess of the sturdy English middle class, this conscientious Protestant Dissenter, so strong, so self-reliant, so fully persuaded in his own mind, have his way, he would be capable, with his want of light,—or, to use the language of the religious world, with his zeal without knowledge,—of stirring up strife which neither he nor any one else could easily compose.

And then comes in, as it did also with the aristocracy, the honesty of our race, and by the voice of another middle-class man, Alderman of the City of London and Colonel of the City of London Militia, proclaims that it has twinges of conscience, and that it will not attempt to cope with our social disorders, and to deal with a business which it feels to be too high for it. Every one remembers how this virtuous Alderman-Colonel, or Colonel-Alderman, led his militia through the London streets; how the bystanders gathered to see him pass; how the London roughs, asserting an Englishman's best and most blissful right of doing what he likes, robbed and beat the bystanders; and how the blameless warrior-magistrate refused to let his troops interfere. 'The crowd,' he touchingly said afterwards, 'was mostly composed of fine healthy strong men, bent on mischief; if he had allowed his soldiers to interfere they might have been overpowered, their rifles taken from them and used against them by the mob; a riot, in fact, might have ensued, and been attended with bloodshed, compared with which the assaults and loss of property that actually occurred would have been as nothing.' Honest and affecting testimony of the English middle class to its own inadequacy for the authoritative part one's admiration would sometimes incline one to assign to it! 'Who are we,' they say by the voice of their Alderman-Colonel, 'that we should not be overpowered if we attempt to cope with social anarchy, our rifles taken from us and used against us by the mob, and we, perhaps, robbed and beaten ourselves? Or what light have we, beyond a free-born Englishman's impulse to do as he likes, which could justify us in preventing, at the cost of bloodshed, other free-born Englishmen from doing as they like, and robbing and beating us as much as they please?'

This distrust of themselves as an adequate centre of authority does not mark the working class, as was shown by their readiness the other day in Hyde Park to take upon themselves all the functions of government. But this comes from the working class being, as I have often said, still an embryo, of which no one can yet quite foresee the final development; and from its not having the same experience and self-knowledge as the aristocratic and middle classes. Honesty it no doubt has, just like the other classes of Englishmen, but honesty in an inchoate and untrained state; and meanwhile its powers of action, which are, as Mr. Frederic Harrison says, exceedingly ready, easily run away with it. That it cannot at present have a sufficiency of light which comes by culture,—that is, by reading, observing, and thinking,—is clear from the very nature of its condition; and, indeed, we saw that Mr. Frederic Harrison, in seeking to make a free stage for its bright powers of sympathy and ready powers of action, had to begin by throwing overboard culture, and flouting it as only fit for a professor of *belles-lettres*. Still, to make it perfectly manifest that no more in the working class than in the aristocratic and middle classes can one find an adequate centre of authority,—that is, as culture teaches us to conceive our required authority, of light,—let us again follow, with this class, the method we have followed with the aristocratic and middle classes, and try to bring before our minds representative men, who may figure to us its virtue and its excess.

We must not take, of course, men like the chiefs of the Hyde Park demonstration, Colonel Dickson or Mr. Beales; because Colonel Dickson, by his martial profession and dashing exterior, seems to belong properly, like Julius Cæsar and Mirabeau and other great popular leaders, to the aristocratic class, and to be carried into the popular ranks only by his ambition or his genius; while Mr. Beales belongs to our solid middle class, and, perhaps, if he had not been a great popular leader, would have been a Philistine. But Mr. Odger, whose speeches we have all read. and of whom his friends relate, besides, much that is favourable, may very well stand for the beautiful and virtuous mean of our present working class; and I think everybody will admit that in Mr. Odger there is manifestly, with all his good points, some insufficiency of light. The excess of the working class, in its present state of development, is perhaps best shown in Mr. Bradlaugh, the iconoclast, who seems to be almost for baptizing us all in blood and fire into his new social dispensation, and to whose reflections, now that I have once been set going on Bishop Wilson's track, I cannot forbear commending this maxim of the good old man: 'Intemperance in talk makes a dreadful havoc in the heart.' Mr. Bradlaugh, like our types of excess in the aristocratic and middle classes, is evidently capable, if he had his head given him, of running us all into great dangers and confusion. I conclude, therefore,—what indeed, few of those who do me the honour to read this disquisition are likely to dispute,—that we can as little find in the working class as in the aristocratic or in the middle class our much-wanted source of authority, as culture suggests it to us.

Well, then, what if we tried to rise above the idea of class to the idea of the whole community, *the State*, and to find our centre of light and authority there? Every one of us has the idea of country, as a sentiment; hardly any one of us has the idea of *the State*, as a working power. And why? Because we habitually live in our ordinary selves, which do not carry us beyond the ideas and wishes of the class to which we happen to belong. And we are all afraid of giving to the State too much power, because we only conceive of the State as something equivalent to the class in occupation of the executive government, and are afraid of that class abusing power to its own purposes. If we strengthen the State with the aristocratic class in occupation of the executive government, we imagine we are delivering ourselves up

captive to the ideas and wishes of our fierce aristocratical baronet ; if with the middle class in occupation of the executive government, to those of our truculent middle-class Dissenting minister ; if with the working class, to those of its notorious tribune, Mr. Bradlaugh. And with much justice ; owing to the exaggerated notion which we English, as I have said, entertain of the right and blessedness of the mere doing as one likes, of the affirming oneself, and oneself just as it is. People of the aristocratic class want to affirm their ordinary selves, their likings and dislikings ; people of the middle class the same ; people of the working class the same. By our everyday selves, however, we are separate, personal, at war ; we are only safe from one another's tyranny when no one has any power ; and this safety, in its turn, cannot save us from anarchy. And when, therefore, anarchy presents itself as a danger to us, we know not where to turn.

But by our *best self* we are united, impersonal, at harmony. We are in no peril from giving authority to this, because it is the truest friend we all of us can have ; and when anarchy is a danger to us, to this authority we may turn with sure trust. Well, and this is the very self which culture, or the study of perfection, seeks to develop in us ; at the expense of our old untransformed self, taking pleasure only in doing what it likes or is used to do, and exposing us

to the risk of clashing with every one else who is doing the same! So that our poor culture, which is flouted as so unpractical, leads us to the very ideas capable of meeting the great want of our present embarrassed times! We want an authority, and we find nothing but jealous classes, checks, and a deadlock; culture suggests the idea of *the State*. We find no basis for a firm State-power in our ordinary selves; culture suggests one to us in our *best self*.

It cannot but acutely try a tender conscience to be accused, in a practical country like ours, of keeping aloof from the work and hope of a multitude of earnest-hearted men, and of merely toying with poetry and æsthetics. So it is with no little sense of relief that I find myself thus in the position of one who makes a contribution in aid of the practical necessities of our times. The great thing, it will be observed, is to find our *best* self, and to seek to affirm nothing but that; not,—as we English with our over-value for merely being free and busy have been so accustomed to do,—resting satisfied with a self which comes uppermost long before our best self, and affirming that with blind energy. In short,—to go back yet once more to Bishop Wilson,—of these two excellent rules of Bishop Wilson's for a man's guidance: 'Firstly, never go against the best light you have; secondly, take care that your light be not darkness,' we English have followed with praiseworthy zeal the first rule, but we have not given so much heed to the second. We have gone manfully according to the best light we have; but we have not taken enough care that this should be really the best light possible for us, that it should not be darkness. And, our honesty being very great, conscience has whispered to us that the light we were following, our ordinary self, was, indeed, perhaps, only an inferior self, only darkness; and that it would not do to impose this seriously on all the world.

But our best self inspires faith, and is capable of affording a serious principle of authority. For example. We are on our way to what the late Duke of Wellington, with his strong sagacity, foresaw and admirably described as 'a revolution by due course of law.' This is undoubtedly,—if we are still to live and grow, and this famous nation is not to stagnate and dwindle away on the one hand, or, on the other, to perish miserably in mere anarchy and confusion,—what we are on the way to. Great changes there must be, for a revolution cannot accomplish itself without great changes; yet order there must be, for without order a revolution cannot accomplish itself by due course of law. So whatever brings risk of tumult and disorder, multitudinous processions in the streets of our crowded towns, multitudinous meetings in their public places and parks,—demonstrations perfectly unnecessary in the present course of our affairs,—our best self, or right reason, plainly enjoins us to set our faces against. It enjoins us to encourage and uphold the occupants of the executive power, whoever they may be, in firmly prohibiting them. But it does this clearly and resolutely, and is thus a real principle of authority, because it does it with a free conscience; because in thus provisionally strengthening the executive power, it knows that it is not doing this merely to enable our aristocratical baronet to affirm himself as against our working-men's tribune, or our middle-class Dissenter to affirm himself as against both. It knows that it is establishing *the State*, or organ of our collective best self, of our national right reason. And it has the testimony of conscience that it is stablishing the State on behalf of whatever great changes are needed, just as much as on behalf of order; stablishing it to deal just as stringently, when the time comes, with our baronet's aristocratical prejudices, or with the fanaticism of our middle-class Dissenter, as it deals with Mr. Bradlaugh's street-processions.

CHAPTER III

BARBARIANS, PHILISTINES, POPULACE

FROM a man without a philosophy no one can expect philosophical completeness. Therefore I may observe without shame, that in trying to get a distinct notion of our aristocratic, our middle, and our working class, with a view of testing the claims of each of these classes to become a centre of authority, I have omitted, I find, to complete the old-fashioned analysis which I had the fancy of applying, and have not shown in these classes, as well as the virtuous mean and the excess, the defect also. I do not know that the omission very much matters. Still, as clearness is the one merit which a plain, unsystematic writer, without a philosophy, can hope to have, and as our notion of the three great English classes may perhaps be made clearer if we see their distinctive qualities in the defect, as well as in the excess and in the mean, let us try, before proceeding further, to remedy this omission.

It is manifest, if the perfect and virtuous

mean of that fine spirit which is the distinctive quality of aristocracies, is to be found in a high, chivalrous style, and its excess in a fierce turn for resistance, that its defect must lie in a spirit not bold and high enough, and in an excessive and pusillanimous unaptness for resistance. If, again, the perfect and virtuous mean of that force by which our middle class has done its great works, and of that self-reliance with which it contemplates itself and them, is to be seen in the performances and speeches of our commercial member of Parliament, and the excess of that force and of that self-reliance in the performances and speeches of our fanatical Dissenting minister, then it is manifest that their defect must lie in a helpless inaptitude for the great works of the middle class, and in a poor and despicable lack of its self-satisfaction.

To be chosen to exemplify the happy mean of a good quality, or set of good qualities, is evidently a praise to a man ; nay, to be chosen to exemplify even their excess, is a kind of praise. Therefore I could have no hesitation in taking actual personages to exemplify, respectively, the mean and the excess of aristocratic and middle-class qualities. But perhaps there might be a want of urbanity in singling out this or that personage as the representative of defect. Therefore I shall leave the defect of aristocracy unillustrated by any representative man. But with oneself one may always, without impropriety, deal quite freely; and, indeed, this sort of plain-dealing with oneself has in it, as all the moralists tell us, something very wholesome. So I will venture to humbly offer myself as an illustration of defect in those forces and qualities which make our middle class what it is. The too well founded reproaches of my opponents declare how little I have lent a hand to the great works of the middle class; for it is evidently these works, and my slackness at them, which are meant, when I am said to 'refuse to lend a hand to the humble operation of uprooting certain definite evils' (such as church-rates and others), and that therefore 'the believers in action grow impatient' with me. The line, again, of a still unsatisfied seeker which I have followed, the idea of self-transformation, of growing towards some measure of sweetness and light not yet reached, is evidently at clean variance with the perfect self-satisfaction current in my class, the middle class, and may serve to indicate in me, therefore, the extreme defect of this feeling. But these confessions, though salutary, are bitter and unpleasant.

To pass, then, to the working class. The defect of this class would be the falling short in what Mr. Frederic Harrison calls those 'bright powers of sympathy and ready powers of action,' of which we saw in Mr. Odger the virtuous mean, and in Mr. Bradlaugh the excess. The working class is so fast growing and rising at the present time, that instances of this defect cannot well be now very common. Perhaps Canning's 'Needy Knife-Grinder' (who is dead, and therefore cannot be pained at my taking him for an illustration) may serve to give us the notion of defect in the essential quality of a working class; or I might even cite (since, though he is alive in the flesh, he is dead to all heed of criticism) my poor old poaching friend, Zephaniah Diggs, who, between his hare-snaring and his gin-drinking, has got his powers of sympathy quite dulled and his powers of action in any great movement of his class hopelessly impaired. But examples of this defect belong, as I have said, to a bygone age rather than to the present.

The same desire for clearness, which has led me thus to extend a little my first analysis of the three great classes of English society, prompts me also to improve my nomenclature for them a little, with a view to making it thereby more manageable. It is awkward and tiresome to be always saying the aristocratic class, the middle class, the working class. For the middle class, for that great body which, as we know, 'has done all the great things that have been done in all departments,' and which is to be conceived as moving between its two cardinal points of our commercial member of Parliament and our fanatical Protestant Dissenter,—for this class we have a designation which now has become pretty well known, and which we may as well still keep for them, the designation of Philistines. What this term means I have so often explained that I need not repeat it here. For the aristocratic class, conceived mainly as a body moving between the two cardinal points of our chivalrous lord and our defiant baronet, we have as yet got no special designation. Almost all my attention has naturally been concentrated on my own class, the middle class, with which I am in closest sympathy, and which has been, besides, the great power of our day, and has had its praises sung by all speakers and newspapers.

Still the aristocratic class is so important in itself, and the weighty functions which Mr. Carlyle proposes at the present critical time to commit to it, must add so much to its importance, that it seems neglectful, and a strong instance of that want of coherent philosophic method for which Mr. Frederic Harrison blames me, to leave the aristocratic class so much without notice and denomination. It may be thought that the characteristic which I have occasionally mentioned as proper to aristocracies,—their natural inaccessibility, as children of the established fact, to ideas,—points to our extending to this class also the designation of Philistines; the Philistine being, as is well known, the enemy of the children of light or servants of the idea. Nevertheless, there seems to be an inconvenience in thus giving one and the same designation to two very different classes; and besides, if we look into the thing closely, we shall find that the term Philistine conveys a sense which makes it more peculiarly appropriate to our middle class than to our aristocratic. For *Philistine* gives the notion of something particularly stiff-necked and perverse in the resistance to light and its children; and therein it specially suits our middle class, who not only do not pursue sweetness and light, but who even prefer to them that sort of machinery of business, chapels, tea-meetings, and addresses from Mr. Murphy, which makes up the dismal and illiberal life on which I have so often touched. But the aristocratic class has actually, as we have seen, in its well-known politeness, a kind of image or shadow of sweetness; and as for light, if it does not pursue light, it is not that it perversely cherishes some dismal and illiberal existence in preference to light, but it is lured off from following light by those mighty and eternal seducers of our race which weave for this class their most irresistible charms,—by worldly splendour, security, power, and pleasure. These seducers are exterior goods, but in a way they are goods; and he who is hindered by them from caring for light and ideas, is not so much doing what is perverse as what is too natural.

Keeping this in view, I have in my own mind often indulged myself with the fancy of employing, in order to designate our aristocratic class, the name of *The Barbarians*. The Barbarians, to whom we all owe so much, and who reinvigorated and renewed our worn-out Europe, had, as is well known, eminent merits; and in this country, where we are for the most part sprung from the Barbarians, we have never had the prejudice against them which prevails among the races of Latin origin. The Barbarians brought with them that staunch individualism, as the modern phrase is, and that passion for doing as one likes, for the assertion of personal liberty, which appears to Mr. Bright the central idea of English life, and of which we have, at any rate, a very rich supply. The stronghold and natural seat of this passion was in the nobles of whom our aristocratic class are the inheritors; and this class, accordingly, have signally manifested it, and have done much by their example to recommend it to the body of the nation, who already, indeed, had it in their blood. The Barbarians, again, had the passion for field-sports; and they have handed it on to our aristocratic class, who of this passion too, as of the passion for asserting one's personal liberty, are the great natural stronghold. The care of the Barbarians for the body, and for all manly exercises; the vigour, good looks, and fine complexion which they acquired and perpetuated in their families by these means,—all this may be observed still in our aristocratic class. The chivalry of the Barbarians, with its characteristics of high spirit, choice manners, and distinguished bearing,—what is this but the attractive commencement of the politeness of our aristocratic class? In some Barbarian noble, no doubt, one would have admired, if one could have been then alive to see it, the rudiments of our politest peer. Only, all this culture (to call it by that name) of the Barbarians was an exterior culture mainly. It consisted principally in outward gifts and graces, in looks, manners, accomplishments, prowess. The chief inward gifts which had part in it were the most exterior, so to speak, of inward gifts, those which come nearest to outward ones; they were courage, a high spirit, self-confidence. Far within, and unawakened, lay a whole range of powers of thought and feeling, to which these interesting productions of nature had, from the circumstances of their life, no access. Making allowances for the difference of the times, surely we can observe precisely the same thing now in our aristocratic class. In general its culture is exterior chiefly; all the exterior graces and accomplishments, and the more external of the inward virtues, seem to be principally its portion. It now, of course, cannot but be often in contact with those studies by which, from the world of thought and feeling, true culture teaches us to fetch sweetness and light; but its hold upon these very studies appears remarkably external, and unable to exert any deep power upon its spirit. Therefore the one insufficiency which we noted in the perfect mean of this class was an insufficiency of light. And owing to the same causes, does not a subtle criticism lead us to make, even on the good looks and politeness of our aristocratic class, and of even the most fascinating half of that class, the feminine half, the one qualifying remark, that in these charming gifts there should perhaps be, for ideal perfection, a shade more *soul?*

I often, therefore, when I want to distinguish clearly the aristocratic class from the Philistines proper, or middle class, name the former, in my own mind, *the Barbarians.* And when I go through the country, and see this and that beautiful and imposing seat of theirs crowning the landscape, 'There,' I say to myself, 'is a great fortified post of the Barbarians.'

It is obvious that that part of the working class which, working diligently by the light of Mrs. Gooch's Golden Rule, looks forward to the happy day when it will sit on thrones with commercial members of Parliament and other middle-class potentates, to survey, as Mr. Bright beautifully says, 'the cities it has built, the railroads it has made, the manufactures it has produced, the cargoes which freight the ships of the greatest mercantile navy the world has ever seen,'—it is obvious, I say, that this part of the working class is, or is in a fair way to be, one in spirit with the industrial middle class.

It is notorious that our middle-class Liberals have long looked forward to this consummation, when the working class shall join forces with them, aid them heartily to carry forward their great works, go in a body to their tea-meetings, and, in short, enable them to bring about their millennium. That part of the working class, therefore, which does really seem to lend itself to these great aims, may, with propriety, be numbered by us among the Philistines. That part of it, again, which so much occupies the attention of philanthropists at present,—the part which gives all its energies to organising itself, through trades' unions and other means, so as to constitute, first, a great working-class power independent of the middle and aristocratic classes, and then, by dint of numbers, give the law to them and itself reign absolutely,—this lively and promising part must also, according to our definition, go with the Philistines; because it is its class and its class instinct which it seeks to affirm—its ordinary self, not its best self; and it is a machinery, an industrial machinery, and power and pre-eminence and other external goods, which fill its thoughts, and not an inward perfection. It is wholly occupied, according to Plato's subtle expression, with the things of itself and not its real self, with the things of the State and not the real State. But that vast portion, lastly, of the working class which, raw and half-developed, has long lain half-hidden amidst its poverty and squalor, and is now issuing from its hiding-place to assert an Englishman's heaven-born privilege of doing as he likes, and is beginning to perplex us by marching where it likes, meeting where it likes, bawling what it likes, breaking what it likes,—to this vast residuum we may with great propriety give the name of *Populace*.

Thus we have got three distinct terms, *Barbarians*, *Philistines*, *Populace*, to denote roughly the three great classes into which our society is divided; and though this humble attempt at a scientific nomenclature falls, no doubt, very far short in precision of what might be required from a writer equipped with a complete and coherent philosophy, yet, from a notoriously unsystematic and unpretending writer, it will, I trust, be accepted as sufficient.

But in using this new, and, I hope, convenient division of English society, two things are to be borne in mind. The first is, that since, under all our class divisions, there is a common basis of human nature, therefore, in every one of us, whether we be properly Barbarians, Philistines, or Populace, there exist, sometimes only in germ and potentially, sometimes more or less developed, the same tendencies and passions which have made our fellow-citizens of other classes what they are. This consideration is very important, because it has great influence in begetting that spirit of indulgence which is a necessary part of sweetness, and which, indeed, when our culture is complete, is, as I have said, inexhaustible. Thus, an English Barbarian who examines himself will, in general, find himself to be not so entirely a Barbarian but that he has in him, also, something of the Philistine, and even something of the Populace as well. And the same with Englishmen of the two other classes.

This is an experience which we may all verify every day. For instance, I myself (I again take myself as a sort of *corpus vile* to serve for illustration in a matter where serving for illustration may not by every one be thought agreeable), I myself am properly a Philistine,—Mr. Swinburne would add, the son of a Philistine. And although, through circumstances which will perhaps one day be known if ever the affecting history of my conversion comes to be written, I have, for the most part, broken with the ideas and the tea-meetings of my own class, yet I have not, on that account, been brought much the nearer to the ideas and works of the Barbarians or of the Populace. Nevertheless, I never take a gun or a fishing-rod in my hands without feeling that I have in the ground of my nature the self-same seeds which, fostered by circumstances, do so much to make the Barbarian; and that, with the Barbarian's advantages, I might have rivalled him. Place me in one of his great fortified posts, with these seeds of a love for field-sports sown in my nature, with all the means of developing them, with all pleasures at my command, with most whom I met deferring to me, every one I met smiling on me, and with every appearance of permanence and security before me and behind me,—then I too might have grown, I feel, into a very passable child of the established fact, of commendable spirit and politeness, and, at the same time, a little inaccessible to ideas and light; not, of course, with either the eminent fine spirit of our type of aristocratic perfection, or the eminent turn for resistance of our type of aristocratic excess, but, according to the measure of the common run of mankind, something between the two. And as to the Populace, who, whether he be Barbarian or Philistine, can look at them without sympathy, when he remembers how often,—every time that we snatch up a vehement opinion in ignorance and passion, every time that we long to crush an adversary by sheer violence, every time that we are envious, every time that we are brutal, every time that we adore mere power or success, every time that we add our voice to swell a blind clamour against some unpopular personage, every time that we trample savagely on the fallen,—he has found in his own bosom the eternal spirit of the Populace, and that there needs only a little help from circumstances to make it triumph in him untamably.

The second thing to be borne in mind I have indicated several times already. It is this. All of us, so far as we are Barbarians, Philistines, or Populace, imagine happiness to consist in doing what one's ordinary self likes. What one's ordinary self likes differs according to the class to which one belongs, and has its severer and its lighter side; always, however, remaining machinery, and nothing more. The graver self of the Barbarian likes honours and consideration; his more relaxed self, field-sports and pleasure. The graver self of one kind of Philistine likes fanaticism, business, and money-making; his more relaxed self, comfort and tea-meetings. Of another kind of Philistine, the graver self likes rattening; the relaxed self, deputations, or hearing Mr. Odger speak. The sterner self of the Populace likes bawling, hustling, and smashing; the lighter self, beer. But in each class there are born a certain number of natures with a curiosity about their best self, with a bent for seeing things as they are, for disentangling themselves from machinery, for simply concerning themselves with reason and the will of God, and doing their best to make these prevail;—for the pursuit, in a word, of perfection. To certain manifestations of this love for perfection mankind have accustomed themselves to give the name of genius; implying, by this name, something original and heaven-bestowed in the passion. But the passion is to be found far beyond those manifestations of it to which the world usually gives the name of genius, and in which there is, for the most part, a *talent* of some kind or other, a special and striking faculty of execution, informed by the heaven-bestowed ardour, or genius. It is to be found in many manifestations besides these, and may best be called, as we have called it, the love and pursuit of perfection; culture being the true nurse of the pursuing love, and sweetness and light the true character of the pursued perfection. Natures with this bent emerge in all classes,—among the Barbarians, among the Philistines, among the Populace. And this bent always tends to take them out of their class, and to make their distinguishing characteristic not their Barbarianism or their Philistinism, but their *humanity*. They have, in general, a rough time of it in their lives; but they are sown more abundantly than one might think, they appear where and when one least expects it, they set up a fire which enfilades, so to speak, the class with which they are ranked; and, in general, by the extrication of their best self as the self to develop, and by the simplicity of the ends fixed by them as paramount, they hinder the unchecked predominance of that class-life which is the affirmation of our ordinary self, and seasonably disconcert mankind in their worship of machinery.

Therefore, when we speak of ourselves as divided into Barbarians, Philistines, and Populace, we must be understood always to imply that within each of these classes there are a certain number of *aliens*, if we may so call them,—persons who are mainly led, not by their class spirit, but by a general *humane* spirit, by the love of human perfection ; and that this number is capable of being diminished or augmented. I mean, the number of those who will succeed in developing this happy instinct will be greater or smaller, in proportion both to the force of the original instinct within them, and to the hindrance or encouragement which it meets with from without. In almost all who have it, it is mixed with some infusion of the spirit of an ordinary self, some quantity of class-instinct, and even, as has been shown, of more than one class-instinct at the same time ; so that, in general, the extrication of the best self, the predominance of the *humane* instinct, will very much depend upon its meeting, or not, with what is fitted to help and elicit it. At a moment, therefore, when it is agreed that we want a source of authority, and when it seems probable that the right source is our best self, it becomes of vast importance to see whether or not the things around us are, in general, such as to help and elicit our best self, and if they are not, to see why they are not, and the most promising way of mending them.

Now, it is clear that the very absence of any powerful authority amongst us, and the prevalent doctrine of the duty and happiness of doing as one likes, and asserting our personal lib[illegible] must tend to prevent the erection of any very strict standard of excellence, the belief in any very paramount authority of right reason, the recognition of our best self as anything very recondite and hard to come at. It may be, as I have said, a proof of our honesty that we do not attempt to give to our ordinary self, as we have it in action, predominant authority, and to impose its rule upon other people. But it is evident also, that it is not easy, with our style of proceeding, to get beyond the notion of an ordinary self at all, or to get the paramount authority of a commanding best self, or right reason, recognised. The learned Martinus Scriblerus well says:—'The taste of the bathos is implanted by nature itself in the soul of man; till, perverted by custom or example, he is taught, or rather compelled, to relish the sublime.' But with us everything seems directed to prevent any such perversion of us by custom or example as might compel us to relish the sublime; by all means we are encouraged to keep our natural taste for the bathos unimpaired.

I have formerly pointed out how in literature the absence of any authoritative centre, like an Academy, tends to do this. Each section of the public has its own literary organ, and the mass of the public is without any suspicion that the value of these organs is relative to their being nearer a certain ideal centre of correct information, taste, and intelligence, or farther away from it. I have said that within certain limits, which any one who is likely to read this will have no difficulty in drawing for himself, my old adversary, the *Saturday Review*, may, on matters of literature and taste, be fairly enough regarded, relatively to the mass of newspapers which treat these matters, as a kind of organ of reason. But I remember once conversing with a company of Nonconformist admirers of some lecturer who had let off a great firework, which the *Saturday Review* said was all noise and false lights, and feeling my way as tenderly as I could about the effect of this unfavourable judgment upon those with whom I was conversing. 'Oh,' said one who was their spokesman, with the most tranquil air of conviction, 'it is true the *Saturday Review* abuses the lecture, but the *British Banner*' (I am not quite sure it was the *British Banner*, but it was some newspaper of that stamp) 'says that the *Saturday Review* is quite wrong.' The speaker had evidently no notion that there was a scale of value for judgments on these topics, and that the judgments of the *Saturday Review* ranked high on this scale, and those of the *British Banner* low; the taste of the bathos implanted by nature in the literary judgments of man had never, in my friend's case, encountered any let or hindrance.

Just the same in religion as in literature. We have most of us little idea of a high standard to choose our guides by, of a great and profound spirit which is an authority while inferior spirits are none. It is enough to give importance to things that this or that person says them decisively, and has a large following of some strong kind when he says them. This habit of ours is very well shown in that able and interesting work of Mr. Hepworth Dixon's, which we were all reading lately, *The Mormons, by One of Themselves*. Here, again, I am not quite sure that my memory serves me as to the exact title, but I mean the well-known book in which Mr. Hepworth Dixon described the Mormons, and other similar religious bodies in America, with so much detail and such warm sympathy. In this work it seems enough for Mr. Dixon that this or that doctrine has its Rabbi, who talks big to him, has a staunch body of disciples, and, above all, has plenty of rifles. That there are any further stricter tests to be applied to a doctrine, before it is pronounced important, never seems to occur to him. 'It is easy to say,' he writes of the Mormons, 'that these saints are dupes and fanatics, to laugh at Joe Smith and his church, but what then? *The great facts remain.* Young and his people are at Utah; a church of 200,000 souls; an army of 20,000 rifles.' But if the followers of a doctrine are really dupes, or worse, and its promulgators are really fanatics, or worse, it gives the doctrine no seriousness or authority the more that there should be found 200,000 souls,—200,000 of the innumerable multitude with a natural taste for the bathos,—to hold it, and 20,000 rifles to defend it. And again, of another religious organisation in America: 'A fair and open field is not to be refused when hosts so mighty throw down wager of battle on behalf of what they hold to be true, however strange their faith may seem.' A fair and open field is not to be refused to any speaker; but this solemn way of heralding him is quite out of place, unless he has, for the best reason and spirit of man, some significance. 'Well, but,' says Mr. Hepworth Dixon, 'a theory which has been accepted by men like Judge Edmonds, Dr. Hare, Elder Frederick, and Professor Bush!' And again: 'Such are, in brief, the bases of what Newman Weeks, Sarah Horton, Deborah Butler, and the associated brethren, proclaimed in Rolt's Hall as the new covenant!' If he was summing up an account of the doctrine of Plato, or of St. Paul, and of its followers, Mr. Hepworth Dixon could not be more earnestly reverential. But the question is, Have personages like Judge Edmonds, and Newman Weeks, and Elderess Polly, and Elderess Antoinette, and the rest of Mr. Hepworth Dixon's heroes and heroines, anything of the weight and significance for the best reason and spirit of man that Plato and St. Paul have? Evidently they, at present, have not; and a very small taste of them and their doctrines ought to have convinced Mr. Hepworth Dixon that they never could have. 'But,' says he, 'the magnetic power which Shakerism is exercising on American thought would of itself compel us,'—and so on. Now, so far as real thought is concerned,—thought which affects the best reason and spirit of man, the scientific or the imaginative thought of the world, the only thought which deserves speaking of in this solemn way,—America has up to the present time been hardly more than a province of England, and even now would not herself claim to be more than abreast of England; and of this only real human thought, English thought itself is not just now, as we must all admit, the most significant factor. Neither, then, can American thought be; and the magnetic power which Shakerism exercises on American thought is about as important, for the best reason and spirit of man, as the magnetic power which Mr. Murphy exercises on Birmingham Protestantism. And as we shall never get rid of our natural taste for the bathos in religion, —never get access to a best self and right reason which may stand as a serious authority,—by treating Mr. Murphy as his own disciples treat him, seriously, and as if he was as much an authority as any one else: so we shall never get rid of it while our able and popular writers treat their Joe Smiths and Deborah Butlers, with their so many thousand souls and so many thousand rifles, in the like exaggerated and misleading manner, and so do their best to confirm us in a bad mental habit to which we are already too prone.

If our habits make it hard for us to come at the idea of a high best self, of a paramount authority, in literature or religion, how much more do they make this hard in the sphere of politics! In other countries the governors, not depending so immediately on the favour of the governed, have everything to urge them, if they know anything of right reason (and it is at least supposed that governors should know more of this than the mass of the governed), to set it authoritatively before the community. But our whole scheme of government being representative, every one of our governors has all possible temptation, instead of setting up before the governed who elect him, and on whose favour he depends, a high standard of right reason, to accommodate himself as much as possible to their natural taste for the bathos; and even if he tries to go counter to it, to proceed in this with so much flattering and coaxing, that they shall not suspect their ignorance and prejudices to be anything very unlike right reason, or their natural taste for the bathos to differ much from a relish for the sublime. Every one is thus in every possible way encouraged to trust in his own heart; but, 'he that trusteth in his own heart,' says the Wise Man, 'is a fool'; and at any rate this, which Bishop Wilson says, is undeniably true: 'The number of those who need to be awakened is far greater than that of those who need comfort.'

But in our political system everybody is comforted. Our guides and governors who have to be elected by the influence of the Barbarians, and who depend on their favour, sing the praises of the Barbarians, and say all the smooth things that can be said of them. With Mr. Tennyson, they celebrate 'the great broad-shouldered genial Englishman,' with his 'sense of duty,' his 'reverence for the laws,' and his 'patient force,' who saves us from the 'revolts, republics, revolutions, most no graver than a schoolboy's barring out,' which upset other and less broad-shouldered nations. Our guides who are chosen by the Philistines and who have to look to their favour, tell the Philistines how 'all the world knows that the great middle class of this country supplies the mind, the will, and the power requisite for all the great and good things that have to be done,' and congratulate them on their 'earnest good sense, which penetrates through sophisms, ignores commonplaces, and gives to conventional illusions their true value.' Our guides who look to the favour of the Populace, tell them that 'theirs are the brightest powers of sympathy, and the readiest powers of action.'

Harsh things are said too, no doubt, against all the great classes of the community; but these things so evidently come from a hostile class, and are so manifestly dictated by the passions and prepossessions of a hostile class, and not by right reason, that they make no serious impression on those at whom they are launched, but slide easily off their minds. For instance, when the Reform League orators inveigh against our cruel and bloated aristocracy, these invectives so evidently show the passions and point of view of the Populace, that they do not sink into the minds of those at whom they are addressed, or awaken any thought or self-examination in them. Again, when our aristocratical baronet describes the Philistines and the Populace as influenced with a kind of hideous mania for emasculating the aristocracy, that reproach so clearly comes from the wrath and excited imagination of the Barbarians, that it does not much set the Philistines and the Populace thinking. Or when Mr. Lowe calls the Populace drunken and venal, he so evidently calls them this in an agony of apprehension for his Philistine or middle-class Parliament, which has done so many great and heroic works, and is now threatened with mixture and debasement, that the Populace do not lay his words seriously to heart.

So the voice which makes a permanent impression on each of our classes is the voice of its friends, and this is from the nature of things, as I have said, a comforting voice. The Barbarians remain in the belief that the great broad-shouldered genial Englishman may be well satisfied with himself; the Philistines remain in the belief that the great middle class of this country, with its earnest common-sense penetrating through sophisms and ignoring commonplaces, may be well satisfied with itself; the Populace, that the working man, with his bright powers of sympathy and ready powers of action, may be well satisfied with himself. What hope, at this rate, of extinguishing the taste of the bathos implanted by nature itself in the soul of man, or of inculcating the belief that excellence dwells among high and steep rocks, and can only be reached by those who sweat blood to reach her?

But it will be said, perhaps, that candidates for political influence and leadership, who thus caress the self-love of those whose suffrages they desire, know quite well that they are not saying the sheer truth as reason sees it, but that they are using a sort of conventional language, or what we call clap-trap, which is essential to the working of representative institutions. And therefore, I suppose, we ought rather to say with Figaro: *Qui est-ce qu'on trompe ici?* Now, I admit that often, but not always, when our governors say smooth things to the self-love of the class whose political support they want, they know very well that they are overstepping, by a long stride, the bounds of truth and soberness; and while they talk, they in a manner, no doubt, put their tongue in their cheek. Not always; because, when a Barbarian appeals to his own class to make him their representative and give him political power, he, when he pleases their self-love by extolling broad-shouldered genial Englishmen with their sense of duty, reverence for the laws, and patient force, pleases his own self-love and extols himself, and is, therefore, himself ensnared by his own smooth words. And so, too, when a Philistine wants to be sent to Parliament by his brother Philistines, and extols the earnest good sense which characterises Manchester and supplies the mind, the will, and the power, as the *Daily News* eloquently says, requisite for all the great and good things that have to be done, he intoxicates and deludes himself as well as his brother Philistines who hear him.

But it is true that a Barbarian often wants the political support of the Philistines; and he unquestionably, when he flatters the self-love of Philistinism, and extols, in the approved fashion, its energy, enterprise, and self-reliance, knows that he is talking clap-trap, and so to say, puts his tongue in his cheek. On all matters where Nonconformity and its catchwords are concerned, this insincerity of Barbarians needing Nonconformist support, and, therefore, flattering the self-love of Nonconformity and repeating its catchwords without the least real belief in them, is very noticeable. When the Nonconformists, in a transport of blind zeal, threw out Sir James Graham's useful Education Clauses in 1843, one-half of their Parliamentary advocates, no doubt, who cried aloud against 'trampling on the religious liberty of the Dissenters by taking the money of Dissenters to teach the tenets of the Church of England,' put their tongue in their cheek while they so cried out. And perhaps there is even a sort of motion of Mr. Frederic Harrison's tongue towards his cheek when he talks of 'the shriek of superstition,' and tells the working class that 'theirs are the brightest powers of sympathy and the readiest powers of action.' But the point on which I would insist is, that this involuntary tribute to truth and soberness on the part of certain of our governors and guides never reaches at all the mass of us governed, to serve as a lesson to us, to abate our self-love, and to awaken in us a suspicion that our favourite prejudices may be, to a higher reason, all nonsense. Whatever by-play goes on among the more intelligent of our leaders, we do not see it; and we are left to believe that, not only in our own eyes, but in the eyes of our representative and ruling men, there is nothing more admirable than our ordinary self, whatever our ordinary self happens to be, Barbarian, Philistine, or Populace.

Thus everything in our political life tends to hide from us that there is anything wiser than our ordinary selves, and to prevent our getting the notion of a paramount right reason. Royalty itself, in its idea the expression of the collective nation, and a sort of constituted witness to its best mind, we try to turn into a kind of grand advertising van, meant to give publicity and credit to the inventions, sound or unsound, of the ordinary self of individuals.

I remember, when I was in North Germany, having this very strongly brought to my mind in the matter of schools and their institution. In Prussia, the best schools are Crown patronage schools, as they are called ; schools which have been established and endowed (and new ones are to this day being established and endowed) by the Sovereign himself out of his own revenues, to be under the direct control and management of him or of those representing him, and to serve as types of what schools should be. The Sovereign, as his position raises him above many prejudices and littlenesses, and as he can always have at his disposal the best advice, has evident advantages over private founders in well planning and directing a school ; while at the same time his great means and his great influence secure, to a well-planned school of his, credit and authority. This is what, in North Germany, the governors do in the matter of education for the governed ; and one may say that they thus give the governed a lesson, and draw out in them the idea of a right reason higher than the suggestions of an ordinary man's ordinary self.

But in England how different is the part which in this matter our governors are accustomed to play! The Licensed Victuallers or the Commercial Travellers propose to make a school for their children; and I suppose, in the matter of schools, one may call the Licensed Victuallers or the Commercial Travellers ordinary men, with their natural taste for the bathos still strong; and a Sovereign with the advice of men like Wilhelm von Humboldt or Schleiermacher may, in this matter, be a better judge, and nearer to right reason. And it will be allowed, probably, that right reason would suggest that, to have a sheer school of Licensed Victuallers' children, or a sheer school of Commercial Travellers' children, and to bring them all up, not only at home but at school too, in a kind of odour of licensed victualism or of bagmanism, is not a wise training to give to these children. And in Germany, I have said, the action of the national guides or governors is to suggest and provide a better. But, in England, the action of the national guides or governors is, for a Royal Prince or a great Minister to go down to the opening of the Licensed Victuallers' or of the Commercial Travellers' school, to take the chair, to extol the energy and self-reliance of the Licensed Victuallers or the Commercial Travellers, to be all of their way of thinking, to predict full success to their schools, and never so much as to hint to them that they are probably doing a very foolish thing, and that the right way to go to work with their children's education is quite different. And it is the same in almost every department of affairs. While, on the Continent, the idea prevails that it is the business of the heads and representatives of the nation, by virtue of their superior means, power, and information, to set an example and to provide suggestions of right reason, among us the idea is that the business of the heads and representatives of the nation is to do nothing of the kind, but to applaud the natural taste for the bathos showing itself vigorously in any part of the community, and to encourage its works.

Now I do not say that the political system of foreign countries has not inconveniences which may outweigh the inconveniences of our own political system; nor am I the least proposing to get rid of our own political system and to adopt theirs. But a sound centre of authority being what, in this disquisition, we have been led to seek, and right reason, or our best self, appearing alone to offer such a sound centre of authority, it is necessary to take note of the chief impediments which hinder, in this country, the extrication or recognition of this right reason as a paramount authority, with a view to afterwards trying in what way they can best be removed.

This being borne in mind, I proceed to remark how not only do we get no suggestions of right reason, and no rebukes of our ordinary self, from our governors, but a kind of philosophical theory is widely spread among us to the effect that there is no such thing at all as a best self and a right reason having claim to paramount authority, or, at any rate, no such thing ascertainable and capable of being made use of; and that there is nothing but an infinite number of ideas and works of our ordinary selves, and suggestions of our natural taste for the bathos, pretty nearly equal in value, which are doomed either to an irreconcilable conflict, or else to a perpetual give and take; and that wisdom consists in choosing the give and take rather than the conflict, and in sticking to our choice with patience and good humour.

And, on the other hand, we have another philosophical theory rife among us, to the effect that without the labour of perverting ourselves by custom or example to relish right reason, but by continuing all of us to follow freely our natural taste for the bathos, we shall, by the mercy of Providence, and by a kind of natural tendency of things, come in due time to relish and follow right reason.

The great promoters of these philosophical theories are our newspapers, which, no less than our Parliamentary representatives, may be said to act the part of guides and governors to us; and these favourite doctrines of theirs I call,—or should call, if the doctrines were not preached by authorities I so much respect,—the first, a peculiarly British form of Atheism, the second, a peculiarly British form of Quietism. The first-named melancholy doctrine is preached in the *Times* with great clearness and force of style; indeed, it is well known, from the example of the poet Lucretius and others, what great masters of style the atheistic doctrine has always counted among its promulgators. 'It is of no use,' says the *Times*, 'for us to attempt to force upon our neighbours our several likings and dislikings. We must take things as they are. Everybody has his own little vision of religious or civil perfection. Under the evident impossibility of satisfying everybody, we agree to take our stand on equal laws and on a system as open and liberal as is possible. The result is that everybody has more liberty of action and of speaking here than anywhere else in the Old World.' We come again here upon Mr. Roebuck's celebrated definition of happiness, on which I have so often commented: 'I look around me and ask what is the state of England? Is not every man able to say what he likes? I ask you whether the world over, or in past history, there is anything like it? Nothing. I pray that our unrivalled happiness may last.' This is the old story of our system of checks and every Englishman doing as he likes, which we have already seen to have been convenient enough so long as there were only the Barbarians and the Philistines to do what they liked, but to be getting inconvenient, and productive of anarchy, now that the Populace wants to do what it likes too.

But for all that, I will not at once dismiss this famous doctrine, but will first quote another passage from the *Times*, applying the doctrine to a matter of which we have just been speaking,—education. 'The difficulty here' (in providing a national system of education), says the *Times*, 'does not reside in any removable arrangements. It is inherent and native in the actual and inveterate state of things in this country. All these powers and personages, all these conflicting influences and varieties of character, exist, and have long existed among us; they are fighting it out, and will long continue to fight it out, without coming to that happy consummation when some one element of the British character is to destroy or to absorb all the rest.' There it is! the various promptings of the natural taste for the bathos in this man and that amongst us are fighting it out; and the day will never come (and, indeed, why should we wish it to come?) when one man's particular sort of taste for the bathos shall tyrannise over another man's; nor when right reason (if that may be called an element of the British character) shall absorb and rule them all. 'The whole system of this country, like the constitution we boast to inherit, and are glad to uphold, is made up of established facts, prescriptive authorities, existing usages, powers that be, persons in possession, and communities or classes that have won dominion for themselves, and will hold it against all comers.' Every force in the world, evidently, except the one reconciling force, right reason! Barbarian here, Philistine there, Mr. Bradlaugh and Populace striking in!—pull devil, pull baker! Really, presented with the mastery of style of our leading journal, the sad picture, as one gazes upon it, assumes the iron and inexorable solemnity of tragic Destiny.

After this, the milder doctrine of our other philosophical teacher, the *Daily News*, has, at first, something very attractive and assuaging. The *Daily News* begins, indeed, in appearance, to weave the iron web of necessity round us like the *Times*. 'The alternative is between a man's doing what he likes and his doing what some one else, probably not one whit wiser than himself, likes.' This points to the tacit compact, mentioned in my last paper, between the Barbarians and the Philistines, and into which it is hoped that the Populace will one day enter; the compact, so creditable to English honesty, that since each class has only the ideas and aims of its ordinary self to give effect to, none of them shall, if it exercise power, treat its ordinary self too seriously, or attempt to impose it on others; but shall let these others,—the fanatical Protestant, for instance, in his Papist-baiting, and the popular tribune in his Hyde Park anarchy-mongering,—have their fling. But then the *Daily News* suddenly lights up the gloom of necessitarianism with bright beams of hope. 'No doubt,' it says, 'the common reason of society ought to check the aberrations of individual eccentricity.' This common reason of society looks very like our best self or right reason, to which we want to give authority, by making the action of the *State*, or nation in its collective character, the expression of it. But of this project of ours, the *Daily News*, with its subtle dialectics, makes havoc. 'Make the State the organ of the common reason?'—it says. 'You make it the organ of something or other, but how can you be certain that reason will be the quality which will be embodied in it?' You cannot be certain of it, undoubtedly, if you never try to bring the thing about; but the question is, the action of the State being the action of the collective nation, and the action of the collective nation carrying naturally great publicity, weight, and force of example with it, whether we should not try to put into the action of the State as much as possible of right reason or our best self, which may, in this manner, come back to us with new force and authority; may have visibility, form, and influence; and help to confirm us, in the many moments when we are tempted to be our ordinary selves merely, in resisting our natural taste of the bathos rather than in giving way to it?

But no! says our teacher: 'It is better there should be an infinite variety of experiments in human action; the common reason of society will in the main check the aberrations of individual eccentricity well enough, if left to its natural operation.' This is what I call the specially British form of Quietism, or a devout, but excessive reliance on an over-ruling Providence. Providence, as the moralists are careful to tell us, generally works in human affairs by human means; so, when we want to make right reason act on individual inclination, our best self on our ordinary self, we seek to give it more power of doing so by giving it public recognition and authority, and embodying it, so far as we can, in the State. It seems too much to ask of Providence, that while we, on our part, leave our congenital taste for the bathos to its natural operation and its infinite variety of experiments, Providence should mysteriously guide it into the true track, and compel it to relish the sublime. At any rate, great men and great institutions have hitherto seemed necessary for producing any considerable effect of this kind. No doubt we have an infinite variety of experiments and an ever-multiplying multitude of explorers. Even in these few chapters I have enumerated many: the *British Banner*, Judge Edmonds, Newman Weeks, Deborah Butler, Elderess Polly, Brother Noyes, Mr. Murphy, the Licensed Victuallers, the Commercial Travellers, and I know not how many more ; and the members of the noble army are swelling every day. But what a depth of Quietism, or rather, what an over-bold call on the direct interposition of Providence, to believe that these interesting explorers will discover the true track, or at any rate, 'will do so in the main well enough' (whatever that may mean) if left to their natural operation ; that is, by going on as they are! Philosophers say, indeed, that we learn virtue by performing acts of virtue ; but to say that we shall learn virtue by performing any acts to which our natural taste for the bathos carries us, that the fanatical Protestant comes at his best self by Papist-baiting, or Newman Weeks and Deborah Butler at right reason by following their noses, this certainly does appear over-sanguine.

It is true, what we want is to make right reason act on individual reason, the reason of individuals ; all our search for authority has that for its end and aim. The *Daily News* says, I observe, that all my argument for authority 'has a non-intellectual root' ; and from what I know of my own mind and its poverty I think this so probable, that I should be inclined easily to admit it, if it were not that, in the first place, nothing of this kind, perhaps, should be admitted without examination ; and, in the second, a way of accounting for the charge being made, in this particular instance, without good grounds, appears to present itself. What seems to me to account here, perhaps, for the charge, is the want of flexibility of our race, on which I have so often remarked. I mean, it being admitted that the conformity of the individual reason of the fanatical Protestant or the popular rioter with right reason is our true object, and not the mere restraining them, by the strong arm of the State, from Papist-baiting, or railing-breaking,—admitting this, we English have so little flexibility that we cannot readily perceive that the State's restraining them from these indulgences may yet fix clearly in their minds that, to the collective nation, these indulgences appear irrational and unallowable, may make them pause and reflect, and may contribute to bringing, with time, their individual reason into harmony with right reason. But in no country, owing to the want of intellectual flexibility above mentioned, is the leaning which is our natural one, and, therefore, needs no recommending to us, so sedulously recommended, and the leaning which is not our natural one, and, therefore, does not need dispraising to us, so sedulously dispraised, as in ours. To rely on the individual being, with us, the natural leaning, we will hear of nothing but the good of relying on the individual; to act through the collective nation on the individual being not our natural leaning, we will hear nothing in recommendation of it. But the wise know that we often need to hear most of that to which we are least inclined, and even to learn to employ, in certain circumstances, that which is capable, if employed amiss, of being a danger to us.

Elsewhere this is certainly better understood than here. In a recent number of the *Westminster Review*, an able writer, but with precisely our national want of flexibility of which I have been speaking, has unearthed, I see, for our present needs, an English translation, published some years ago, of Wilhelm von Humboldt's book, *The Sphere and Duties of Government.* Humboldt's object in this book is to show that the operation of government ought to be severely limited to what directly and immediately relates to the security of person and property. Wilhelm von Humboldt, one of the most beautiful souls that have ever existed, used to say that one's business in life was first to perfect one's self by all the means in one's power, and secondly, to try and create in the world around one an aristocracy, the most numerous that one possibly could, of talents and characters. He saw, of course, that, in the end, everything comes to this,—that the individual must act for himself, and must be perfect in himself; and he lived in a country, Germany, where people were disposed to act too little for themselves, and to rely too much on the Government. But even thus, such was his flexibility, so little was he in bondage to a mere abstract maxim, that he saw very well that for his purpose itself, of enabling the individual to stand perfect on his own foundations and to do without the State, the action of the State would for long, long years be necessary. And soon after he wrote his book on *The Sphere and Duties of Government*, Wilhelm von Humboldt became Minister of Education in Prussia ; and from his ministry all the great reforms which give the control of Prussian education to the State,—the transference of the management of public schools from their old boards of trustees to the State, the obligatory State-examination for schoolmasters, and the foundation of the great State-University of Berlin,—take their origin. This his English reviewer says not a word of. But, writing for a people whose dangers lie, as we have seen, on the side of their unchecked and unguided individual action, whose dangers none of them lie on the side of an over-reliance on the State, he quotes just so much of Wilhelm von Humboldt's example as can flatter them in their propensities, and do them no good ; and just what might make them think, and be of use to them, he leaves on one side. This precisely recalls the manner, it will be observed, in which we have seen that our royal and noble personages proceed with the Licensed Victuallers.

In France the action of the State on individuals is yet more preponderant than in Germany ; and the need which friends of human perfection feel for what may enable the individual to stand perfect on his own foundations is all the stronger. But what says one of the staunchest of these friends, M. Renan, on State action; and even State action in that very sphere where in France it is most excessive, the sphere of education? Here are his words:—'A Liberal believes in liberty, and liberty signifies the non-intervention of the State. *But such an ideal is still a long way off from us, and the very means to remove it to an indefinite distance would be precisely the State's withdrawing its action too soon.*' And this, he adds, is even truer of education than of any other department of public affairs.

We see, then, how indispensable to that human perfection which we seek is, in the opinion of good judges, some public recognition and establishment of our best self, or right reason. We see how our habits and practice oppose themselves to such a recognition, and the many inconveniences which we therefore suffer. But now let us try to go a little deeper, and to find, beneath our actual habits and practice, the very ground and cause out of which they spring.

CHAPTER IV

HEBRAISM AND HELLENISM

This fundamental ground is our preference of doing to thinking. Now this preference is a main element in our nature, and as we study it we find ourselves opening up a number of large questions on every side.

Let me go back for a moment to Bishop Wilson, who says: 'First, never go against the best light you have; secondly, take care that your light be not darkness.' We show, as a nation, laudable energy and persistence in walking according to the best light we have, but are not quite careful enough, perhaps, to see that our light be not darkness. This is only another version of the old story that energy is our strong point and favourable characteristic, rather than intelligence. But we may give to this idea a more general form still, in which it will have a yet larger range of application. We may regard this energy driving at practice, this paramount sense of the obligation of duty, self-control, and work, this earnestness in going manfully with the best light we have, as one force. And we may regard the intelligence driving at those ideas which are, after all, the basis of right practice, the ardent sense for all the new and changing combinations of them which man's development brings with it, the indomitable impulse to know and adjust them perfectly, as another force. And these two forces we may regard as in some sense rivals,—rivals not by the necessity of their own nature, but as exhibited in man and his history,—and rivals dividing the empire of the world between them. And to give these forces names from the two races of men who have supplied the most signal and splendid manifestations of them, we may call them respectively the forces of Hebraism and Hellenism. Hebraism and Hellenism,—between these two points of influence moves our world. At one time it feels more powerfully the attraction of one of them, at another time of the other; and it ought to be, though it never is, evenly and happily balanced between them.

The final aim of both Hellenism and Hebraism, as of all great spiritual disciplines, is no doubt the same: man's perfection or salvation. The very language which they both of them use in schooling us to reach this aim is often identical. Even when their language indicates by variation,—sometimes a broad variation, often a but slight and subtle variation,—the different courses of thought which are uppermost in each discipline, even then the unity of the final end and aim is still apparent. To employ the actual words of that discipline with which we ourselves are all of us most familiar, and the words of which, therefore, come most home to us, that final end and aim is 'that we might be partakers of the divine nature.' These are the words of a Hebrew apostle, but of Hellenism and Hebraism alike this is, I say, the aim. When the two are confronted, as they very often are confronted, it is nearly always with what I may call a rhetorical purpose; the speaker's whole design is to exalt and enthrone one of the two, and he uses the other only as a foil and to enable him the better to give effect to his purpose. Obviously, with us, it is usually Hellenism which is thus reduced to minister to the triumph of Hebraism. There is a sermon on Greece and the Greek spirit by a man never to be mentioned without interest and respect, Frederick Robertson, in which this rhetorical use of Greece and the Greek spirit, and the inadequate exhibition of them necessarily consequent upon this, is almost ludicrous, and would be censurable if it were not to be explained by the exigencies of a sermon. On the other hand, Heinrich Heine, and other writers of his sort, give us the spectacle of the tables completely turned, and of Hebraism brought in just as a foil and contrast to Hellenism, and to make the superiority of Hellenism more manifest. In both these cases there is injustice and misrepresentation. The aim and end of both Hebraism and Hellenism is, as I have said, one and the same, and this aim and end is august and admirable.

Still, they pursue this aim by very different courses. The uppermost idea with Hellenism is to see things as they really are; the uppermost idea with Hebraism is conduct and obedience. Nothing can do away with this ineffaceable difference. The Greek quarrel with the body and its desires is, that they hinder right thinking; the Hebrew quarrel with them is, that they hinder right acting. 'He that keepeth the law, happy is he'; 'Blessed is the man that feareth the Eternal, that delighteth greatly in his commandments';—that is the Hebrew notion of felicity; and, pursued with passion and tenacity, this notion would not let the Hebrew rest till, as is well known, he had at last got out of the law a network of prescriptions to enwrap his whole life, to govern every moment of it, every impulse, every action. The Greek notion of felicity, on the other hand, is perfectly conveyed in these words of a great French moralist: '*C'est le bonheur des hommes*,'—when? when they abhor that which is evil?—no; when they exercise themselves in the law of the Lord day and night?—no; when they die daily?—no; when they walk about the New Jerusalem with palms in their hands?—no; but when they think aright, when their thought hits: '*quand ils pensent juste*.'

At the bottom of both the Greek and the Hebrew notion is the desire, native in man, for reason and the will of God, the feeling after the universal order,—in a word, the love of God. But, while Hebraism seizes upon certain plain, capital intimations of the universal order, and rivets itself, one may say, with unequalled grandeur of earnestness and intensity on the study and observance of them, the bent of Hellenism is to follow, with flexible activity, the whole play of the universal order, to be apprehensive of missing any part of it, of sacrificing one part to another, to slip away from resting in this or that intimation of it, however capital. An unclouded clearness of mind, an unimpeded play of thought, is what this bent drives at. The governing idea of Hellenism is *spontaneity of consciousness;* that of Hebraism, *strictness of conscience.*

Christianity changed nothing in this essential bent of Hebraism to set doing above knowing. Self-conquest, self-devotion, the following not our own individual will, but the will of God, *obedience*, is the fundamental idea of this form, also, of the discipline to which we have attached the general name of Hebraism. Only, as the old law and the network of prescriptions with which it enveloped human life were evidently a motive-power not driving and searching enough to produce the result aimed at,—patient continuance in well-doing, self-conquest,—Christianity substituted for them boundless devotion to that inspiring and affecting pattern of self-conquest offered by Jesus Christ ; and by the new motive-power, of which the essence was this, though the love and admiration of Christian churches have for centuries been employed in varying, amplifying, and adorning the plain description of it, Christianity, as St. Paul truly says, 'establishes the law,' and in the strength of the ampler power which she has thus supplied to fulfil it, has accomplished the miracles, which we all see, of her history.

So long as we do not forget that both Hellenism and Hebraism are profound and admirable manifestations of man's life, tendencies, and powers, and that both of them aim at a like final result, we can hardly insist too strongly on the divergence of line and of operation with which they proceed. It is a divergence so great that it most truly, as the prophet Zechariah says, 'has raised up thy sons, O Zion, against thy sons, O Greece !' The difference whether it is by doing or by knowing that we set most store, and the practical consequences which follow from this difference, leave their mark on all the history of our race and of its development. Language may be abundantly quoted from both Hellenism and Hebraism to make it seem that one follows the same current as the other towards the same goal. They are, truly, borne towards the same goal ; but the currents which bear them are infinitely different. It is true, Solomon will praise knowing: 'Understanding is a well-spring of life unto him that hath it.' And in the New Testament, again, Jesus Christ is a 'light,' and 'truth makes us free.' It is true, Aristotle will undervalue knowing: 'In what concerns virtue,' says he, 'three things are necessary—knowledge, deliberate will, and perseverance; but, whereas the two last are all-important, the first is a matter of little importance.' It is true that with the same impatience with which St. James enjoins a man to be not a forgetful hearer, but a *doer of the work*, Epictetus exhorts us to *do* what we have demonstrated to ourselves we ought to do; or he taunts us with futility, for being armed at all points to prove that lying is wrong, yet all the time continuing to lie. It is true, Plato, in words which are almost the words of the New Testament or the Imitation, calls life a learning to die. But underneath the superficial agreement the fundamental divergence still subsists. The understanding of Solomon is 'the walking in the way of the commandments'; this is 'the way of peace,' and it is of this that blessedness comes. In the New Testament, the truth which gives us the peace of God and makes us free, is the love of Christ constraining us to crucify, as he did, and with a like purpose of moral regeneration, the flesh with its affections and lusts, and thus establishing, as we have seen, the law. The moral virtues, on the other hand, are with Aristotle but the porch and access to the intellectual, and with these last is blessedness. That partaking of the divine life, which both Hellenism and Hebraism, as we have said, fix as their crowning aim, Plato expressly denies to the man of practical virtue merely, of self-conquest with any other motive than that of perfect intellectual vision. He reserves it for the lover of pure knowledge, of seeing things as they really are,—the φιλομαθής.

Both Hellenism and Hebraism arise out of the wants of human nature, and address themselves to satisfying those wants. But their methods are so different, they lay stress on such different points, and call into being by their respective disciplines such different activities, that the face which human nature presents when it passes from the hands of one of them to those of the other, is no longer the same. To get rid of one's ignorance, to see things as they are, and by seeing them as they are to see them in their beauty, is the simple and attractive ideal which Hellenism holds out before human nature ; and from the simplicity and charm of this ideal, Hellenism, and human life in the hands of Hellenism, is invested with a kind of aërial ease, clearness, and radiancy ; they are full of what we call sweetness and light. Difficulties are kept out of view, and the beauty and rationalness of the ideal have all our thoughts. 'The best man is he who most tries to perfect himself, and the happiest man is he who most feels that he *is* perfecting himself,' —this account of the matter by Socrates, the true Socrates of the *Memorabilia*, has something so simple, spontaneous, and unsophisticated about it, that it seems to fill us with clearness and hope when we hear it. But there is a saying which I have heard attributed to Mr. Carlyle about Socrates,—a very happy saying, whether it is really Mr. Carlyle's or not,—which excellently marks the essential point in which Hebraism differs from Hellenism. 'Socrates,' this saying goes, 'is terribly *at ease in Zion.*' Hebraism,—and here is the source of its wonderful strength,—has always been severely preoccupied with an awful sense of the impossibility of being at ease in Zion; of the difficulties which oppose themselves to man's pursuit or attainment of that perfection of which Socrates talks so hopefully, and, as from this point of view one might almost say, so glibly. It is all very well to talk of getting rid of one's ignorance, of seeing things in their reality, seeing them in their beauty; but how is this to be done when there is something which thwarts and spoils all our efforts?

This something is *sin*; and the space which sin fills in Hebraism, as compared with Hellenism, is indeed prodigious. This obstacle to perfection fills the whole scene, and perfection appears remote and rising away from earth, in the background. Under the name of sin, the difficulties of knowing oneself and conquering oneself which impede man's passage to perfection, become, for Hebraism, a positive, active entity hostile to man, a mysterious power which I heard Dr. Pusey the other day, in one of his impressive sermons, compare to a hideous hunchback seated on our shoulders, and which it is the main business of our lives to hate and oppose. The discipline of the Old Testament may be summed up as a discipline teaching us to abhor and flee from sin; the discipline of the New Testament, as a discipline teaching us to die to it. As Hellenism speaks of thinking clearly, seeing things in their essence and beauty, as a grand and precious feat for man to achieve, so Hebraism speaks of becoming conscious of sin, of awakening to a sense of sin, as a feat of this kind. It is obvious to what wide divergence these differing tendencies, actively followed, must lead. As one passes and repasses from Hellenism to Hebraism, from Plato to St. Paul, one feels inclined to rub one's eyes and ask oneself whether man is indeed a gentle and simple being, showing the traces of a noble and divine nature; or an unhappy chained captive, labouring with groanings that cannot be uttered to free himself from the body of this death.

Apparently it was the Hellenic conception of human nature which was unsound, for the world could not live by it. Absolutely to call it unsound, however, is to fall into the common error of its Hebraising enemies; but it was unsound at that particular moment of man's development, it was premature. The indispensable basis of conduct and self-control, the platform upon which alone the perfection aimed at by Greece can come into bloom, was not to be reached by our race so easily; centuries of probation and discipline were needed to bring us to it. Therefore the bright promise of Hellenism faded, and Hebraism ruled the world. Then was seen that astonishing spectacle, so well marked by the often-quoted words of the prophet Zechariah, when men of all languages and nations took hold of the skirt of him that was a Jew, saying:—'*We will go with you, for we have heard that God is with you.*' And the Hebraism which thus received and ruled a world all gone out of the way and altogether become unprofitable, was, and could not but be, the later, the more spiritual, the more attractive development of Hebraism. It was Christianity; that is to say, Hebraism aiming at self-conquest and rescue from the thrall of vile affections, not by obedience to the letter of a law, but by conformity to the image of a self-sacrificing example. To a world stricken with moral enervation Christianity offered its spectacle of an inspired self-sacrifice; to men who refused themselves nothing, it showed one who refused himself everything;—'*my Saviour banished joy!*'

says George Herbert. When the *alma Venus*, the life-giving and joy-giving power of nature, so fondly cherished by the Pagan world, could not save her followers from self-dissatisfaction and ennui, the severe words of the apostle came bracingly and refreshingly: 'Let no man deceive you with vain words, for because of these things cometh the wrath of God upon the children of disobedience.' Through age after age, and generation after generation, our race, or all that part of our race which was most living and progressive, was *baptized into a death*; and endeavoured, by suffering in the flesh, to cease from sin. Of this endeavour, the animating labours and afflictions of early Christianity, the touching asceticism of mediæval Christianity, are the great historical manifestations. Literary monuments of it, each in its own way incomparable, remain in the Epistles of St. Paul, in St. Augustine's Confessions, and in the two original and simplest books of the Imitation.[1]

Of two disciplines laying their main stress, the one, on clear intelligence, the other, on firm obedience; the one, on comprehensively knowing the grounds of one's duty, the other, on diligently practising it; the one, on taking all possible care (to use Bishop Wilson's words again) that the light we have be not darkness, the other, that according to the best light we have we diligently walk,—the priority naturally

[1] The two first books.

belongs to that discipline which braces all man's moral powers, and founds for him an indispensable basis of character. And, therefore, it is justly said of the Jewish people, who were charged with setting powerfully forth that side of the divine order to which the words *conscience* and *self-conquest* point, that they were 'entrusted with the oracles of God'; as it is justly said of Christianity, which followed Judaism and which set forth this side with a much deeper effectiveness and a much wider influence, that the wisdom of the old Pagan world was foolishness compared to it. No words of devotion and admiration can be too strong to render thanks to these beneficent forces which have so borne forward humanity in its appointed work of coming to the knowledge and possession of itself; above all, in those great moments when their action was the wholesomest and the most necessary.

But the evolution of these forces, separately and in themselves, is not the whole evolution of humanity,—their single history is not the whole history of man; whereas their admirers are always apt to make it stand for the whole history. Hebraism and Hellenism are, neither of them, the *law* of human development, as their admirers are prone to make them; they are, each of them, *contributions* to human development,—august contributions, invaluable contributions; and each showing itself to us more august, more invaluable, more preponderant over the other, according to the moment in which we take them, and the relation in which we stand to them. The nations of our modern world, children of that immense and salutary movement which broke up the Pagan world, inevitably stand to Hellenism in a relation which dwarfs it, and to Hebraism in a relation which magnifies it. They are inevitably prone to take Hebraism as the law of human development, and not as simply a contribution to it, however precious. And yet the lesson must perforce be learned, that the human spirit is wider than the most priceless of the forces which bear it onward, and that to the whole development of man Hebraism itself is, like Hellenism, but a contribution.

Perhaps we may help ourselves to see this clearer by an illustration drawn from the treatment of a single great idea which has profoundly engaged the human spirit, and has given it eminent opportunities for showing its nobleness and energy. It surely must be perceived that the idea of immortality, as this idea rises in its generality before the human spirit, is something grander, truer, and more satisfying, than it is in the particular forms by which St. Paul, in the famous fifteenth chapter of the Epistle to the Corinthians, and Plato, in the *Phaedo*, endeavour to develop and establish it. Surely we cannot but feel, that the argumentation with which the Hebrew apostle goes about to expound this great idea is, after all, confused and inconclusive ; and that the reasoning, drawn from analogies of likeness and equality, which is employed upon it by the Greek philosopher, is over-subtle and sterile. Above and beyond the inadequate solutions which Hebraism and Hellenism here attempt, extends the immense and august problem itself, and the human spirit which gave birth to it. And this single illustration may suggest to us how the same thing happens in other cases also.

But meanwhile, by alternations of Hebraism and Hellenism, of a man's intellectual and moral impulses, of the effort to see things as they really are, and the effort to win peace by self-conquest, the human spirit proceeds ; and each of these two forces has its appointed hours of culmination and seasons of rule. As the great movement of Christianity was a triumph of Hebraism and man's moral impulses, so the great movement which goes by the name of the Renascence[1] was an uprising and re-instatement of man's intellectual impulses and of Hellenism. We in England, the devoted children of Protestantism, chiefly know the Renascence by its subordinate and secondary side of the Reformation. The Reformation has been often called a Hebraising revival, a return to the ardour and sincereness of

[1] I have ventured to give to the foreign word *Renaissance*,—destined to become of more common use amongst us as the movement which it denotes comes, as it will come, increasingly to interest us,—an English form.

primitive Christianity. No one, however, can study the development of Protestantism and of Protestant churches without feeling that into the Reformation too,—Hebraising child of the Renascence and offspring of its fervour, rather than its intelligence, as it undoubtedly was,—the subtle Hellenic leaven of the Renascence found its way, and that the exact respective parts, in the Reformation, of Hebraism and of Hellenism, are not easy to separate. But what we may with truth say is, that all which Protestantism was to itself clearly conscious of, all which it succeeded in clearly setting forth in words, had the characters of Hebraism rather than of Hellenism. The Reformation was strong, in that it was an earnest return to the Bible and to doing from the heart the will of God as there written. It was weak, in that it never consciously grasped or applied the central idea of the Renascence,—the Hellenic idea of pursuing, in all lines of activity, the law and science, to use Plato's words, of things as they really are. Whatever direct superiority, therefore, Protestantism had over Catholicism was a moral superiority, a superiority arising out of its greater sincerity and earnestness,—at the moment of its apparition at any rate,—in dealing with the heart and conscience. Its pretensions to an intellectual superiority are in general quite illusory. For Hellenism, for the thinking side in man as distinguished from the acting side, the attitude of mind of Protestantism towards the Bible in no respect differs from the attitude of mind of Catholicism towards the Church. The mental habit of him who imagines that Balaam's ass spoke, in no respect differs from the mental habit of him who imagines that a Madonna of wood or stone winked; and the one, who says that God's Church makes him believe what he believes, and the other, who says that God's Word makes him believe what he believes, are for the philosopher perfectly alike in not really and truly knowing, when they say *God's Church* and *God's Word*, what it is they say, or whereof they affirm.

In the sixteenth century, therefore, Hellenism re-entered the world, and again stood in presence of Hebraism,—a Hebraism renewed and purged. Now, it has not been enough observed, how, in the seventeenth century, a fate befell Hellenism in some respects analogous to that which befell it at the commencement of our era. The Renascence, that great re-awakening of Hellenism, that irresistible return of humanity to nature and to seeing things as they are, which in art, in literature, and in physics, produced such splendid fruits, had, like the anterior Hellenism of the Pagan world, a side of moral weakness and of relaxation or insensibility of the moral fibre, which in Italy showed itself with the most startling plainness, but which in France, England, and other countries was very apparent too. Again this loss of spiritual balance, this exclusive

Spiritual balance.

preponderance given to man's perceiving and knowing side, this unnatural defect of his feeling and acting side, provoked a reaction. Let us trace that reaction where it most nearly concerns us.

Science has now made visible to everybody the great and pregnant elements of difference which lie in race, and in how signal a manner they make the genius and history of an Indo-European people vary from those of a Semitic people. Hellenism is of Indo-European growth, Hebraism is of Semitic growth ; and we English, a nation of Indo-European stock, seem to belong naturally to the movement of Hellenism. But nothing more strongly marks the essential unity of man, than the affinities we can perceive, in this point or that, between members of one family of peoples and members of another. And no affinity of this kind is more strongly marked than that likeness in the strength and prominence of the moral fibre, which, notwithstanding immense elements of difference, knits in some special sort the genius and history of us English, and our American descendants across the Atlantic, to the genius and history of the Hebrew people. Puritanism, which has been so great a power in the English nation, and in the strongest part of the English nation, was originally the reaction in the seventeenth century of the conscience and moral sense of our race, against the moral indifference and lax rule of conduct which in the sixteenth century came in with the Renascence. It was a reaction of Hebraism against Hellenism; and it powerfully manifested itself, as was natural, in a people with much of what we call a Hebraising turn, with a signal affinity for the bent which was the master-bent of Hebrew life. Eminently Indo-European by its *humour*, by the power it shows, through this gift, of imaginatively acknowledging the multiform aspects of the problem of life, and of thus getting itself unfixed from its own over-certainty, of smiling at its own over-tenacity, our race has yet (and a great part of its strength lies here), in matters of practical life and moral conduct, a strong share of the assuredness, the tenacity, the intensity of the Hebrews. This turn manifested itself in Puritanism, and has had a great part in shaping our history for the last two hundred years. Undoubtedly it checked and changed amongst us that movement of the Renascence which we see producing in the reign of Elizabeth such wonderful fruits. Undoubtedly it stopped the prominent rule and direct development of that order of ideas which we call by the name of Hellenism, and gave the first rank to a different order of ideas. Apparently, too, as we said of the former defeat of Hellenism, if Hellenism was defeated, this shows that Hellenism was imperfect, and that its ascendency at that moment would not have been for the world's good.

Yet there is a very important difference

between the defeat inflicted on Hellenism by Christianity eighteen hundred years ago, and the check given to the Renascence by Puritanism. The greatness of the difference is well measured by the difference in force, beauty, significance, and usefulness, between primitive Christianity and Protestantism. Eighteen hundred years ago it was altogether the hour of Hebraism. Primitive Christianity was legitimately and truly the ascendant force in the world at that time, and the way of mankind's progress lay through its full development. Another hour in man's development began in the fifteenth century, and the main road of his progress then lay for a time through Hellenism. Puritanism was no longer the central current of the world's progress, it was a side stream crossing the central current and checking it. The cross and the check may have been necessary and salutary, but that does not do away with the essential difference between the main stream of man's advance and a cross or side stream. For more than two hundred years the main stream of man's advance has moved towards knowing himself and the world, seeing things as they are, spontaneity of consciousness; the main impulse of a great part, and that the strongest part, of our nation has been towards strictness of conscience. They have made the secondary the principal at the wrong moment, and the principal they have at the wrong moment treated as secondary. This contravention of the natural order has produced, as such contravention always must produce, a certain confusion and false movement, of which we are now beginning to feel, in almost every direction, the inconvenience. In all directions our habitual causes of action seem to be losing efficaciousness, credit, and control, both with others and even with ourselves. Everywhere we see the beginnings of confusion, and we want a clue to some sound order and authority. This we can only get by going back upon the actual instincts and forces which rule our life, seeing them as they really are, connecting them with other instincts and forces, and enlarging our whole view and rule of life.

CHAPTER V

PORRO UNUM EST NECESSARIUM

THE matter here opened is so large, and the trains of thought to which it gives rise are so manifold, that we must be careful to limit ourselves scrupulously to what has a direct bearing upon our actual discussion. We have found that at the bottom of our present unsettled state, so full of the seeds of trouble, lies the notion of its being the prime right and happiness, for each of us, to affirm himself, and his ordinary self; to be doing, and to be doing freely and as he likes. We have found at the bottom of it the disbelief in right reason as a lawful authority. It was easy to show from our practice and current history that this is so; but it was impossible to show why it is so without taking a somewhat wider sweep and going into things a little more deeply. Why, in fact, should good, well-meaning, energetic, sensible people, like the bulk of our countrymen, come to have such light belief in right reason, and such an exaggerated value for their own independent doing, however crude? The answer is: because of an exclusive and excessive development in them, without due allowance for time, place, and circumstance, of that side of human nature, and that group of human forces, to which we have given the general name of Hebraism. Because they have thought their real and only important homage was owed to a power concerned with obedience rather than with their intelligence, a power interested in the moral side of their nature almost exclusively. Thus they have been led to regard in themselves, as the one thing needful, *strictness of conscience*, the staunch adherence to some fixed law of doing we have got already, instead of *spontaneity of consciousness*, which tends continually to enlarge our whole law of doing. They have fancied themselves to have in their religion a sufficient basis for the whole of their life fixed and certain for ever, a full law of conduct and a full law of thought, so far as thought is needed, as well; whereas what they really have is a law of conduct, a law of unexampled power for enabling them to war against the law of sin in their members and not to serve it in the lusts thereof. The book which contains this invaluable law they call the Word of God, and attribute to it, as I have said, and as, indeed, is perfectly well known, a reach and sufficiency coextensive with all the wants of human nature.

This might, no doubt, be so, if humanity

were not the composite thing it is, if it had only, or in quite overpowering eminence, a moral side, and the group of instincts and powers which we call moral. But it has besides, and in notable eminence, an intellectual side, and the group of instincts and powers which we call intellectual. No doubt, mankind makes in general its progress in a fashion which gives at one time full swing to one of these groups of instincts, at another time to the other; and man's faculties are so intertwined, that when his moral side, and the current of force which we call Hebraism, is uppermost, this side will manage somehow to provide, or appear to provide, satisfaction for his intellectual needs; and when his intellectual side, and the current of force which we call Hellenism, is uppermost, this again will provide, or appear to provide, satisfaction for men's moral needs. But sooner or later it becomes manifest that when the two sides of humanity proceed in this fashion of alternate preponderance, and not of mutual understanding and balance, the side which is uppermost does not really provide in a satisfactory manner for the needs of the side which is undermost, and a state of confusion is, sooner or later, the result. The Hellenic half of our nature, bearing rule, makes a sort of provision for the Hebrew half, but it turns out to be an inadequate provision; and again the Hebrew half of our nature, bearing rule, makes a sort of provision for the Hellenic half, but this, too, turns out to be an inadequate provision. The true and smooth order of humanity's development is not reached in either way. And therefore, while we willingly admit with the Christian apostle that the world by wisdom,—that is, by the isolated preponderance of its intellectual impulses,—knew not God, or the true order of things, it is yet necessary, also, to set up a sort of converse to this proposition, and to say likewise (what is equally true) that the world by Puritanism knew not God. And it is on this converse of the apostle's proposition that it is particularly needful to insist in our own country just at present.

Here, indeed, is the answer to many criticisms which have been addressed to all that we have said in praise of sweetness and light. Sweetness and light evidently have to do with the bent or side in humanity which we call Hellenic. Greek intelligence has obviously for its essence the instinct for what Plato calls the true, firm, intelligible law of things; the law of light, of seeing things as they are. Even in the natural sciences, where the Greeks had not time and means adequately to apply this instinct, and where we have gone a great deal further than they did, it is this instinct which is the root of the whole matter and the ground of all our success; and this instinct the world has mainly learnt of the Greeks, inasmuch as they are humanity's most signal manifestation of it. Greek art, again, Greek beauty, have their root in the same impulse to see things as they really are, inasmuch as Greek art and beauty rest on fidelity to nature,—the *best* nature,—and on a delicate discrimination of what this best nature is. To say we work for sweetness and light, then, is only another way of saying that we work for Hellenism. But, oh! cry many people, sweetness and light are not enough; you must put strength or energy along with them, and make a kind of trinity of strength, sweetness and light, and then, perhaps, you may do some good. That is to say, we are to join Hebraism, strictness of the moral conscience, and manful walking by the best light we have, together with Hellenism, inculcate both, and rehearse the praises of both.

Or, rather, we may praise both in conjunction, but we must be careful to praise Hebraism most. 'Culture,' says an acute, though somewhat rigid critic, Mr. Sidgwick, 'diffuses sweetness and light. I do not undervalue these blessings, but religion gives fire and strength, and the world wants fire and strength even more than sweetness and light.' By religion, let me explain, Mr. Sidgwick here means particularly that Puritanism on the insufficiency of which I have been commenting and to which he says I am unfair. Now, no doubt, it is possible to be a fanatical partisan of light and the instincts which push us to it, a fanatical enemy of strictness of moral conscience and the instincts which push us to it. A fanaticism of this sort deforms and vulgarises the well-known work, in some respects so remarkable, of the late Mr. Buckle. Such a fanaticism carries its own mark with it, in lacking sweetness; and its own penalty, in that, lacking sweetness, it comes in the end to lack light too. And the Greeks,—the great exponents of humanity's bent for sweetness and light united, of its perception that the truth of things must be at the same time beauty,—singularly escaped the fanaticism which we moderns, whether we Hellenise or whether we Hebraise, are so apt to show. They arrived,—though failing, as has been said, to give adequate practical satisfaction to the claims of man's moral side,—at the idea of a comprehensive adjustment of the claims of both the sides in man, the moral as well as the intellectual, of a full estimate of both, and of a reconciliation of both; an idea which is philosophically of the greatest value, and the best of lessons for us moderns. So we ought to have no difficulty in conceding to Mr. Sidgwick that manful walking by the best light one has, —fire and strength as he calls it,—has its high value as well as culture, the endeavour to see things in their truth and beauty, the pursuit of sweetness and light. But whether at this or that time, and to this or that set of persons, one ought to insist most on the praises of fire and strength, or on the praises of sweetness and light, must depend, one would think, on the circumstances and needs of that particular time and those particular persons. And all that we have been saying, and indeed any glance at the world around us shows that with us, with the most respectable and strongest part of us, the ruling force is now, and long has been, a Puritan force,—the care for fire and strength, strictness of conscience, Hebraism, rather than the care for sweetness and light, spontaneity of consciousness, Hellenism.

Well, then, what is the good of our now rehearsing the praises of fire and strength to ourselves, who dwell too exclusively on them already? When Mr. Sidgwick says so broadly, that the world wants fire and strength even more than sweetness and light, is he not carried away by a turn for broad generalisation? does he not forget that the world is not all of one piece, and every piece with the same needs at the same time? It may be true that the Roman world at the beginning of our era, or Leo the Tenth's Court at the time of the Reformation, or French society in the eighteenth century, needed fire and strength even more than sweetness and light. But can it be said that the Barbarians who overran the empire needed fire and strength even more than sweetness and light; or that the Puritans needed them more; or that Mr. Murphy, the Birmingham lecturer, and his friends, need them more?

The Puritan's great danger is that he imagines

himself in possession of a rule telling him the *unum necessarium*, or one thing needful, and that he then remains satisfied with a very crude conception of what this rule really is and what it tells him, thinks he has now knowledge and henceforth needs only to act, and, in this dangerous state of assurance and self-satisfaction, proceeds to give full swing to a number of the instincts of his ordinary self. Some of the instincts of his ordinary self he has, by the help of his rule of life, conquered; but others which he has not conquered by this help he is so far from perceiving to need subjugation, and to be instincts of an inferior self, that he even fancies it to be his right and duty, in virtue of having conquered a limited part of himself, to give unchecked swing to the remainder. He is, I say, a victim of Hebraism, of the tendency to cultivate strictness of conscience rather than spontaneity of consciousness. And what he wants is a larger conception of human nature, showing him the number of other points at which his nature must come to its best, besides the points which he himself knows and thinks of. There is no *unum necessarium*, or one thing needful, which can free human nature from the obligation of trying to come to its best at all these points. The real *unum necessarium* for us is to come to our best at all points. Instead of our 'one thing needful,' justifying in us vulgarity, hideousness, ignorance, violence,—our vulgarity, hideousness, ignorance, violence, are really so many touchstones which try our one thing needful, and which prove that in the state, at any rate, in which we ourselves have it, it is not all we want. And as the force which encourages us to stand staunch and fast by the rule and ground we have is Hebraism, so the force which encourages us to go back upon this rule, and to try the very ground on which we appear to stand, is Hellenism,—a turn for giving our consciousness free play and enlarging its range. And what I say is, not that Hellenism is always for everybody more wanted than Hebraism, but that for Mr. Murphy at this particular moment, and for the great majority of us his fellow-countrymen, it is more wanted.

Nothing is more striking than to observe in how many ways a limited conception of human nature, the notion of a one thing needful, a one side in us to be made uppermost, the disregard of a full and harmonious development of ourselves, tells injuriously on our thinking and acting. In the first place, our hold upon the rule or standard, to which we look for our one thing needful, tends to become less and less near and vital, our conception of it more and more mechanical, and more and more unlike the thing itself as it was conceived in the mind where it originated. The dealings of Puritanism with the writings of St. Paul, afford a noteworthy illustration of this. Nowhere so much as in the writings of St. Paul, and in that great apostle's greatest work, the Epistle to the Romans, has Puritanism found what seemed to furnish it with the one thing needful, and to give it canons of truth absolute and final. Now all writings, as has been already said, even the most precious writings and the most fruitful, must inevitably, from the very nature of things, be but contributions to human thought and human development, which extend wider than they do. Indeed, St. Paul, in the very Epistle of which we are speaking, shows, when he asks, 'Who hath known the mind of the Lord?'—who hath known, that is, the true and divine order of things in its entirety,—that he himself acknowledges this fully. And we have already pointed out in another Epistle of St. Paul a great and vital idea of the human spirit,—the idea of immortality,—transcending and overlapping, so to speak, the expositor's power to give it adequate definition and expression.

But quite distinct from the question whether St. Paul's expression, or any man's expression, can be a perfect and final expression of truth, comes the question whether we rightly seize and understand his expression as it exists. Now, perfectly to seize another man's meaning, as it stood in his own mind, is not easy; especially when the man is separated from us by such differences of race, training, time, and circumstances as St. Paul. But there are degrees of nearness in getting at a man's meaning; and though we cannot arrive quite at what St. Paul had in his mind, yet we may come near it. And who, that comes thus near it, must not feel how terms which St. Paul employs, in trying to follow with his analysis of such profound power and originality some of the most delicate, intricate, obscure, and contradictory workings and states of the human spirit, are detached and employed by Puritanism, not in the connected and fluid way in which St. Paul employs them, and for which alone words are really meant, but in an isolated, fixed, mechanical way, as if they were talismans; and how all trace and sense of St. Paul's true movement of ideas, and sustained masterly analysis, is thus lost? Who, I say, that has watched Puritanism,—the force which so strongly Hebraises, which so takes St. Paul's writings as something absolute and final, containing the one thing needful,—handle such terms as *grace*, *faith*, *election*, *righteousness*, but must feel, not only that these terms have for the mind of Puritanism a sense false and misleading, but also that this sense is the most monstrous and grotesque caricature of the sense of St. Paul, and that his true meaning is by these worshippers of his words altogether lost?

Or to take another eminent example, in which not Puritanism only, but, one may say, the whole religious world, by their mechanical use of St. Paul's writings, can be shown to miss or change his real meaning. The whole religious world, one may say, use now the word *resurrection*,—a word which is so often in their thoughts and on their lips, and which they find so often in St. Paul's writings,—in one sense only. They use it to mean a rising again after the physical death of the body. Now it is quite true that St. Paul speaks of resurrection in this sense, that he tries to describe and explain it, and that he condemns those who doubt and deny it. But it is true, also, that in nine cases out of ten where St. Paul thinks and speaks of resurrection, he thinks and speaks of it in a sense different from this;—in the sense of a rising to a new life before the physical death of the body, and not after it. The idea on which we have already touched, the profound idea of being baptized into the death of the great exemplar of self-devotion and self-annulment, of repeating in our own person, by virtue of identification with our exemplar, his course of self-devotion and self-annulment, and of thus coming, within the limits of our present life, to a new life, in which, as in the death going before it, we are identified with our exemplar,—this is the fruitful and original conception of being *risen with Christ* which possesses the mind of St. Paul, and this is the central point round which, with such incomparable emotion and eloquence, all his teaching moves. For him, the life after our physical death is really in the main but a consequence and continuation of the inexhaustible energy of the new life thus originated on this side the grave. This grand Pauline idea of Christian resurrection is worthily rehearsed in one of the noblest collects of the Prayer-Book, and is destined, no doubt, to fill a more and more important place in the Christianity of the future. But meanwhile, almost as signal as the essentialness of this characteristic idea in St. Paul's teaching, is the completeness with which the worshippers of St. Paul's words as an absolute final expression of saving truth have lost it, and have substituted for the apostle's living and near conception of a resurrection now, their mechanical and remote conception of a resurrection hereafter.

In short, so fatal is the notion of possessing, even in the most precious words or standards, the one thing needful, of having in them, once for all, a full and sufficient measure of light to guide us, and of there being no duty left for us except to make our practice square exactly with them,—so fatal, I say, is this notion to the right knowledge and comprehension of the very words or standards we thus adopt, and to such strange distortions and perversions of them does it inevitably lead, that whenever we hear that commonplace which Hebraism, if we venture to inquire what a man knows, is so apt to bring out against us, in disparagement of what we call culture, and in praise of a man's sticking to the one thing needful,—*he knows*, says Hebraism, *his Bible!*—whenever we hear this said, we may, without any elaborate defence of culture, content ourselves with answering simply: 'No man, who knows nothing else, knows even his Bible.'

Now the force which we have so much neglected, Hellenism, may be liable to fail in moral strength and earnestness, but by the law of its nature,—the very same law which makes it sometimes deficient in intensity when intensity is required,—it opposes itself to the notion of cutting our being in two, of attributing to one part the dignity of dealing with the one thing needful, and leaving the other part to take its chance, which is the bane of Hebraism. Essential in Hellenism is the impulse to the development of the whole man, to connecting and harmonising all parts of him, perfecting all, leaving none to take their chance.

The characteristic bent of Hellenism, as has been said, is to find the intelligible law of things, to see them in their true nature and as they really are. But many things are not seen in their true nature and as they really are, unless they are seen as beautiful. Behaviour is not intelligible, does not account for itself to the mind and show the reason for its existing, unless it is beautiful. The same with discourse, the same with song, the same with worship, all of them modes in which man proves his activity and expresses himself. To think that when one produces in these what is mean, or vulgar, or hideous, one can be permitted to plead that one has that within which passes show; to suppose that the possession of what benefits and satisfies one part of our being can make allowable either discourse like Mr. Murphy's, or poetry like the hymns we all hear, or places of worship like the chapels we all see,—this it is abhorrent to the nature of Hellenism to concede. And to be, like our honoured and justly honoured Faraday, a great natural philosopher with one side of his being and a Sandemanian with the other, would to Archimedes have been impossible.

It is evident to what a many-sided perfecting of man's powers and activities this demand of Hellenism for satisfaction to be given to the mind by everything which we do, is calculated to impel our race. It has its dangers, as has been fully granted. The notion of this sort of equipollency in man's modes of activity may lead to moral relaxation; what we do not make our one thing needful, we may come to treat not enough as if it were needful, though it is indeed very needful and at the same time very hard. Still, what side in us has not its dangers, and which of our impulses can be a talisman to give us perfection outright, and not merely a help to bring us towards it? Has not Hebraism, as we have shown, its dangers as well as Hellenism? or have we used so excessively the tendencies in ourselves to which Hellenism makes appeal, that we are now suffering from it? Are we not, on the contrary, now suffering because we have not enough used these tendencies as a help towards perfection?

For we see whither it has brought us, the long exclusive predominance of Hebraism,—the insisting on perfection in one part of our nature and not in all; the singling out the moral side, the side of obedience and action, for such intent regard; making strictness of the moral conscience so far the principal thing, and putting off for hereafter and for another world the care for being complete at all points, the full and harmonious development of our humanity. Instead of watching and following on its ways the desire which, as Plato says, 'for ever through all the universe tends towards that which is lovely,' we think that the world has settled its accounts with this desire, knows what this desire wants of it, and that all the impulses of our ordinary self which do not conflict with the terms of this settlement, in our narrow view of it, we may follow unrestrainedly, under the sanction of some such text as 'Not slothful in business,' or, 'Whatsoever thy hand findeth to do, do it with all thy might,' or something else of the same kind. And to any of these impulses we soon come to give that same character of a mechanical, absolute law, which we give to our religion; we regard it, as we do our religion, as an object for strictness of conscience, not for spontaneity of consciousness; for unremitting adherence on its own account, not for going back upon, viewing in its connection with other things, and adjusting to a number of changing circumstances. We treat it, in short, just as we treat our religion,—as machinery. It is in this way that the Barbarians treat their bodily exercises, the Philistines their business, Mr. Spurgeon his voluntaryism, Mr. Bright the assertion of personal liberty, Mr. Beales the right of meeting in Hyde Park. In all those cases what is needed is a freer play of consciousness upon the object of pursuit; and in all of them Hebraism, the valuing staunchness and earnestness more than this free play, the entire subordination of thinking to doing, has led to a mistaken and misleading treatment of things.

The newspapers a short time ago contained an account of the suicide of a Mr. Smith, secretary to some insurance company, who, it was said, 'laboured under the apprehension that he would come to poverty, and that he was eternally lost.' And when I read these words, it occurred to me that the poor man who came to such a mournful end was, in truth, a kind of type,—by the selection of his two grand objects of concern, by their isolation from everything else, and their juxtaposition to one another,—of all the strongest, most respectable, and most representative part of our nation. 'He laboured under the apprehension that he would come to poverty, and that he was eternally lost.' The whole middle class have a conception of things,

—a conception which makes us call them Philistines,—just like that of this poor man; though we are seldom, of course, shocked by seeing it take the distressing, violently morbid, and fatal turn, which it took with him. But how generally, with how many of us, are the main concerns of life limited to these two: the concern for making money, and the concern for saving our souls! And how entirely does the narrow and mechanical conception of our secular business proceed from a narrow and mechanical conception of our religious business! What havoc do the united conceptions make of our lives! It is because the second-named of these two master-concerns presents to us the one thing needful in so fixed, narrow, and mechanical a way, that so ignoble a fellow master-concern to it as the first-named becomes possible; and, having been once admitted, takes the same rigid and absolute character as the other.

Poor Mr. Smith had sincerely the nobler master-concern as well as the meaner,—the concern for saving his soul (according to the narrow and mechanical conception which Puritanism has of what the salvation of the soul is), as well as the concern for making money. But let us remark how many people there are, especially outside the limits of the serious and conscientious middle class to which Mr. Smith belonged, who take up with a meaner master-concern,—whether it be pleasure, or field-sports, or bodily exercises, or business, or popular agitation, — who take up with one of these exclusively, and neglect Mr. Smith's nobler master-concern, because of the mechanical form which Hebraism has given to this noble master-concern. Hebraism makes it stand, as we have said, as something talismanic, isolated, and all-sufficient, justifying our giving our ordinary selves free play in bodily exercises, or business, or popular agitation, if we have made our accounts square with this master-concern ; and, if we have not, rendering other things indifferent, and our ordinary self all we have to follow, and to follow with all the energy that is in us, till we do. Whereas the idea of perfection at all points, the encouraging in ourselves spontaneity of consciousness, and letting a free play of thought live and flow around all our activity, the indisposition to allow one side of our activity to stand as so all-important and all-sufficing that it makes other sides indifferent,—this bent of mind in us may not only check us in following unreservedly a mean master-concern of any kind, but may even, also, bring new life and movement into that side of us with which alone Hebraism concerns itself, and awaken a healthier and less mechanical activity there. Hellenism may thus actually serve to further the designs of Hebraism.

Undoubtedly it thus served in the first days of Christianity. Christianity, as has been said, occupied itself, like Hebraism, with the moral side of man exclusively, with his moral affections and moral conduct; and so far it was but a continuation of Hebraism. But it transformed and renewed Hebraism by criticising a fixed rule, which had become mechanical, and had thus lost its vital motive power; by letting the thought play freely around this old rule, and perceive its inadequacy; by developing a new motive power, which men's moral consciousness could take living hold of, and could move in sympathy with. What was this but an importation of Hellenism, as we have defined it, into Hebraism? St. Paul used the contradiction between the Jew's profession and practice, his shortcomings on that very side of moral affection and moral conduct which the Jew and St. Paul, both of them, regarded as all in all ('Thou that sayest a man should not steal, dost thou steal? thou that sayest a man should not commit adultery, dost thou commit adultery?'), for a proof of the inadequacy of the old rule of life in the Jew's mechanical conception of it; and tried to rescue him by making his consciousness play freely around this rule,—that is, by a so far Hellenic treatment of it. Even so we, too, when we hear so much said of the growth of commercial immorality in our serious middle class, of the melting away of habits of strict probity before the temptation to get quickly rich and to cut a figure in the world; when we see, at any rate, so much confusion of thought and of practice in this great representative class of our nation,—may we not be disposed to say, that this confusion shows that his new motive-power of grace and imputed righteousness has become to the Puritan as mechanical, and with as ineffective a hold upon his practice, as the old motive-power of the law was to the Jew? and that the remedy is the same as that which St. Paul employed,—an importation of what we have called Hellenism into his Hebraism, a making his consciousness flow freely round his petrified rule of life and renew it? Only with this difference: that whereas St. Paul imported Hellenism within the limits of our moral part only, this part being still treated by him as all in all; and whereas he well-nigh exhausted, one may say, and used to the very uttermost, the possibilities of fruitfully importing it on that side exclusively; we ought to try and import it,—guiding ourselves by the ideal of a human nature harmoniously perfect in all points,—into all the lines of our activity. Only by so doing can we rightly quicken, refresh, and renew those very instincts, now so much baffled, to which Hebraism makes appeal.

But if we will not be warned by the confusion visible enough at present in our thinking and acting, that we are in a false line in having developed our Hebrew side so exclusively, and our Hellenic side so feebly and at random, in loving fixed rules of action so much more than the intelligible law of things, let us listen to a remarkable testimony which the opinion of the world around us offers. All the world now sets great and increasing value on three objects which have long been very dear to us, and pursues them in its own way, or tries to pursue them. These three objects are industrial enterprise, bodily exercises, and freedom. Certainly we have, before and beyond our neighbours, given ourselves to these three things with ardent passion and with high success. And this our neighbours cannot but acknowledge; and they must needs, when they themselves turn to these things, have an eye to our example, and take something of our practice.

Now, generally, when people are interested in an object of pursuit, they cannot help feeling an enthusiasm for those who have already laboured successfully at it, and for their success. Not only do they study them, they also love and admire them. In this way a man who is interested in the art of war not only acquaints himself with the performance of great generals, but he has an admiration and enthusiasm for them. So, too, one who wants to be a painter or a poet cannot help loving and admiring the great painters or poets, who have gone before him and shown him the way.

But it is strange with how little of love, admiration, or enthusiasm, the world regards us and our freedom, our bodily exercises, and our industrial prowess, much as these things themselves are beginning to interest it. And is not the reason because we follow each of these things in a mechanical manner, as an end in and for itself, and not in reference to a general end of human perfection; and this makes the pursuit of them uninteresting to humanity, and not what the world truly wants? It seems to them mere machinery that we can, knowingly, teach them to worship,—a mere fetish. British freedom, British industry, British muscularity, we work for each of these three things blindly, with no notion of giving each its due proportion and prominence, because we have no ideal of harmonious human perfection before our minds, to set our work in motion, and to guide it. So the rest of the world, desiring industry, or freedom, or bodily strength, yet desiring these not, as we do, absolutely, but as means to something else, imitate, indeed, of our practice what seems useful for them, but us, whose practice they imitate, they seem to entertain neither love nor admiration for.

Let us observe, on the other hand, the love and enthusiasm excited by others who have laboured for these very things. Perhaps of what we call industrial enterprise it is not easy to find examples in former times; but let us consider how Greek freedom and Greek gymnastics have attracted the love and praise of mankind, who give so little love and praise to ours. And what can be the reason of this difference? Surely because the Greeks pursued freedom and pursued gymnastics not mechanically, but with constant reference to some ideal of complete human perfection and happiness. And therefore, in spite of faults and failures, they interest and delight by their pursuit of them all the rest of mankind, who instinctively feel that only as things are pursued with reference to this ideal are they valuable.

Here again, therefore, as in the confusion into which the thought and action of even the steadiest class amongst us is beginning to fall, we seem to have an admonition that we have fostered our Hebraising instincts, our preference of earnestness of doing to delicacy and flexibility of thinking, too exclusively, and have been landed by them in a mechanical and unfruitful routine. And again we seem taught that the development of our Hellenising instincts, seeking ardently the intelligible law of things, and making a stream of fresh thought play freely about our stock notions and habits, is what is most wanted by us at present.

Well, then, from all sides, the more we go into the matter, the currents seem to converge, and together to bear us along towards culture. If we look at the world outside us we find a disquieting absence of sure authority. We discover that only in right reason can we get a source of sure authority; and culture brings us towards right reason. If we look at our own inner world, we find all manner of confusion arising out of the habits of unintelligent routine and one-sided growth, to which a too exclusive worship of fire, strength, earnestness, and action, has brought us. What we want is a fuller harmonious development of our humanity, a free play of thought upon our routine notions, spontaneity of consciousness, sweetness and light; and these are just what culture generates and fosters. We will not stickle for a name, and the name of culture one might easily give up, if only those who decry the frivolous and pedantic sort of culture, but wish at bottom for the same things as we do, would be careful on their part, not, in disparaging and discrediting the false culture, to unwittingly disparage and discredit, among a people with little natural reverence for it, the true also. But what we are concerned for is the thing, not the name; and the thing, call it by what name we will, is simply the enabling ourselves, by getting to know, whether through reading, observing, or thinking, the best that can at present be known in the world, to come as near as we can to the firm intelligible law of things, and thus to get a basis for a less confused action and a more complete perfection than we have at present.

And now, therefore, when we are accused of preaching up a spirit of cultivated inaction, of provoking the earnest lovers of action, of refusing to lend a hand at uprooting certain definite evils, of despairing to find any lasting truth to minister to the diseased spirit of our time, we shall not be so much confounded and embarrassed what to answer for ourselves. We shall say boldly that we do not at all despair of finding some lasting truth to minister to the diseased spirit of our time; but that we have discovered the best way of finding this to be not so much by lending a hand to our friends and countrymen in their actual operations for the removal of certain definite evils, but rather in getting our friends and countrymen to seek culture, to let their consciousness play freely round their present operations and the stock notions on which they are founded, show what these are like, and how related to the intelligible law of things, and auxiliary to true human perfection.

CHAPTER VI

OUR LIBERAL PRACTITIONERS

But an unpretending writer, without a philosophy based on inter-independent, subordinate, and coherent principles, must not presume to indulge himself too much in generalities. He must keep close to the level ground of common fact, the only safe ground for understandings without a scientific equipment. Therefore, since I have spoken so slightingly of the practical operations in which my friends and countrymen are at this moment engaged for the removal of certain definite evils, I am bound to take, before concluding, some of those operations, and to make them, if I can, show the truth of what I have advanced.

Probably I could hardly give a greater proof of my confessed inexpertness in reasoning and arguing, than by taking, for my first example of an operation of this kind, the proceedings for the disestablishment of the Irish Church, which we are now witnessing.[1] It seems so clear that

[1] Written in 1869.

this is surely one of those operations for the uprooting of a certain definite evil in which one's Liberal friends engage, and have a right to complain, and to get impatient, and to reproach one with delicate Conservative scepticism and cultivated inaction, if one does not lend a hand to help them. This does, indeed, seem evident; and yet this operation comes so prominently before us at this moment,[1] — it so challenges everybody's regard,—that one seems cowardly in blinking it. So let us venture to try and see whether this conspicuous operation is one of those round which we need to let our consciousness play freely and reveal what manner of spirit we are of in doing it; or whether it is one which by no means admits the application of this doctrine of ours, and one to which we ought to lend a hand immediately.

I

Now it seems plain that the present Church-establishment in Ireland is contrary to reason and justice, in so far as the Church of a very small minority of the people there takes for itself all the Church-property of the Irish people. And one would think, that property, assigned for the purpose of providing for a people's religious worship when that worship

[1] 1869.

was one, the State should, when that worship is split into several forms, apportion between those several forms. But the apportionment should be made with due regard to circumstances, taking account only of great differences, which are likely to be lasting, and of considerable communions, which are likely to represent profound and widespread religious characteristics. It should overlook petty differences, which have no serious reason for lasting, and inconsiderable communions, which can hardly be taken to express any broad and necessary religious lineaments of our common nature. This is just in accordance with that maxim about the State which we have more than once used : *The State is of the religion of all its citizens, without the fanaticism of any of them.* Those who deny this, either think so poorly of the State that they do not like to see religion condescend to touch the State, or they think so poorly of religion that they do not like to see the State condescend to touch religion. But no good statesman will easily think thus unworthily either of the State or of religion.

Our statesmen of both parties were inclined, one may say, to follow the natural line of the State's duty, and to make in Ireland some fair apportionment of Church - property between large and radically divided religious communions in that country. But then it was discovered that in Great Britain the national mind, as it is called, is grown averse to endowments for religion and will make no new ones; and though this in itself looks general and solemn enough, yet there were found political philosophers to give it a look of more generality and more solemnity still, and to elevate, by their dexterous command of powerful and beautiful language, this supposed edict of the British national mind into a sort of formula for expressing a great law of religious transition and progress for all the world.

But we, who, having no coherent philosophy, must not let ourselves philosophise, only see that the English and Scotch Nonconformists have a great horror of establishments and endowments for religion, which, they assert, were forbidden by Jesus Christ when he said: 'My kingdom is not of this world'; and that the Nonconformists will be delighted to aid statesmen in disestablishing any church, but will suffer none to be established or endowed if they can help it. Then we see that the Nonconformists make the strength of the Liberal Majority in the House of Commons; and that, therefore, the leading Liberal statesmen, to get the support of the Nonconformists, forsake the notion of fairly apportioning Church-property in Ireland among the chief religious communions, declare that the national mind has decided against new endowments, and propose simply to disestablish and disendow the present establishment in

Ireland without establishing or endowing any other. The actual power, in short, by virtue of which the Liberal party in the House of Commons is now trying to disestablish the Irish Church, is not the power of reason and justice, it is the power of the Nonconformists' antipathy to Church establishments.

Clearly it is this ; because Liberal statesmen, relying on the power of reason and justice to help them, proposed something quite different from what they now propose ; and they proposed what they now propose, and talked of the decision of the national mind, because they had to rely on the English and Scotch Nonconformists. And clearly the Nonconformists are actuated by antipathy to establishments, not by antipathy to the injustice and irrationality of the present appropriation of Church-property in Ireland ; because Mr. Spurgeon, in his eloquent and memorable letter, expressly avowed that he would sooner leave things as they are in Ireland, that is, he would sooner let the injustice and irrationality of the present appropriation continue, than do anything to set up the Roman image,—that is, than give the Catholics their fair and reasonable share of Church-property. Most indisputably, therefore, we may affirm that the real moving power by which the Liberal party are now operating the overthrow of the Irish establishment is the antipathy of the Nonconformists to Church-establishments, and not the sense of reason or justice, except so far as reason and justice may be contained in this antipathy. And thus the matter stands at present.

Now surely we must all see many inconveniences in performing the operation of uprooting this evil, the Irish Church-establishment, in this particular way. As was said about industry and freedom and gymnastics, we shall never awaken love and gratitude by this mode of operation; for it is pursued, not in view of reason and justice and human perfection and all that enkindles the enthusiasm of men, but it is pursued in view of a certain stock notion, or fetish, of the Nonconformists, which proscribes Church-establishments. And yet, evidently, one of the main benefits to be got by operating on the Irish Church is to win the affections of the Irish people. Besides this, an operation performed in virtue of a mechanical rule, or fetish, like the supposed decision of the English national mind against new endowments, does not easily inspire respect in its adversaries, and make their opposition feeble and hardly to be persisted in, as an operation evidently done in virtue of reason and justice might. For reason and justice have in them something persuasive and irresistible; but a fetish or mechanical maxim, like this of the Nonconformists, has in it nothing at all to conciliate either the affections or the understanding. Nay, it provokes the counter-employment of other fetishes or mechanical maxims on the opposite side, by which the confusion and hostility already prevalent are heightened. Only in this way can be explained the apparition of such fetishes as are beginning to be set up on the Conservative side against the fetish of the Nonconformists :—*The Constitution in danger! The bulwark of British freedom menaced! The lamp of the Reformation put out! No Popery!* —and so on. To elevate these against an operation relying on reason and justice to back it, is not so easy, or so tempting to human infirmity, as to elevate them against an operation relying on the Nonconformists' antipathy to Church-establishments to back it. For after all, *No Popery!* is a rallying-cry which touches the human spirit quite as vitally as *No Church-establishments!*—that is to say, neither the one nor the other, in themselves, touch the human spirit vitally at all.

Ought the believers in action, then, to be so impatient with us, if we say, that even for the sake of this operation of theirs itself and its satisfactory accomplishment, it is more important to make our consciousness play freely round the stock notion or habit on which their operation relies for aid, than to lend a hand to it straight away? Clearly they ought not; because nothing is so effectual for operating as reason and justice, and a free play of thought will either disengage the reason and justice lying hid in the Nonconformist fetish, and make them effectual, or else it will help to get this fetish out of the way, and to let statesmen go freely where reason and justice take them.

So, suppose we take this absolute rule, this mechanical maxim of Mr. Spurgeon and the Nonconformists, that Church-establishments are bad things because Jesus Christ said: 'My kingdom is not of this world.' Suppose we try and make our consciousness bathe and float this piece of petrifaction,—for such it now is,—and bring it within the stream of the vital movement of our thought, and into relation with the whole intelligible law of things. An enemy and a disputant might probably say that much of the machinery which Nonconformists themselves employ,—the Liberation Society which exists already, and the Nonconformist Union which Mr. Spurgeon desires to see existing,—come within the scope of Christ's words as well as Church-establishments. This, however, is merely a negative and contentious way of dealing with the Nonconformist maxim; whereas what we desire is to bring this maxim within the positive and vital movement of our thought. We say, therefore, that Jesus Christ's words mean that his religion is a force of inward persuasion acting on the soul, and not a force of outward constraint acting on the body; and if the Nonconformist maxim against Church-establishments and Church-endowments has warrant given to it from what Christ thus meant, then their maxim is good, even though their own practice in the matter of the Liberation Society may be at variance with it.

And here we cannot but remember what we have formerly said about religion, Miss Cobbe, and the British College of Health in the New Road. In religion there are two parts, the part of thought and speculation, and the part of worship and devotion. Jesus Christ certainly meant his religion, as a force of inward persuasion acting on the soul, to employ both parts as perfectly as possible. Now thought and speculation is eminently an individual matter, and worship and devotion is eminently a collective matter. It does not help me to think a thing more clearly that thousands of other people are thinking the same; but it does help me to worship with more emotion that thousands of other people are worshipping with me. The consecration of common consent, antiquity, public establishment, long-used rites, national edifices, is everything for religious worship. 'Just what makes worship impressive,' says Joubert, 'is its publicity, its external manifestation, its sound, its splendour, its observance universally and visibly holding its sway through all the details both of our outward and of our inward life.' Worship, therefore, should have in it as little as possible of what divides us, and should be as much as possible a common and public act; as Joubert says again: 'The best prayers are those which have nothing distinct about them, and which are thus of the nature of simple adoration.' For, 'the same devotion,' as he says in another place, 'unites men far more than the same thought and knowledge.' Thought and knowledge, as we have said before, is eminently something individual, and of our own; the more we possess it as strictly of our own, the more power it has on us. Man worships best, therefore, with the community; he philosophises best alone.

So it seems that whoever would truly give effect to Jesus Christ's declaration that his religion is a force of inward persuasion acting on the soul, would leave our thought on the intellectual aspects of Christianity as individual as possible, but would make Christian worship as collective as possible. Worship, then, appears to be eminently a matter for public and national establishment; for even Mr. Bright, who, when he stands in Mr. Spurgeon's great Tabernacle, is so ravished with admiration, will hardly say that the great Tabernacle and its worship are in themselves, as a temple and service of religion, so impressive and affecting as the public and national Westminster Abbey, or Notre Dame, with their worship. And when, immediately after the great Tabernacle, one comes plump down to the mass of private and individual establishments of religious worship, establishments falling, like the British College of Health in the New Road, conspicuously short of what a public and national establishment might be, then one cannot but feel that Jesus Christ's command to make his religion a force of persuasion to the soul, is, so far as one main source of persuasion is concerned, altogether set at nought.

But perhaps the Nonconformists worship so unimpressively because they philosophise so keenly; and one part of religion, the part of public national worship, they have subordinated to the other part, the part of individual thought and knowledge? This, however, their organisation in congregations forbids us to admit. They are members of congregations, not isolated thinkers; and a free play of individual thought is at least as much impeded by membership of a small congregation as by membership of a great Church. Thinking by batches of fifties is to the full as fatal to free thought as thinking by batches of thousands. Accordingly, we have had occasion already to notice that Nonconformity does not at all differ from the Established Church by having worthier or more philosophical ideas about God, and the ordering of the world, than the Established Church has. It has very much the same ideas about these as the Established Church has, but it differs from the Established Church in that its worship is a much less collective and national affair.

So Mr. Spurgeon and the Nonconformists seem to have misapprehended the true meaning of Christ's words, *My kingdom is not of this world.* Because, by these words, Christ meant that his religion was to work on the soul. And of the two parts of the soul on which religion works,—the thinking and speculative part, and the feeling and imaginative part,—Nonconformity satisfies the first no better than the Established Churches, which Christ by these words is supposed to have condemned, satisfy it; and the second part it satisfies even worse than the Established Churches. And thus the balance of advantage seems to rest with the Established Churches; and they seem to have apprehended and applied Christ's words, if not with perfect adequacy, at least less inadequately than the Nonconformists.

Might it not, then, be urged with great force that the way to do good, in presence of this operation for uprooting the Church-establishment in Ireland by the power of the Nonconformists' antipathy to publicly establishing or endowing religious worship, is not by lending a hand straight away to the operation, and Hebraising,—that is, in this case, taking an uncritical interpretation of certain Bible words as our absolute rule of conduct,—with the Nonconformists? It may be very well for born Hebraisers, like Mr. Spurgeon, to Hebraise; but for Liberal statesmen to Hebraise is surely unsafe, and to see poor old Liberal hacks Hebraising, whose real self belongs to a kind of negative Hellenism,—a state of moral indifferency without intellectual ardour,—is even painful. And when, by our Hebraising, we neither do what the better mind of statesmen prompted them to do, nor win the affections of the people we want to conciliate, nor yet reduce the opposition of our adversaries but rather heighten it, surely it may not be unreasonable to Hellenise a little, to let our thought and consciousness play freely about our proposed operation and its motives, dissolve these motives if they are unsound,—which certainly they have some appearance, at any rate, of being,—and create in their stead, if they are, a set of sounder and more persuasive motives conducting to a more solid operation. May not the man who promotes this be giving the best help towards finding some lasting truth to minister to the diseased spirit of his time, and does he really deserve that the believers in action should grow impatient with him?

II

But now to take another operation which does not at this moment so excite people's feelings as the disestablishment of the Irish Church, but which, I suppose, would also be called exactly one of those operations of simple, practical, common-sense reform, aiming at the removal of some particular abuse, and rigidly restricted to that object, to which a Liberal ought to lend a hand, and deserves that other Liberals should grow impatient with him if he does not. This operation I had the great advantage of with my own ears hearing discussed in the House of Commons, and recommended by a powerful speech from that famous speaker, Mr. Bright. So that the effeminate horror which, it is alleged, I have of practical reforms of this kind, was put to a searching test; and if it survived, it must have, one would think, some reason or other to support it, and can hardly quite merit the stigma of its present name.

The operation I mean was that which the Real Estate Intestacy Bill aimed at accomplishing, and the discussion on this bill I heard in the House of Commons. The bill proposed, as every one knows, to prevent the land of a man who dies intestate from going, as it goes now, to his eldest son, and was thought, by its friends and by its enemies, to be a step towards abating the now almost exclusive possession of the land of this country by the people whom we call the Barbarians. Mr. Bright, and other speakers on his side, seemed to hold that there is a kind of natural law or fitness of things which assigns to all a man's children a right to equal shares in the enjoyment of his property after his death; and that if, without depriving a man of an Englishman's prime privilege of doing what he likes by making what will he chooses, you provide that when he makes none his land shall be divided among his family, then you give the sanction of the law to the natural fitness of things, and inflict a sort of check on the present violation of this by the Barbarians.

It occurred to me, when I saw Mr. Bright and his friends proceeding in this way, to ask myself a question. If the almost exclusive possession of the land of this country by the Barbarians is a bad thing, is this practical operation of the Liberals, and the stock notion, on which it seems to rest, about the natural right of children to share equally in the enjoyment of their father's property after his death, the best and most effective means of dealing with it? Or is it best dealt with by letting one's thought and consciousness play freely and naturally upon the Barbarians, this Liberal operation, and the stock notion at the bottom of it, and trying to get as near as we can to the intelligible law of things as to each of them?

Now does any one, if he simply and naturally reads his consciousness, discover that he has any rights at all? For my part, the deeper I go in my own consciousness, and the more simply I abandon myself to it, the more it seems to tell me that I have no rights at all, only duties; and that men get this notion of rights from a process of abstract reasoning, inferring that the obligations they are conscious of towards others,

others must be conscious of towards them, and not from any direct witness of consciousness at all. But it is obvious that the notion of a right, arrived at in this way, is likely to stand as a formal and petrified thing, deceiving and misleading us; and that the notions got directly from our consciousness ought to be brought to bear upon it, and to control it. So it is unsafe and misleading to say that our children have rights against us; what is true and safe to say is, that we have duties towards our children. But who will find among these natural duties, set forth to us by our consciousness, the obligation to leave to all our children an equal share in the enjoyment of our property? Or, though consciousness tells us we ought to provide for our children's welfare, whose consciousness tells him that the enjoyment of property is in itself welfare? Whether our children's welfare is best served by their all sharing equally in our property, depends on circumstances and on the state of the community in which we live. With this equal sharing, society could not, for example, have organised itself afresh out of the chaos left by the fall of the Roman Empire; and to have an organised society to live in is more for a child's welfare than to have an equal share of his father's property.

So we see how little convincing force the stock notion on which the Real Estate Intestacy Bill was based,—the notion that in the nature and fitness of things all a man's children have a right to an equal share in the enjoyment of what he leaves,—really has ; and how powerless, therefore, it must of necessity be to persuade and win any one who has habits and interests which disincline him to it. On the other hand, the practical operation proposed relies entirely, if it is to be effectual in altering the present practice of the Barbarians, on the power of truth and persuasiveness in the notion which it seeks to consecrate ; for it leaves to the Barbarians full liberty to continue their present practice, to which all their habits and interests incline them, unless the promulgation of a notion, which we have seen to have no vital efficacy and hold upon our consciousness, shall hinder them.

Are we really to adorn an operation of this kind, merely because it proposes to *do* something, with all the favourable epithets of simple, practical common-sense, definite ; to enlist on its side all the zeal of the believers in action, and to call indifference to it an effeminate horror of useful reforms? It seems to me quite easy to show that a free disinterested play of thought on the Barbarians and their land-holding is a thousand times more really practical, a thousand times more likely to lead to some effective result, than an operation such as that of which we have been now speaking. For if, casting aside the impediments of stock notions and mechanical action, we try to find the intelligible law of things respecting a great land-owning class such as we have in this country, does not our consciousness readily tell us that whether the perpetuation of such a class is for its own real good and for the real good of the community, depends on the actual circumstances of this class and of the community; does it not readily tell us that wealth, power, and consideration are,—and above all when inherited and not earned,—in themselves trying and dangerous things? as Bishop Wilson excellently says: 'Riches are almost always abused without a very extraordinary grace.' But this extraordinary grace was in great measure supplied by the circumstances of the feudal epoch, out of which our land-holding class, with its rules of inheritance, sprang. The labour and contentions of a rude, nascent, and struggling society supplied it. These perpetually were trying, chastising, and forming the class whose predominance was then needed by society to give it points of cohesion, and was not so harmful to themselves because they were thus sharply tried and exercised. But in a luxurious, settled and easy society, where wealth offers the means of enjoyment a thousand times more, and the temptation to abuse them is thus made a thousand times greater, the exercising discipline is at the same time taken away, and the feudal class is left exposed to the full operation of the natural law well put by the French moralist: *Pouvoir sans savoir est fort dangereux.* And, for my part, when I regard the young people of this class, it is above all by the trial and shipwreck made of their own welfare by the circumstances in which they live that I am struck. How far better it would have been for nine out of every ten among them, if they had had their own way to make in the world, and not been tried by a condition for which they had not the extraordinary grace requisite!

This, I say, seems to be what a man's consciousness, simply consulted, would tell him about the actual welfare of our Barbarians themselves. Then, as to the effect upon the welfare of the community, how can that be salutary, if a class which, by the very possession of wealth, power and consideration, becomes a kind of ideal or standard for the rest of the community, is tried by ease and pleasure more than it can well bear, and almost irresistibly carried away from excellence and strenuous virtue? This must certainly be what Solomon meant when he said: 'As he who putteth a stone in a sling, so is he that giveth honour to a fool.'

For any one can perceive how this honouring of a false ideal, not of intelligence and strenuous virtue, but of wealth and station, pleasure and ease, is as a stone from a sling to kill in our great middle class, in us who are called Philistines, the desire before spoken of, which by nature for ever carries all men towards that which is lovely; and to leave instead of it only a blind deteriorating pursuit, for ourselves also, of the false ideal. And in those among us Philistines whom the desire does not wholly abandon, yet, having no excellent ideal set forth to nourish and to steady it, it meets with that natural bent for the bathos which together with this desire itself is implanted at birth in the breast of man, and is by that force twisted awry, and borne at random hither and thither, and at last flung upon those grotesque and hideous forms of popular religion which the more respectable part among us Philistines mistake for the true goal of man's desire after all that is lovely. And for the Populace this false idea is a stone which kills the desire before it can even arise; so impossible and unattainable for them do the conditions of that which is lovely appear according to this ideal to be made, so necessary to the reaching of them by the few seems the falling short of them by the many. So that, perhaps, of the actual vulgarity of our Philistines and brutality of our Populace, the Barbarians and their feudal habits of succession, enduring out of their due time and place, are involuntarily the cause in a great degree; and they hurt the welfare of the rest of the community at the same time that, as we have seen, they hurt their own.

But must not, now, the working in our minds

of considerations like these, to which culture, that is, the disinterested and active use of reading, reflection, and observation, in the endeavour to know the best that can be known, carries us, be really much more effectual to the dissolution of feudal habits and rules of succession in land than an operation like the Real Estate Intestacy Bill, and a stock notion like that of the natural right of all a man's children to an equal share in the enjoyment of his property; since we have seen that this mechanical maxim is unsound, and that, if it is unsound, the operation relying upon it cannot possibly be effective? If truth and reason have, as we believe, any natural, irresistible effect on the mind of man, it must. These considerations, when culture has called them forth and given them free course in our minds, will live and work. They will work gradually, no doubt, and will not bring us ourselves to the front to sit in high place and put them into effect; but so they will be all the more beneficial. Everything teaches us how gradually nature would have all profound changes brought about; and we can even see, too, where the absolute abrupt stoppage of feudal habits has worked harm. And appealing to the sense of truth and reason, these considerations will, without doubt, touch and move all those of even the Barbarians themselves, who are (as are some of us Philistines also, and some of the Populace) beyond their fellows quick of feeling for truth and reason. For indeed this is just one of the advantages of sweetness and light over fire and strength, that sweetness and light make a feudal class quietly and gradually drop its feudal habits because it sees them at variance with truth and reason, while fire and strength are for tearing them passionately off, because this class applauded Mr. Lowe when he called, or was supposed to call, the working class drunken and venal.

III

But when once we have begun to recount the practical operations by which our Liberal friends work for the removal of definite evils, and in which if we do not join them they are apt to grow impatient with us, how can we pass over that very interesting operation,—the attempt to enable a man to marry his deceased wife's sister? This operation, too, like that for abating the feudal customs of succession in land, I have had the advantage of myself seeing and hearing my Liberal friends labour at.

I was lucky enough to be present when Mr. Chambers brought forward in the House of Commons his bill for enabling a man to marry his deceased wife's sister, and I heard the speech which Mr. Chambers then made in support of his bill. His first point was that God's law, —the name he always gave to the Book of

Leviticus,—did not really forbid a man to marry his deceased wife's sister. God's law not forbidding it, the Liberal maxim, that a man's prime right and happiness is to do as he likes, ought at once to come into force, and to annul any such check upon the assertion of personal liberty as the prohibition to marry one's deceased wife's sister. A distinguished Liberal supporter of Mr. Chambers, in the debate which followed the introduction of the bill, produced a formula of much beauty and neatness for conveying in brief the Liberal notions on this head: 'Liberty,' said he, 'is the law of human life.' And, therefore, the moment it is ascertained that God's law, the Book of Leviticus, does not stop the way, man's law, the law of liberty, asserts its right, and makes us free to marry our deceased wife's sister.

And this exactly falls in with what Mr. Hepworth Dixon, who may almost be called the Colenso of love and marriage,—such a revolution does he make in our ideas on these matters, just as Dr. Colenso does in our ideas on religion,—tells us of the notions and proceedings of our kinsmen in America. With that affinity of genius to the Hebrew genius which we have already noticed, and with the strong belief of our race that liberty is the law of human life, so far as that fixed, perfect, and paramount rule of conscience, the Bible, does not expressly control it, our American kinsmen go again, Mr. Hepworth Dixon tells us, to their Bible, the Mormons to the patriarchs and the Old Testament, Brother Noyes to St. Paul and the New, and having never before read anything else but their Bible, they now read their Bible over again, and make all manner of great discoveries there. All these discoveries are favourable to liberty, and in this way is satisfied that double craving so characteristic of our Philistine, and so eminently exemplified in that crowned Philistine, Henry the Eighth,—the craving for forbidden fruit and the craving for legality.

Mr. Hepworth Dixon's eloquent writings give currency, over here, to these important discoveries; so that now, as regards love and marriage, we seem to be entering, with all our sails spread, upon what Mr. Hepworth Dixon, its apostle and evangelist, calls a Gothic Revival, but what one of the many newspapers that so greatly admire Mr. Hepworth Dixon's lithe and sinewy style and form their own style upon it, calls, by a yet bolder and more striking figure, 'a great sexual insurrection of our Anglo-Teutonic race.' For this end we have to avert our eyes from everything Hellenic and fanciful, and to keep them steadily fixed upon the two cardinal points of the Bible and liberty. And one of those practical operations in which the Liberal party engage, and in which we are summoned to join them, directs itself entirely, as we have seen, to these cardinal points, and may almost be regarded, perhaps, as a kind of first instalment, or public and parliamentary pledge, of the great sexual insurrection of our Anglo-Teutonic race.

But here, as elsewhere, what we seek is the Philistine's perfection, the development of his best self, not mere liberty for his ordinary self. And we no more allow absolute validity to his stock maxim, *Liberty is the law of human life*, than we allow it to the opposite maxim, which is just as true, *Renouncement is the law of human life*. For we know that the only perfect freedom is, as our religion says, a service; not a service to any stock maxim, but an elevation of our best self, and a harmonising in subordination to this, and to the idea of a perfected humanity, all the multitudinous, turbulent, and blind impulses of our ordinary selves. Now, the Philistine's great defect being a defect in delicacy of perception, to cultivate in him this delicacy, to render it independent of external and mechanical rule, and a law to itself, is what seems to make most for his perfection, his true humanity. And his true humanity, and therefore his happiness, appears to lie much more, so far as the relations of love and marriage are concerned, in becoming alive to the finer shades of feeling which arise within these relations, in being able to enter with tact and sympathy into the subtle instinctive propensions and repugnances of the person with whose life his own life is bound up, to make them his own, to direct and govern in harmony with them the arbitrary range of his personal action, and thus to enlarge his spiritual and intellectual life and liberty, than in remaining insensible to these finer shades of feeling and this delicate sympathy, in giving unchecked range, so far as he can, to his mere personal action, in allowing no limits or government to this except such as a mechanical external law imposes, and in thus really narrowing, for the satisfaction of his ordinary self, his spiritual and intellectual life and liberty.

Still more must this be so when his fixed eternal rule, his God's law, is supplied to him from a source which is less fit, perhaps, to supply final and absolute instructions on this particular topic of love and marriage than on any other relation of human life. Bishop Wilson, who is full of examples of that fruitful Hellenising within the limits of Hebraism itself, of that renewing of the stiff and stark notions of Hebraism by turning upon them a stream of fresh thought and consciousness, which we have already noticed in St. Paul,—Bishop Wilson gives an admirable lesson to rigid Hebraisers, like Mr. Chambers, asking themselves: Does God's law (that is, the Book of Leviticus) forbid us to marry our wife's sister?—Does

God's law (that is, again, the Book of Leviticus) allow us to marry our wife's sister?—when he says: 'Christian duties are founded on reason, not on the sovereign authority of God commanding what He pleases; God cannot command us what is not fit to be believed or done, all his commands being founded in the necessities of our nature.' And, immense as is our debt to the Hebrew race and its genius, incomparable as is its authority on certain profoundly important sides of our human nature, worthy as it is to be described as having uttered, for those sides, the voice of the deepest necessities of our nature, the statutes of the divine and eternal order of things, the law of God,—who, that is not manacled and hoodwinked by his Hebraism, can believe that, as to love and marriage, our reason and the necessities of our humanity have their true, sufficient, and divine law expressed for them by the voice of any Oriental and polygamous nation like the Hebrews? Who, I say, will believe, when he really considers the matter, that where the feminine nature, the feminine ideal, and our relations to them, are brought into question, the delicate and apprehensive genius of the Indo-European race, the race which invented the Muses, and chivalry, and the Madonna, is to find its last word on this question in the institutions of a Semitic people, whose wisest king had seven hundred wives and three hundred concubines?

IV

If here again, therefore, we minister better to the diseased spirit of our time by leading it to think about the operation our Liberal friends have in hand, than by lending a hand to this operation ourselves, let us see, before we dismiss from our view the practical operations of our Liberal friends, whether the same thing does not hold good as to their celebrated industrial and economical labours also. Their great work of this kind is, of course, their free-trade policy. This policy, as having enabled the poor man to eat untaxed bread, and as having wonderfully augmented trade, we are accustomed to speak of with a kind of thankful solemnity. It is chiefly on their having been our leaders in this policy that Mr. Bright founds for himself and his friends the claim, so often asserted by him, to be considered guides of the blind, teachers of the ignorant, benefactors slowly and laboriously developing in the Conservative party and in the country that which Mr. Bright is fond of calling *the growth of intelligence*,—the object, as is well known, of all the friends of culture also, and the great end and aim of the culture that we preach.

Now, having first saluted free-trade and its doctors with all respect, let us see whether even here, too, our Liberal friends do not pursue their operations in a mechanical way, without reference to any firm intelligible law of things, to human life as a whole, and human happiness; and whether it is not more for our good, at this particular moment at any rate, if, instead of worshipping free-trade with them Hebraistically, as a kind of fetish, and helping them to pursue it as an end in and for itself, we turn the free stream of our thought upon their treatment of it, and see how this is related to the intelligible law of human life, and to national well-being and happiness. In short, suppose we Hellenise a little with free-trade, as we Hellenised with the Real Estate Intestacy Bill, and with the disestablishment of the Irish Church by the power of the Nonconformists' antipathy to religious establishments, and see whether what our reprovers beautifully call ministering to the diseased spirit of our time is best done by the Hellenising method of proceeding, or by the other.

But first let us understand how the policy of free-trade really shapes itself for our Liberal friends, and how they practically employ it as an instrument of national happiness and salvation. For as we said that it seemed clearly right to prevent the Church-property of Ireland from being all taken for the benefit of the Church of a small minority, so it seems clearly right that the poor man should eat untaxed bread, and, generally, that restrictions and regulations which, for the supposed benefit of some particular person or class of persons, make the price of things artificially high here, or artificially low there, and interfere with the natural flow of trade and commerce, should be done away with. But in the policy of our Liberal friends free-trade means more than this, and is specially valued as a stimulant to the production of wealth, as they call it, and to the increase of the trade, business, and population of the country. We have already seen how these things,—trade, business, and population,—are mechanically pursued by us as ends precious in themselves, and are worshipped as what we call fetishes; and Mr. Bright, I have already said, when he wishes to give the working class a true sense of what makes glory and greatness, tells it to look at the cities it has built, the railroads it has made, the manufactures it has produced. So to this idea of glory and greatness the free-trade which our Liberal friends extol so solemnly and devoutly, has served,—to the increase of trade, business, and population; and for this it is prized. Therefore, the untaxing of the poor man's bread has, with this view of national happiness, been used not so much to make the existing poor man's bread cheaper or more abundant, but rather to create more poor men to eat it; so that we cannot precisely say that we have fewer poor men than we had before free-trade, but we can say with truth that we have many more centres of industry, as they are called, and much more business, population, and manufactures. And if we are sometimes a little troubled by our multitude of poor men, yet we know the increase of manufactures and population to be such a salutary thing in itself, and our free-trade policy begets such an admirable movement, creating fresh centres of industry and fresh poor men here, while we were thinking about our poor men there, that we are quite dazzled and borne away, and more and more industrial movement is called for, and our social progress seems to become one triumphant and enjoyable course of what is sometimes called, vulgarly, outrunning the constable.

If, however, taking some other criterion of man's well-being than the cities he has built and the manufactures he has produced, we persist in thinking that our social progress would be happier if there were not so many of us so very poor, and in busying ourselves with notions of in some way or other adjusting the poor man and business one to the other, and not multiplying the one and the other mechanically and blindly, then our Liberal friends, the appointed doctors of free-trade, take us up very sharply. 'Art is long,' says the *Times*, 'and life is short; for the most part we settle things first and understand them afterwards. Let us have as few theories as possible; what is wanted is not the light of speculation. If nothing worked well of which the theory was not perfectly understood, we should be in sad confusion. The relations of labour and capital, we are told, are not understood, yet trade and commerce, on the whole, work satisfactorily.' I quote from the *Times* of only the other day.[1] But thoughts like these, as I have often pointed out, are thoroughly British thoughts, and we have been familiar with them for years.

Or, if we want more of a philosophy of the matter than this, our free-trade friends have two axioms for us, axioms laid down by their justly esteemed doctors, which they think ought to satisfy us entirely. One is, that, other things being equal, the more population increases, the more does production increase to keep pace with it; because men by their numbers and contact call forth all manner of activities and resources in one another and in nature, which, when men are few and sparse, are never developed. The other is, that, although population always tends to equal the means of subsistence, yet people's notions of what subsistence is enlarge as civilisation advances, and take in a number of things beyond the bare necessaries of life; and thus, therefore, is supplied whatever check on population is needed. But the error of our friends is precisely, perhaps, that they apply axioms of this sort as if they were self-acting laws which will put themselves into operation without trouble or planning on our part, if we will only pursue free-trade, business, and population

[1] Written in 1869.

zealously and staunchly. Whereas the real truth is, that, however the case might be under other circumstances, yet in fact, as we now manage the matter, the enlarged conception of what is included in *subsistence* does not operate to prevent the bringing into the world of numbers of people who but just attain to the barest necessaries of life or who even fail to attain to them ; while, again, though production may increase as population increases, yet it seems that the production may be of such a kind, and so related, or rather non-related, to population, that the population may be little the better for it.

For instance, with the increase of population since Queen Elizabeth's time the production of silk-stockings has wonderfully increased, and silk-stockings have become much cheaper, and procurable in greater abundance by many more people, and tend perhaps, as population and manufactures increase, to get cheaper and cheaper, and at last to become, according to Bastiat's favourite image, a common free property of the human race, like light and air. But bread and bacon have not become much cheaper with the increase of population since Queen Elizabeth's time, nor procurable in much greater abundance by many more people ; neither do they seem at all to promise to become, like light and air, a common free property of the human race. And if bread and bacon have not kept pace with our population, and we have many more people in want of them now than in Queen Elizabeth's time, it seems vain to tell us that silk-stockings have kept pace with our population, or even more than kept pace with it, and that we are to get our comfort out of that.

In short, it turns out that our pursuit of free-trade, as of so many other things, has been too mechanical. We fix upon some object, which in this case is the production of wealth, and the increase of manufactures, population, and commerce through free-trade as a kind of one thing needful, or end in itself; and then we pursue it staunchly and mechanically, and say that it is our duty to pursue it staunchly and mechanically, not to see how it is related to the whole intelligible law of things and to full human perfection, or to treat it as the piece of machinery, of varying value as its relations to the intelligible law of things vary, which it really is.

So it is of no use to say to the *Times*, and to our Liberal friends rejoicing in the possession of their talisman of free-trade, that about one in nineteen of our population is a pauper,[1] and that, this being so, trade and commerce can hardly be said to prove by their satisfactory working that it matters nothing whether the relations between labour and capital are understood or not; nay, that we can hardly be said not to be in sad confusion. For here our faith in the staunch mechanical pursuit of a fixed object comes in,

[1] This was in 1869.

and covers itself with that imposing and colossal necessitarianism of the *Times* which we have before noticed. And this necessitarianism, taking for granted that an increase in trade and population is a good in itself, one of the chiefest of goods, tells us that disturbances of human happiness caused by ebbs and flows in the tide of trade and business, which, on the whole, steadily mounts, are inevitable and not to be quarrelled with. This firm philosophy I seek to call to mind when I am in the East of London, whither my avocations often lead me ; and, indeed, to fortify myself against the depressing sights which on these occasions assail us, I have transcribed from the *Times* one strain of this kind, full of the finest economical doctrine, and always carry it about with me. The passage is this :—

'The East End is the most commercial, the most industrial, the most fluctuating region of the metropolis. It is always the first to suffer ; for it is the creature of prosperity, and falls to the ground the instant there is no wind to bear it up. The whole of that region is covered with huge docks, shipyards, manufactories, and a wilderness of small houses, all full of life and happiness in brisk times, but in dull times withered and lifeless, like the deserts we read of in the East. Now their brief spring is over. There is no one to blame for this ; it is the result of Nature's simplest laws !' We must all agree that it is impossible that anything can be firmer than this, or show a surer faith in the working of free-trade, as our Liberal friends understand and employ it.

But, if we still at all doubt whether the indefinite multiplication of manufactories and small houses can be such an absolute good in itself as to counterbalance the indefinite multiplication of poor people, we shall learn that this multiplication of poor people, too, is an absolute good in itself, and the result of divine and beautiful laws. This is indeed a favourite thesis with our Philistine friends, and I have already noticed the pride and gratitude with which they receive certain articles in the *Times*, dilating in thankful and solemn language on the majestic growth of our population. But I prefer to quote now, on this topic, the words of an ingenious young Scotch writer, Mr. Robert Buchanan, because he invests with so much imagination and poetry this current idea of the blessed and even divine character which the multiplying of population is supposed in itself to have. 'We move to multiplicity,' says Mr. Robert Buchanan. 'If there is one quality which seems God's, and his exclusively, it seems that divine philoprogenitiveness, that passionate love of distribution and expansion into living forms. Every animal added seems a new ecstasy to the Maker; every life added, a new embodiment of his love. He would *swarm* the earth with beings. There are never enough. Life, life, life,—faces gleaming, hearts beating, must fill every cranny. Not a corner is suffered to remain empty. The whole earth breeds, and God glories.'

It is a little unjust, perhaps, to attribute to the Divinity exclusively this philoprogenitiveness, which the British Philistine, and the poorer class of Irish, may certainly claim to share with him; yet how inspiriting is here the whole strain of thought! and these beautiful words, too, I carry about with me in the East of London, and often read them there. They are quite in agreement with the popular language one is accustomed to hear about children and large families, which describes children as *sent*. And a line of poetry, which Mr. Robert Buchanan throws in presently after the poetical prose I have quoted,—

> ''Tis the old story of the fig-leaf time'—

this fine line, too, naturally connects itself, when one is in the East of London, with the idea of God's desire to *swarm* the earth with beings; because the swarming of the earth with beings does indeed, in the East of London, so seem to revive *the old story of the fig-leaf time*, such a number of the people one meets there having hardly a rag to cover them; and the more the swarming goes on, the more it promises to revive this old story. And when the story is perfectly revived, the swarming quite completed, and every cranny choke-full, then, too, no doubt, the faces in the East of London will be gleaming faces, which Mr. Robert Buchanan says it is God's desire they should be, and which every one must perceive they are not at present, but, on the contrary, very miserable.

But to prevent all this philosophy and poetry from quite running away with us, and making us think with the *Times*, and our practical Liberal free-traders, and the British Philistines generally, that the increase of houses and manufactories, or the increase of population, are absolute goods in themselves, to be mechanically pursued, and to be worshipped like fetishes,—to prevent this, we have got that notion of ours immovably fixed, of which I have long ago spoken, the notion that culture, or the study of perfection, leads us to conceive of no perfection as being real which is not a *general* perfection, embracing all our fellow-men with whom we have to do. Such is the sympathy which binds humanity together, that we are, indeed, as our religion says, members of one body, and if one member suffer, all the members suffer with it. Individual perfection is impossible so long as the rest of mankind are not perfected along with us. 'The *multitude* of the wise is the welfare of the world,' says the wise man. And to this effect that excellent and often-quoted guide of ours, Bishop Wilson, has some striking words:—'It is not,' says he, 'so much our neighbour's interest as our own that we love him.' And again he

says: 'Our salvation does in some measure depend upon that of others.' And the author of the *Imitation* puts the same thing admirably when he says:—'*Obscurior etiam via ad coelum videbatur quando tam pauci regnum coelorum quaerere curabant;* the fewer there are who follow the way to perfection, the harder that way is to find.' So all our fellow-men, in the East of London and elsewhere, we must take along with us in the progress towards perfection, if we ourselves really, as we profess, want to be perfect; and we must not let the worship of any fetish, any machinery, such as manufactures or population,—which are not, like perfection, absolute goods in themselves, though we think them so,—create for us such a multitude of miserable, sunken, and ignorant human beings, that to carry them all along with us is impossible, and perforce they must for the most part be left by us in their degradation and wretchedness. But evidently the conception of free-trade, on which our Liberal friends vaunt themselves, and in which they think they have found the secret of national prosperity,—evidently, I say, the mere unfettered pursuit of the production of wealth, and the mere mechanical multiplying, for this end, of manufactures and population, threatens to create for us, if it has not created already, those vast, miserable, unmanageable masses of sunken people, to the existence of which we are, as we have seen, absolutely forbidden to reconcile ourselves, in spite of all that the philosophy of the *Times* and the poetry of Mr. Robert Buchanan may say to persuade us.

Hebraism in general seems powerless, almost as powerless as our free-trading Liberal friends, to deal efficaciously with our ever-accumulating masses of pauperism, and to prevent their accumulating still more. Hebraism builds churches, indeed, for these masses, and sends missionaries among them; above all, it sets itself against the social necessitarianism of the *Times*, and refuses to accept their degradation as inevitable. But with regard to their ever-increasing accumulation, it seems to be led to the very same conclusions, though from a point of view of its own, as our free-trading Liberal friends. Hebraism, with that mechanical and misleading use of the letter of Scripture on which we have already commented, is governed by such texts as: *Be fruitful and multiply*, the edict of God's law, as Mr. Chambers would say; or by the declaration of what he would call God's word in the Psalms, that the man who has a great number of children is thereby made happy. And in conjunction with such texts as these, Hebraism is apt to place another text: *The poor shall never cease out of the land*. Thus Hebraism is conducted to nearly the same notion as the popular mind and as Mr. Robert Buchanan, that children are *sent*, and that the divine nature takes a delight in swarming the East End of

London with paupers. Only, when they are perishing in their helplessness and wretchedness, it asserts the Christian duty of succouring them, instead of saying, like the *Times*: 'Now their brief spring is over; there is nobody to blame for this; it is the result of Nature's simplest laws!' But, like the *Times*, Hebraism despairs of any help from knowledge and says that 'what is wanted is not the light of speculation.'

I remember, only the other day, a good man looking with me upon a multitude of children who were gathered before us in one of the most miserable regions of London,—children eaten up with disease, half-sized, half-fed, half-clothed, neglected by their parents, without health, without home, without hope,—said to me: 'The one thing really needful is to teach these little ones to succour one another, if only with a cup of cold water; but now, from one end of the country to the other, one hears nothing but the cry for knowledge, knowledge, knowledge!' And yet surely, so long as these children are there in these festering masses, without health, without home, without hope, and so long as their multitude is perpetually swelling, charged with misery they must still be for themselves, charged with misery they must still be for us, whether they help one another with a cup of cold water or no; and the knowledge how to prevent their accumulating is necessary, even to give their moral life and growth a fair chance!

May we not, therefore, say, that neither the true Hebraism of this good man, willing to spend and be spent for these sunken multitudes, nor what I may call the spurious Hebraism of our free-trading Liberal friends,—mechanically worshipping their fetish of the production of wealth and of the increase of manufactures and population, and looking neither to the right nor left so long as this increase goes on,—avail us much here; and that here, again, what we want is Hellenism, the letting our consciousness play freely and simply upon the facts before us, and listening to what it tells us of the intelligible law of things as concerns them? And surely what it tells us is, that a man's children are not really *sent*, any more than the pictures upon his wall, or the horses in his stable are *sent*; and that to bring people into the world, when one cannot afford to keep them and oneself decently and not too precariously, or to bring more of them into the world than one can afford to keep thus, is, whatever the *Times* and Mr. Robert Buchanan may say, by no means an accomplishment of the divine will or a fulfilment of Nature's simplest laws, but is just as wrong, just as contrary to reason and the will of God, as for a man to have horses, or carriages, or pictures, when he cannot afford them, or to have more of them than he can afford; and that, in the one case as in the other, the larger the scale on which the violation of reason's law is practised, and the longer it is persisted in, the greater must be the confusion and final trouble. Surely no laudations of free-trade, no meetings of bishops and clergy in the East End of London, no reading of papers and reports, can tell us anything about our social condition which it more concerns us to know than that! and not only to know, but habitually to have the knowledge present, and to act upon it as one acts upon the knowledge that water wets and fire burns! And not only the sunken populace of our great cities are concerned to know it, and the pauper twentieth of our population; we Philistines of the middle class, too, are concerned to know it, and all who have to set themselves to make progress in perfection.

But we all know it already! some one will say; it is the simplest law of prudence. But how little reality must there be in our knowledge of it; how little can we be putting it in practice; how little is it likely to penetrate among the poor and struggling masses of our population, and to better our condition, so long as an unintelligent Hebraism of one sort keeps repeating as an absolute eternal word of God the psalm-verse which says that the man who has a great many children is happy; or an unintelligent Hebraism of another sort,—that is to say, a blind following of certain stock notions as infallible,—keeps assigning as an absolute proof of national prosperity the multiplying of manufactures and population! Surely, the one set of Hebraisers have to learn that their psalm-verse was composed at the resettlement of Jerusalem after the Captivity, when the Jews of Jerusalem were a handful, an undermanned garrison, and every child was a blessing; and that the word of God, or the voice of the divine order of things, declares the possession of a great many children to be a blessing only when it really is so! And the other set of Hebraisers, have they not to learn that if they call their private acquaintances imprudent or unlucky, when, with no means of support for them or with precarious means, they have a large family of children, then they ought not to call the State well managed and prosperous merely because its manufactures and its citizens multiply, if the manufactures, which bring new citizens into existence just as much as if they had actually begotten them, bring more of them into existence than they can maintain, or are too precarious to go on maintaining those whom for a while they maintained?

Hellenism, surely, or the habit of fixing our mind upon the intelligible law of things, is most salutary if it makes us see that the only absolute good, the only absolute and eternal object prescribed to us by God's law, or the divine order of things, is the progress towards perfection, —our own progress towards it and the progress of humanity. And therefore, for every individual man, and for every society of men, the possession and multiplication of children, like the possession and multiplication of horses and pictures, is to be accounted good or bad, not in itself, but with reference to this object and the progress towards it. And as no man is to be excused in having horses or pictures, if his having them hinders his own or others' progress towards perfection and makes them lead a servile and ignoble life, so is no man to be excused for having children if his having them makes him or others lead this. Plain thoughts of this kind are surely the spontaneous product of our consciousness, when it is allowed to play freely and disinterestedly upon the actual facts of our social condition, and upon our stock notions and stock habits in respect to it. Firmly grasped and simply uttered, they are more likely, one cannot but think, to better that condition, than is the mechanical pursuit of free-trade by our Liberal friends.

V

So that, here as elsewhere, the practical operations of our Liberal friends, by which they set so much store, and in which they invite us to join them and to show what Mr. Bright calls a commendable interest, do not seem to us so practical for real good as they think ; and our Liberal friends seem to us themselves to need to Hellenise, as we say, a little,—that is, to examine into the nature of real good, and to listen to what their consciousness tells them about it,—rather than to pursue with such heat and confidence their present practical operations. And it is clear that they have no just cause, so far as regards several operations of theirs which we have canvassed, to reproach us with delicate Conservative scepticism. For often by Hellenising we seem to subvert stock Conservative notions and usages more effectually than they subvert them by Hebraising. But, in truth, the free spontaneous play of consciousness with which culture tries to float our stock habits of thinking and acting, is by its very nature, as has been said, disinterested. Sometimes the result of floating them may be agreeable to this party, sometimes to that; now it may be unwelcome to our so-called Liberals, now to our so-called Conservatives; but what culture seeks is, above all, to *float* them, to prevent their being stiff and stark pieces of petrifaction any longer. It is mere Hebraising, if we stop short, and refuse to let our consciousness play freely, whenever we or our friends do not happen to like what it discovers to us. This is to make the Liberal party, or the Conservative party, our one thing needful, instead of human perfection; and we have seen what mischief arises from making an even greater thing than the Liberal or the Conservative party,—the predominance of the moral side in man,—our one thing needful. But wherever the free play of our consciousness leads us, we shall follow; believing that in this way we shall tend to make good at all points what is wanting to us, and so shall be brought nearer to our complete human perfection.

Everything, in short, confirms us in the doctrine, so unpalatable to the believers in action, that our main business at the present moment is not so much to work away at certain crude reforms of which we have already the scheme in our own mind, as to create, through the help of that culture which at the very outset we began by praising and recommending, a frame of mind out of which the schemes of really fruitful reforms may with time grow. At any rate, we ourselves must put up with our friends' impatience, and with their reproaches against cultivated inaction, and must still decline to lend a hand to their practical operations, until we, for our own part, at least, have grown a little clearer about the nature of real good, and have arrived nearer to a condition of mind out of which really fruitful and solid operations may spring.

In the meanwhile, since our Liberal friends keep loudly and resolutely assuring us that their actual operations at present are fruitful and solid, let us in each case keep testing these operations in the simple way we have indicated, by letting the natural stream of our consciousness flow over them freely; and if they stand this test successfully, then let us give them our interest, but not else.

CONCLUSION

And so we bring to an end what we had to say in praise of culture, and in evidence of its special utility for the circumstances in which we find ourselves, and the confusion which environs us. Through culture seems to lie our way, not only to perfection, but even to safety. Resolutely refusing to lend a hand to the imperfect operations of our Liberal friends, disregarding their impatience, taunts, and reproaches, firmly bent on trying to find in the intelligible laws of things a firmer and sounder basis for future practice than any which we have at present, and believing this search and discovery to be, for our generation and circumstances, of yet more vital and pressing importance than practice itself, we nevertheless may do more, perhaps, we poor disparaged followers of culture, to make the actual present, and the frame of society in which we live, solid and seaworthy, than all which our bustling politicians can do.

For we have seen how much of our disorders and perplexities is due to the disbelief, among the classes and combinations of men, Barbarian or Philistine, which have hitherto governed our society, in right reason, in a paramount best self; to the inevitable decay and break-up of the organisations by which, asserting and expressing in these organisations their ordinary self only, they have so long ruled us; and to their irresolution, when the society, which their conscience tells them they have made and still manage not with right reason but with their ordinary self, is rudely shaken, in offering resistance to its subverters. But for us,—who believe in right reason, in the duty and possibility of extricating and elevating our best self, in the progress of humanity towards perfection,—for us the framework of society, that theatre on which this august drama has to unroll itself, is sacred; and whoever administers it, and however we may seek to remove them from their tenure of administration, yet, while they administer, we steadily and with undivided heart support them in repressing anarchy and disorder; because without order there can be no society, and without society there can be no human perfection.

And this opinion of the intolerableness of anarchy we can never forsake, however our Liberal friends may think a little rioting, and what they call popular demonstrations, useful sometimes to their own interests and to the interests of the valuable practical operations they have in hand, and however they may preach the right of an Englishman to be left to do as far as possible what he likes, and the duty of his government to indulge him and connive as much as possible and abstain from all harshness of repression. And even when they artfully show us operations which are undoubtedly precious, such as the abolition of the slave-trade, and ask us if, for their sake, foolish and obstinate governments may not wholesomely be frightened by a little disturbance, the good design in view and the difficulty of overcoming opposition to it being considered,—still we say no, and that monster-processions in the streets and forcible irruptions into the parks, even in professed support of this good design, ought to be unflinchingly forbidden and repressed; and that far more is lost than is gained by permitting them. Because a State in which law is authoritative and sovereign, a firm and settled course of public order, is requisite if man is to bring to maturity anything precious and lasting now, or to found anything precious and lasting for the future.

Thus, in our eyes, the very framework and exterior order of the State, whoever may administer the State, is sacred; and culture is the most resolute enemy of anarchy, because of the great hopes and designs for the State which culture teaches us to nourish. But as, believing in right reason, and having faith in the progress of humanity towards perfection, and ever labouring for this end, we grow to have clearer sight of the ideas of right reason, and of the elements and helps of perfection, and come gradually to fill the framework of the State with them, to fashion its internal composition and all its laws and institutions conformably to them, and to make the State more and more the expression, as we say, of our best self, which is not manifold, and vulgar, and unstable, and contentious, and ever-varying, but one, and noble, and secure, and peaceful, and the same for all mankind,—with what aversion shall we not *then* regard anarchy, with what firmness shall we not check it, when there is so much that is so precious which it will endanger!

So that, for the sake of the present, but far more for the sake of the future, the lovers of culture are unswervingly and with a good conscience the opposers of anarchy. And not as the Barbarians and Philistines, whose honesty and whose sense of humour make them shrink, as we have seen, from treating the State as too serious a thing, and from giving it too much power;—for indeed the only State they know of, and think they administer, is the expression of their ordinary self. And though the headstrong and violent extreme among them might gladly arm this with full authority, yet their virtuous mean is, as we have said, pricked in conscience at doing this; and as our Barbarian Secretaries of State let the Park railings be broken down, and our Philistine Alderman-Colonels let the London roughs rob and beat the bystanders. But we, beholding in the State no expression of our ordinary self, but even already, as it were, the appointed frame and prepared vessel of our best self, and, for the future, our best self's powerful, beneficent, and sacred expression and organ,—we are willing and resolved, even now, to strengthen against anarchy the trembling hands of our Barbarian Home Secretaries, and the feeble knees of our Philistine Alderman-Colonels ; and to tell them, that it is not really in behalf of their own ordinary self that they are called to protect the Park railings, and to suppress the London roughs, but in behalf of the best self both of themselves and of all of us in the future.

Nevertheless, though for resisting anarchy the lovers of culture may prize and employ fire and strength, yet they must, at the same time, bear constantly in mind that it is not at this moment true, what the majority of people tell us, that the world wants fire and strength more than sweetness and light, and that things are for the most part to be settled first and understood afterwards. We have seen how much of our present perplexities and confusion this untrue notion of the majority of people amongst us has caused, and tends to perpetuate. Therefore the true business of the friends of culture now is, to dissipate this false notion, to spread the belief in right reason and in a firm intelligible law of things, and to get men to try, in preference to staunchly acting with imperfect knowledge, to obtain some sounder basis of knowledge on which to act. This is what the friends and lovers of culture have to do, however the believers in action may grow impatient with us for saying so, and may insist on our lending a hand to their practical operations and showing a commendable interest in them.

To this insistence we must indeed turn a deaf ear. But neither, on the other hand, must the friends of culture expect to take the believers in action by storm, or to be visibly and speedily important, and to rule and cut a figure in the world. Aristotle says that those for whom alone ideas and the pursuit of the intelligible law of things can, in general, have much attraction, are principally the young, filled with generous spirit and with a passion for perfection; but the mass of mankind, he says, follow seeming goods for real, bestowing hardly a thought upon true sweetness and light;—'and to *their* lives,' he adds mournfully, 'who can give another and a better rhythm?' But, although those chiefly attracted by sweetness and light will probably always be the young and enthusiastic, and culture must not hope to take the mass of mankind by storm, yet we will not therefore, for our own day and for our own people, admit and rest in the desponding sentence of Aristotle. For is not this the right crown of the long discipline of Hebraism, and the due fruit of mankind's centuries of painful schooling in self-conquest, and the just reward, above all, of the strenuous energy of our own nation and kindred in dealing honestly with itself and walking steadfastly according to the best light it knows,—that when in the fulness of time it has reason and beauty offered to it, and the law of things as they really are, it should at last walk by this true light with the same staunchness and zeal with which it formerly walked by its imperfect light? And thus man's two great natural forces, Hebraism and Hellenism, will no longer be dissociated and rival, but will be a joint force of right thinking and strong doing to carry him on towards perfection. This is what the lovers of culture may perhaps dare to augur for such a nation as ours.

Therefore, however great the changes to be accomplished, and however dense the array of Barbarians, Philistines, and Populace, we will neither despair on the one hand, nor, on the other, threaten violent revolution and change. But we will look forward cheerfully and hopefully to 'a revolution,' as the Duke of Wellington said, 'by due course of law'; though not exactly such laws as our Liberal friends are now, with their actual lights, fond of offering to us.

But if despondency and violence are both of them forbidden to the believer in culture, yet neither, on the other hand, is public life and direct political action much permitted to him. For it is his business, as we have seen, to get the present believers in action, and lovers of political talking and doing, to make a return upon their own minds, scrutinise their stock notions and habits much more, value their present talking and doing much less; in order that, by learning to think more clearly, they may come at last to act less confusedly. But how shall we persuade our Barbarian to hold lightly to his feudal usages; how shall we persuade our Nonconformist that his time spent in agitating for the abolition of church-establishments would have been better spent in getting worthier ideas of God and the ordering of the world, or his time spent in battling for voluntaryism in education better spent in learning to value and found a public and national culture; how shall we persuade, finally, our Alderman-Colonel not to be content with sitting in the hall of judgment or marching at the head of his men of war, without some knowledge how to perform judgment and how to direct men of war,—how, I say, shall we persuade all these of this, if our Alderman-Colonel sees that we want to get his leading-staff and his scales of justice for our own hands; or the Nonconformist, that we want for ourselves his platform; or the Barbarian, that we want for ourselves his pre-eminency and function? Certainly they will be less slow to believe, as we want them to believe, that the intelligible law of things has in itself something desirable and precious, and that all place, function, and bustle are hollow goods without it, if they see that we ourselves can content ourselves with this law, and find in it our satisfaction, without making it an instrument to give us for ourselves place, function, and bustle.

And although Mr. Sidgwick says that social usefulness really means 'losing oneself in a mass of disagreeable, hard, mechanical details,' and though all the believers in action are fond of asserting the same thing, yet, as to lose ourselves is not what we want, but to find ourselves through finding the intelligible law of things, this assertion too we shall not blindly accept, but shall sift and try it a little first. And if we see that because the believers in action, forgetting Goethe's maxim, 'to act is easy, to think is hard,' imagine there is some wonderful virtue in losing oneself in a mass of mechanical details, therefore they excuse themselves from much thought about the clear ideas which ought to govern these details, then we shall give our chief care and pains to seeking out those ideas and to setting them forth ; being persuaded that if we have the ideas firm and clear, the mechanical details for their execution will come a great deal more simply and easily than we now suppose.

At this exciting juncture, then, while so many of the lovers of new ideas, somewhat weary, as we too are, of the stock performances of our Liberal friends upon the political stage, are disposed to rush valiantly upon this public stage themselves, we cannot at all think that for a wise lover of new ideas this stage is the right one. Plenty of people there will be without us,—country gentlemen in search of a club, demagogues in search of a tub, lawyers in search of a place, industrialists in search of gentility,—who will come from the east and from the west, and will sit down at that Thyesteän banquet of clap-trap which English public life for these many years past has been. And, so long as those old organisations, of which we have seen the insufficiency,—those expressions of our ordinary self, Barbarian or Philistine,—have force anywhere, they will have force in Parliament. There, the man whom the Barbarians send, cannot but be impelled to please the Barbarians' ordinary self, and their natural taste for the bathos: and the man whom the Philistines send, cannot but be impelled to please those of the Philistines. Parliamentary Conservatism will and must long mean this, that the Barbarians should keep their heritage; and Parliamentary Liberalism, that the Barbarians should pass away, as they will pass away, and that into their heritage the Philistines should enter. This seems, indeed, to be the true and authentic promise of which our Liberal friends and Mr. Bright believe themselves the heirs, and the goal of that great man's labours. Presently, perhaps, Mr. Odger and Mr. Bradlaugh will be there with their mission to oust both Barbarians and

Philistines, and to get the heritage for the Populace.

We, on the other hand, are for giving the heritage neither to the Barbarians nor to the Philistines, nor yet to the Populace; but we are for the transformation of each and all of these according to the law of perfection. Through the length and breadth of our nation a sense,—vague and obscure as yet,—of weariness with the old organisations, of desire for this transformation, works and grows. In the House of Commons the old organisations must inevitably be most enduring and strongest, the transformation must inevitably be longest in showing itself; and it may truly be averred, therefore, that at the present juncture the centre of movement is not in the House of Commons. It is in the fermenting mind of the nation; and his is for the next twenty years the real influence who can address himself to this.

Pericles was perhaps the most perfect public speaker who ever lived, for he was the man who most perfectly combined thought and wisdom with feeling and eloquence. Yet Plato brings in Alcibiades declaring, that men went away from the oratory of Pericles, saying it was very fine, it was very good, and afterwards thinking no more about it; but they went away from hearing Socrates talk, he says, with the point of what he had said sticking fast in their minds, and they could not get rid of it. Socrates has drunk his hemlock and is dead; but in his own breast does not every man carry about with him a possible Socrates, in that power of a disinterested play of consciousness upon his stock notions and habits, of which this wise and admirable man gave all through his lifetime the great example, and which was the secret of his incomparable influence? And he who leads men to call forth and exercise in themselves this power, and who busily calls it forth and exercises it in himself, is at the present moment, perhaps, as Socrates was in his time, more in concert with the vital working of men's minds, and more effectually significant, than any House of Commons orator, or practical operator in politics.

Every one is now boasting of what he has done to educate men's minds and to give things the course they are taking. Mr. Disraeli educates, Mr. Bright educates, Mr. Beales educates. We, indeed, pretend to educate no one, for we are still engaged in trying to clear and educate ourselves. But we are sure that the endeavour to reach, through culture, the firm intelligible law of things, we are sure that the detaching ourselves from our stock notions and habits, that a more free play of consciousness, an increased desire for sweetness and light, and all the bent which we call Hellenising, is the master impulse even now of the life of our nation and of humanity,—somewhat obscurely perhaps for this actual moment, but decisively and certainly for the immediate future ; and that those who work for this are the sovereign educators.

Docile echoes of the eternal voice, pliant organs of the infinite will, such workers are going along with the essential movement of the world ; and this is their strength, and their happy and divine fortune. For if the believers in action, who are so impatient with us and call us effeminate, had had the same good fortune, they would, no doubt, have surpassed us in this sphere of vital influence by all the superiority of their genius and energy over ours. But now we go the way the human race is going, while they abolish the Irish Church by the power of the Nonconformists' antipathy to establishments, or they enable a man to marry his deceased wife's sister.

FRIENDSHIP'S GARLAND

. . . . *manibus date lilia plenis*

CONTENTS

FRIENDSHIP'S GARLAND

DEDICATORY LETTER

GRUB STREET, *Candlemas Day*, 1871.

MY DEAR LEO,

SHALL I ever forget the evening, at the end of last November, when your feeling letter describing the death of our friend first met my eyes? I was alone in my garret; it was just dark; my landlady opened the door and threw a paper on the table. Selfish creatures that we are! my first thought was: It is a communication from the Literary Fund! The straits to which I am reduced by my long warfare with the Philistines, have at last, I said to myself, become known; they have excited sympathy; this is no doubt a letter from Mr. Octavian Blewitt, enclosing half-a-crown, the promise of my dinner at Christmas, and the kind wishes of Lord Stanhope for my better success in authorship. Hastily I lighted my lamp, and saw the *Pall Mall Gazette*. You know, Leo, how, after vainly knocking at the door of the *Daily Telegraph*, I carried to Northumberland Street my records of the conversations of Arminius. I love to think that the success of the 'Workhouse Casual' had disposed the Editor's heart to be friendly towards Pariahs; my communication was affably accepted, and from that day to this the *Pall Mall Gazette*, whenever there is any mention in it of Arminius, reaches me in Grub Street *gratis*. I took the paper, I opened it; your playful signature caught my eye. I read your letter through to the end, and then . . .

Suffer me, Leo, to draw a veil over those first days of grief. In the tumult of feeling plans were then formed to which I have not energy to give effect. I nourished the design of laying before the public a complete account of Arminius von Thunder-ten-Tronckh, and of the group which was gathered round him. The history of his family has been written by the famous Voltaire in his *Candide;* but I doubt whether an honest man can in conscience send the British public to even the historical works of that dangerous author. Yet a singular fortune brought together in our set the descendants of a number of the personages of *Candide*. Von Thunder-ten-Tronckh is, perhaps, sufficiently made known by the following letters; his curious delusion about the living representative of Pangloss is also fully noticed there. But not a glimpse, alas, do these records give of our poor friend Martin (de Mabille), who has just been shut up in Paris eating rats, the cynical descendant of that great foe of Pangloss's optimism, the Martin of *Candide*. Hardly a glimpse is given of the Marquis Pompeo Pococurante, little Pompey with the soft eyes and dark hair, whose acquaintance you made at Turin under the *portiques du Pô*, and whom you brought to London in the hope of curing, by the spectacle of the *Daily Telegraph*, his hereditary indifference and ennui. Of our English friends, too, the public would, doubtless, be glad to hear more. Mr. Bottles himself fills, in the following letters, by no means that space to which his importance entitles him; the excellent Baptist minister, for whom Mr. Bottles has so high a regard, the Rev. Josiah Jupp, appears far too unfrequently; your *Mary Jane*, Leo, is a name and nothing more; hardly more than names are my good and kind patroness, the late lamented Mrs. Bottles, and her sister and successor, Miss Hannah. It is a small matter, perhaps; but I should have liked, too, the public to know something of my faithful landlady here in Grub Street, Kitty Crone, on whom, after my vain conflict with the Philistines is ended, will probably devolve the pious duty of closing my eyes.

I had imagined a memorial of Arminius, in which all these would have found their place; but my spirits broke down in the attempt to execute my design. All, therefore, that I have done is to collect the stray records of Arminius which have already been published, to illustrate them with notes so far as appeared necessary, and to give myself the melancholy pleasure of dedicating to you, Leo, a collection which owes to your brilliant and facile pen some of its best ornaments.

Our friend had an odd way of showing it, but certainly Arminius had a love for this country. Do you remember, Leo, that conversation in the summer of last year, the last we spent together in his company? It was in the arbour of the garden of the 'Bald-Faced Stag' at Finchley. We had all been to the gallery of the House of Commons to hear Mr. Vernon Harcourt develop a system of unsectarian religion from the Life of Mr. Pickwick; but from some obstacle or other the expected treat did not come off. We adjourned to Finchley, and there, you remember, Arminius began with a discourse on religious education. He exacted from me, as you know, the promise not, as he harshly phrased it, to 'make a hash of his ideas' by reporting them to the public; and the promises of friendship are sacred. But afterwards the conversation became general. It then took a wider range; and I remember Mr. Frederic Harrison beginning to harangue, with his usual fiery eloquence, on the enervation of England, and on the malignancy of all the brute mass of us who are not Comtists. Arminius checked him. 'Enervation!'—said he; 'depend upon it, yours is still the most fighting people in the whole world. Malignancy !—the best character of the English people ever yet given, friendly as the character is, is still this of Burke's: "The ancient and inbred integrity, piety, good-nature, and good-humour of the people of England." Your nation is sound enough, if only it can be taught that being able to do what one likes, and say what one likes, is not sufficient for salvation. Its dangers are from a surfeit of clap-trap, due to the false notion that liberty and publicity are not only valuable for the use to be made of them, but are goods in themselves, nay, are the *summum bonum !*'

To the same effect he wrote to me from before Paris, a week or two before his death. 'You know I do not join in the common dislike of your nation, or in the belief in its certain decay. But no nation can, without danger, go on stuffing its mind with such nonsense as is talked by the newspapers which you are stupid (*sic*) enough to quote with admiration. "The Germans, forsooth," says your precious *Telegraph*, "cannot too soon begin the lesson, of which England has been the special teacher, that national greatness and wealth are to be prized only in so far as they ensure the freedom of the individual citizen, and the right of all to join in free debate. Without that liberty, a German Empire will be only a gilded despotism, politically weak in spite of its military power, barbaric in spite of its schools and universities." "The fall," says your *Daily News*, " of the late Government of France is history's reassertion of the principle of political liberty." Do you not see that, if France, without political liberty, has signally lost, and Germany, without political liberty, has signally won, it is absurd to make the presence or absence of political liberty in themselves the ground of the fall or success of nations? Of the fall or success of nations, certain *virtues* are the ground; political, ay, and social liberty, are, if you like, favourable to those virtues, where a root of them already exists; therefore I am a Republican;—but they by no means ensure them. If you have not these virtues, and imagine that your political liberty will pull you through without them, you will be ruined in spite of your political liberty. I admire England because she has such a root in her of these virtues; not because they have given her, among other good things, political liberty. Your fetish-worship of mere liberty is, on the contrary, just now the gravest danger to you. Your newspapers are every day solemnly saying that the great lesson to be learned from the present war is so and so,—always something which it is not. There are many lessons to be learned from the present war; I will tell you what is for *you* the great lesson to be learned from it:—*obedience*. That, instead of every man airing his self-consequence, thinking it bliss to talk at random about things, and to put his finger in every pie, you should seriously understand that there is a *right* way of doing things, and that the bliss is, without thinking of one's self-consequence, to do them in that way, or to forward their being done,—this is the great lesson your British public, as you call it, has to learn, and may learn, in some degree, from the Germans in this war! Englishmen were once famous for the power of holding their tongues and doing their business, and, therefore, I admire your nation. The business now to be done in the world is harder than ever, and needs far more than has been ever yet needed of thought, study, and seriousness: miscarry you must, if you let your daily doses of clap-trap make you imagine that liberty and publicity can be any substitute for these.'

I doubt whether this is sound, Leo, and, at any rate, the *D. T.* should have been more respectfully mentioned; but it shows that the feeling of Arminius towards this country was at bottom tender. My own patriotism, as you know, never wavered, even while I made myself, in a manner, the mouthpiece of Arminius, and submitted to the predominance which his intellect, I own, exercised over me. My affection for him remains as strong as ever, but now that his life is ended, and his predominance withdrawn, I feel that a new destiny is probably opening for me. My patriotic feelings will henceforth have free play; the iron hand of

Arminius will no longer press them down. Your counsels, Leo, the study of our newspapers, the spectacle of our grandeur, will work with these my natural feelings; I shall earn the public approbation, I shall not be always an Ishmael. I shall ally myself to some of those great Liberal movements which,—however Arminius might choose to call them petty aimless activities, bustle without any *Ernst, der ins Ganze geht*,—seem to me admirably suited to the genius of our national life, and highly productive of enjoyable excitement and honourable importance to their promoters.

We are now on the point of commencing what Arminius, with his fatally carping spirit, called our 'Thyesteän banquet of clap-trap';—we are on the eve of the meeting of Parliament. Mr. T. Chambers will again introduce that enfranchising measure, against which I have had some prejudices, but which you, Leo, have so eloquently upheld,—the bill for enabling a man to marry his deceased wife's sister. Mr. Miall, that Israelite, indeed, will resume, on a more stupendous scale than ever, his labours for making all bitterness, and wrath, and anger, and clamour, and evil-speaking be put away from us, with all malice; and for our enjoyment of the pure milk of Christianity. The devoted adversaries of the Contagious Diseases Act will spread through the length and breadth of the land a salutary discussion of this equivocal measure and of all matters connected with it; and will thus, at the same time that they oppose immorality, enable the followers of even the very straitest sects of Puritanism to see life. Some of these workers will doubtless suffer me to put my hand to their plough. Like the tailor to the poet Cowper, to some one or other of them I may be allowed to make my modest appeal :—

> Say, shall *my* little bark attendant sail,
> Pursue the triumph, and partake the gale?

If not on the hustings or the platform, at least I may do something in the closet, with the pen! My mind full of this new thought, as I passed down Regent Street yesterday, and saw in a shop window, in the frontispiece to one of Mr. Hepworth Dixon's numerous but well-merited editions, the manly and animated features of the author of the immortal *Guide to Mormonism*, I could not help exclaiming with pride: 'I, too, am an author!'

And then, Leo, comes the reaction. I look up and see Arminius's vacant stool; I sniff, and my nostrils no longer catch the scent of his tobacco. The dreams of excitement and ambition fly away; I am left solitary with the remembrance of the past, and with those consolations of piety and religion, which you, Leo, have outgrown. Yet how can I do you such an injustice?—when at this very moment my chief consolation, under our heavy bereavement, is in repeating to myself that glorious passage you read to me the other day from one of your unpublished articles for the *D. T.*:—'*In the Garden of the Hesperides, the inscrutable-eyed Sphinx whispers, with half-parted lips, Mysteries more than Eleusinian of the Happy Dead!*'

Believe me, my dear Leo,

Your faithful admirer,

MATTHEW ARNOLD.

To ADOLESCENS LEO, Esq.
etc. etc. etc.

(The acquaintance of the ever-to-be-lamented Arminius was made by the present Editor on the Continent in the year 1865. The early history of the noble family of Von-Thunder-ten-Tronckh, to which Arminius belonged, their establishment in Westphalia, the sack of their castle in the middle of the last century by the Bulgarians, the fate of their principal dependants (among whom was the famous optimist philosopher, Dr. Pangloss), the adventures of Arminius's grandfather and his deportation to the Jesuits at Rome, are recorded in a well-known treatise of Voltaire. Additional information is supplied in several of the following letters.

Arminius came to England in 1866, and the correspondence now given in a collected form to the public commenced in the summer of that year, at the outbreak of the war between Prussia and Austria. Many will yet remember the thrill with which they originally received, through the unworthy ministry of the present Editor, the communication of the great doctrine of 'Geist.' What, then, must it have been to hear that doctrine in its first newness from the lips of Arminius himself! Yet it will, I hope, be admitted, that even in this position of exceptional privilege, the present Editor succeeded in preserving his coolness, his independent judgment, and his proper feelings as a Briton.)—Ed.

LETTER I

I INTRODUCE ARMINIUS AND 'GEIST' TO THE BRITISH PUBLIC

SIR, GRUB STREET, *July* 19, 1866.

A PRUSSIAN acquaintance of mine, one of the party of foreigners who so offensively criticised my countrymen to me when I was abroad last year, has been over here just now, and for the last week or so he has been favouring me with his remarks on all he hears us say about the present crisis in Germany. In confidence I will own to you that he makes himself intensely disagreeable. He has the harsh, arrogant Prussian way of turning up his nose at things and laying down the law about them; and though, as a lover of intellect, I admire him, and, as a seeker of truth, I value his frankness, yet, as an Englishman, and a member of what the *Daily Telegraph* calls 'the Imperial race,' I feel so uncomfortable under it, that I want, through your kindness, to call to my aid the great British public, which never loses heart and has always a bold front and a rough word ready for its assailants.

My Prussian friend got a little mortification at the beginning of his visit, and as it is my belief this mortification set him wrong from the first, I shall relate what it was. I took him with me down to Reigate by the railroad, and in the carriage was one of our representative industrial men (something in the bottle way), a famous specimen of that great middle class whose energy and self-reliance make England what it is, and who give the tone to our Parliament and to our policy. News had just come of the first bloodshed between the Austrians and Prussians now at war together in Germany. 'So they've begun fighting,' cried my countryman; 'what fools they both are!' And he handed us *Punch* with that masterly picture in it of 'Denmark avenged'; that scathing satire which represents the King of Denmark sitting with his glass of grog and his cigar, to gloat over the terrible retribution falling upon his great enemy Prussia for her misdeeds towards him. My Prussian glared at the striking moral lesson thus brought to his notice, but rage and contempt made him speechless. I hastened, with a few sentences taken from Mr. Gladstone's recent advice to the Roumanians, to pay my homage to the great principles of peaceful, industrial development which were invoked by my countryman. 'Yes; war,' I said, 'interrupts business, and brings intolerable inconvenience with it; whereas people have only to persist steadily in the manufacture of bottles, railways, banks, and finance companies, and all good things will come to them of their own accord.' Before I had finished we reached Reigate, and I got my still speechless Prussian quickly out of the train.

But never shall I forget the flood when speech came at last: 'The dolt! the dunder-head! His ignorance of the situation, his ignorance of Germany, his ignorance of what makes nations great, his ignorance of what makes life worth living, his ignorance of everything except bottles,—those infernal bottles!' I heard so much of all this that I am glad to forget it without going through it again with the British public. I only mention it to make the rudeness of expression in what follows less unaccountable.

The day before yesterday the *Daily News* published that powerful letter from Mr. Goldwin Smith, pronouncing in favour of the Prussian alliance. In great excitement I ran with it to my friend. 'At last I have got something,' I cried, 'which will please you; a declaration by one of our best writers, in one of our best newspapers, for a united Germany under Prussian headship. She and we are thereupon to combine to curb France. Wherever I go, I hear people admiring the letter and approving the idea.' A sardonic smile, such as Alexander von Humboldt used to have when he contemplated the late King of Prussia's missionary deaconesses, came over my Berliner's harsh countenance. 'Good God!' said he, 'the miracles that needle-gun is working! It is only a year ago you were threatening Prussia with France, and suggesting to that great and sagacious ruler, as you called him, the French Emperor, to take the Rhine Province from us; it is not six weeks since I saw him styled in this very newspaper, with the dignity usual in Englishmen at present, "the arbiter of Europe." He has done nothing in the meantime to injure you; he has done his best to keep well with you. How charmed he will be with his friends! But the declaration you are all so pleased at, who is it by?' 'Mr. Goldwin Smith,' I answered. 'I know him,' he said; 'a good writer, but a fanatic.' 'Oh, no, no,' said I; 'a man of genius and virtue.'

Without answering, my Berliner took the newspaper and read the letter. 'He should have served under Nelson,' he said, as he finished it; 'he hates a Frenchman as he does the devil. However, it is true that a preponderance in the world such as the French, thanks to your stupidity, were fast getting, is enough to make any human being, let alone a Frenchman, unbearable; and it is a good thing to have a great Germany in the world as well as a great

France. It would be a good thing to have a great England too, if you would let us. But pray what is to unite Germany and England against France? What is to be the ground of sympathy between actual England and actual Germany?' 'You are a strong Liberal,' said I, 'so I can easily answer you. You are drawn towards England because of her liberalism, and away from the French Emperor because of his despotism.' 'Liberalism and despotism!' cried the Prussian; 'let us get beyond these forms and words. What unites and separates people now is *Geist*.'

I had not the slightest idea what he meant, and my looks told my bewilderment. 'I thought you had read Mr. Grant Duff's chapters on Germany,' said he. 'But Mr. Grant Duff knows what he writes about, so I suppose you have not. Your great Lord Palmerston used to call Germany "that country of d——d professors"; and the English public, which supposes professors to be people who know something, and hates anybody who knows anything, has always kept its mind as clear of my unfortunate country as it could. But I advise you, for the sake of the events now passing, to read Mr. Grant Duff's book. There you will find that in Berlin we oppose "Geist,"—*intelligence*, as you or the French might say,—to "Ungeist." The victory of "Geist" over "Ungeist" we think the great matter in the world. The same idea is at the bottom of democracy; the victory of reason and intelligence over blind custom and prejudice. So we German Liberals who believe in "Geist" have a sympathy with France and its governors, so far as they are believers in democracy. We have no sympathy with English liberalism, whose centre is in the "Ungeist" of such people as your wiseacre in the Reigate train.'

'But then you play,' cried I, 'the game of the Tories; for listen to Mr. Goldwin Smith: "The Tories in Europe, with the sure instinct of a party, recognise the great patron of reaction in the Emperor of the French." You and we are to unite, in order to defeat the Tories and the Emperor of the French.'

The Prussian answered: 'Mr. Goldwin Smith blinds himself with the passions, as the Emperor of the French himself would say, of another age. The Tories of Europe have no real love for the Emperor of the French; they may admire and envy his absolutism and strength, but they hate his fundamental principles: they can have no real sympathy with the Sovereign who says boldly that he detests the actual public law of Europe, and who tells the people that it is among the people he finds the true genius of France, and breathes freely. Such a man works for "Geist" in his way;[1] not, perhaps, through

[1] The indulgence of Arminius for this execrable and unsuccessful tyrant was unworthy of a member of our great Teutonic family. Probably, after Sedan, he changed his opinion of him.—Ed.

a *Daily Telegraph*, or monster meetings in Trafalgar Square, or a Coles's Truss Manufactory standing where it ought not, a glorious monument of individualism and industrialism, to adorn the "finest site in Europe"; but by making the common people feel they are alive and have a human spirit in them. We North-Germans have worked for "Geist" in our way, by loving knowledge, by having the best-educated middle and lower class in the world. You see what this has just done for us. France has "Geist" in her democracy, and Prussia in her education. Where have you got it?—got it as a force, I mean, and not only in a few scattered individuals. Your common people is barbarous; in your middle class "Ungeist" is rampant; and as for your aristocracy, you know "Geist" is forbidden by nature to flourish in an aristocracy.

'So do not,' he continued, 'suffer yourself to be deceived by parallels drawn from times before "Geist." What has won this Austrian battle for Prussia is "Geist"; "Geist" has used the King, and Bismarck, and the Junkers, and "Ungeist in uniform," all for its own ends; and "Geist" will continue so to use them till it has triumphed.[1] It will ally itself with "Geist"

[1] I am unwilling to triumph over Arminius in his grave; but I cannot help remarking that 'Ungeist in uniform,' as Mr. Bottles observes to me, has just given a pretty good account of the 'Geist' in French democracy; and I have a shrewd suspicion it will give an equally good account of the 'Geist' of Arminius's educated

where it finds it, because there it has a ground for mutual respect and understanding ; and where there is no "Geist," it has none.

'And now,' this odious man went on, 'now, my dear friend, I shall soon be leaving you, so one word more. You have lately been writing about the Celts and the Germans, and in the course of your remarks on the Germans you have said, among many impertinences, one thing which is true. You have said that the strength of North Germany lay in this, that the idea of science governed every department of human activity there. You, my dear friend, live in a country where at present the idea of clap-trap governs every department of human activity. Great events are happening in the world, and Mr. Goldwin Smith tells you that "England will be compelled to speak at last." It would be truly sad if, when she does speak, she should talk nonsense. To prevent such a disaster, I will give you this piece of advice, with which I take my leave : "*Get Geist.*"'

Thank God, this d——d professor (to speak as Lord Palmerston) is now gone back to his own *Intelligenz-Staat*. I half hope there may next come a smashing defeat of the Prussians before Vienna, and make my ghostly friend laugh on the wrong side of his mouth. Meanwhile, I shall take care that he hears whatever answers

and liberal friends in Prussia. Perhaps Arminius was taken away from the evil to come !—Ed.

he gets. I know that they will be conclusive, and I hope that they will be speedy, and in this hope,

I am, Sir,

Your obedient servant,

MATTHEW ARNOLD.

To the EDITOR *of the* PALL MALL GAZETTE.

LETTER II

ARMINIUS APPEARS AS HIS OWN INTERPRETER

SIR, BERLIN, *July* 31, 1866.

AN English friend of mine, Mr. Matthew Arnold, seems to have rushed into print with an idea or two he picked up from me when I was in England, and to have made rather a mess of it ; at least, he sends me some newspapers which have answered him, and writes me a helpless sort of a letter at the same time, asking me how he is to parry this, and what he is to say in reply to that. Now, I have a regard for this Mr. Matthew Arnold, but I have taken his measure, and know him to be, as a disputant, rather a poor creature. Again and again I have seen him anxiously ruminating over what his adversary has happened to say against his ideas ; and when I tell him (if the ideas were mine) that his adversary is a *dummkopf*, and that he must stand up to him firm and square, he begins to smile, and tells me that what is probably passing through his adversary's mind is so and so.[1]

I see your hideous truss manufactory in Trafalgar Square comes up in this controversy, and that very manufactory brings to my mind a ridiculous instance of my poor friend's weakness. I had been running over with him a few of the principal violations of æsthetic laws in London, illustrating the lesson by reference to the stucco palaces of my beautiful Berlin. After despatching the Duke of Wellington's statue and the black dome and gray pepper-boxes of your National Gallery, I came to Coles's manufactory. 'Can anything be more atrocious?' I asked. 'It is bad,' answered my poor friend; 'and yet,' he went on, 'and yet, Arminius, I have a tenderness for that manufactory. That manufactory, with other things in London like it, is one of my favourite arguments for the immortality of the soul.' 'What folly have you got in your head now?' said I. 'Remember,' said he, 'what is told us of the statue of the Olympian Zeus by Phidias. It was life enough to have seen it; felicity had then reached its consummation; the spirit could grasp no more, and the man might end. And what therefore, I ask, must not be in store for the British ratepayer, who in his life has only seen the Duke of Wellington's statue and Coles's truss

[1] A very ill-natured and exaggerated description of my (I hope) not unamiable candour.—Ed.

manufactory ? His felicity must surely be yet to come. Somewhere, beyond the grave' . . . and for a good twenty minutes my simple friend went on with stuff like this, which I will not weary you with any more of.

I, Sir, as a true Prussian, have a passion for what is *wissenschaftlich* (I do not say 'scientific,' because then you English will think I mean I have an interest in the sea-bear, or in the blue lights and smells of a chemical lecture). I am, I say, *wissenschaftlich ;* I love to proceed with the stringency of a philosopher, and Mr. Matthew Arnold with his shillyshallying spoils the ideas I confide to him. Therefore I write to you myself, to tell you (since I like your nation for the sake of the great men it has formerly produced, and of its brave-hearted, industrious people) where the pinch of the matter for you really lies.

It lies here—there is in you '*kein Ernst*, *der ins Ganze geht*.' You peck at the mere outside of problems ; you have not got your mind at work upon them ; you fancy they will solve themselves without mind, if only you keep making bottles, and letting every one do what is right in his own eyes, and congratulating yourselves at the top of your voices on your own success. 'Individualism and industrialism will in time replace Coles by a worthier edifice,' says one of your prophets. Not without an '*Ernst*, *der ins Ganze geht*,' I answer. Not without 'Geist' and faith in 'Geist' ; and this is just what your individualism and industrialism has not got. 'A self-administering community is surely an ideal.'—That depends entirely on what the self-administering community is like. If it has 'Geist,' and faith in 'Geist,' yes; if it has not, no. Then another of your prophets asks: 'Why should "Geist" care about democracy? Democracy is government by the masses, by the light of their own vulgar tastes.'—Your democracy perhaps, but this is just what makes your weakness; you have no *demos*, no people, but 'masses with vulgar tastes.' The top part of them are in training to be Philistines like your middle class; the lower part is a rabble. Your democracy has not yet reached even the idea of country; the friends of your northern workmen tell us they read American newspapers, and care more for America than for England. No wonder; they have never been quickened by an '*Ernst, der ins Ganze geht*,' the only baptism that makes masses into a people; they have never been in contact with 'Geist,' only with clap-trap. To abate feudalism by providing that in one insignificant case out of one million land shall not follow the feudal law of descent; to abolish English church-rates because the English Dissenters are strong, and to spare the Irish Church Establishment because the Irish Catholics are weak;[1] to give a man leave to

[1] No doubt this remark of Arminius had some share in producing that great measure which has since abolished the Irish

marry his deceased wife's sister; to give a man who lives in a particular kind of house a vote for members of Parliament—that is the pabulum by which the leaders of your people seek to develop 'Geist' in it, and to awaken an '*Ernst, der ins Ganze geht.*' If this is not spiritual enough, as a final resource there is rioting in the parks, and a despotism of your penny newspapers tempered by the tears of your executive, to hasten the growth of English democracy in dignity and intelligence.

The French are not solid enough for my taste; but, *Gott in Himmel!* that people has had a fire baptism, and the democracy which is born of a fire baptism like theirs, 'Geist' cannot help caring about. They were unripe for the task they in '89 set themselves to do; and yet, by the strength of 'Geist' and their faith in 'Geist,' this 'mere viper brood of canting egotists' did so much that they left their trace in half the beneficial reforms through Europe; and if you ask how, at Naples, a convent became a school, or in Ticino an intolerable oligarchy ceased to govern, or in Prussia Stein was able to carry his land-reforms, you get one answer: *the French!* Till modern society is finally formed, French democracy will still be a power in Europe, and it will manage to have effective leaders at the Tuileries, and not only in

Church by the power of the English Dissenters' enmity to Church establishments.—Ed.

Cayenne. It will live, though the classes above it may rot; because it has faith in 'Geist,' and does not think that people can do without 'Geist' by dint of holding monster meetings, and having their *Star*[1] and *Telegraph* every morning, and paying no church-rates, and marrying their deceased wife's sister.

We Prussians, Sir, have, as a people, no great love for the French, because we were blown into the air by the explosion of their 'Geist' some sixty years ago, and much quarrelling and ill-blood followed. But we saw then what a power the 'Geist' in their democracy gave them; and we set to work to make ourselves strong, not by a sort of wild fire-baptism of the mass, but in our steady German way, by culture, by *forming* our faculties of all kinds, by every man doing the very best he could with himself, by trusting, with an '*Ernst, der ins Ganze geht*,' to mind and not to clap-trap. Your 'earnest Liberal' in England thinks culture all moonshine; he is for the spiritual development of your democracy by rioting in the parks, abolishing church-rates, and marrying a deceased wife's sister; and for leaving your narrow and vulgar middle class (of which I saw an incomparable specimen in a Reigate train

[1] The *Star*, like Arminius himself, has passed from amongst us; but may we not say that its work was done when it had once laid the basis of that admirable and fruitful alliance between Mialism and Millism, which the course of our politics is now every day consolidating?—ED.

when I was over in England) just as it is. On the other hand, Mr. Matthew Arnold writes me word that a club has just been formed among you to do honour to the memory of that great man, Richard Cobden ; that this club has taken for its motto, 'Peace, Retrenchment, and Reform' ; and that these words, by a special command from Mr. Cobden's ghost, are to bear the following interpretation :—'Peace to our nonsense, retrenchment of our profligate expenditure of clap-trap, and reform of ourselves.' Whether this is true, or merely a stroke of my poor friend's so-called playfulness (Heaven save the mark !), I do not feel quite sure ; I hope for your sakes it is true, as this is the very thing you want, and nothing else can save you from certain decline.

Do not be astonished at the aristocratic prefix to my name ; I come of a family which has for three generations rubbed shoulders with philosophy.

Your humble servant,

VON THUNDER-TEN-TRONCKH.

To the EDITOR *of the* PALL MALL GAZETTE.

LETTER III

I EXPOSTULATE WITH ARMINIUS ON HIS REVOLUTIONARY SENTIMENTS

SIR, GRUB STREET, *August* 6, 1866.

I THOUGHT it was very odd I got no answer from Arminius von Thunder-ten-Tronckh (he was christened Hermann, but I call him Arminius, because it is more in the grand style), when I so particularly begged him to write soon, and save what rags he could of his tissue of nonsense about 'Geist,' after my countrymen had riddled it, as I knew they were sure to do. I supposed he had taken service, like the rest of the German Liberals, under Bismarck, and was too busy pillaging the poor Frankfort people to think of intellectual matters; but I now see he has been writing direct to you, and wants to leave me out in the cold altogether. I do not in the least care for his coarse Prussian sneers, but I must say it is rather good that he should not be above sponging on me week after week in Grub Street, swilling beer (none of your Bavarian wash, but sound English Bass) at my expense, filling my garret (for I don't smoke myself) with the smell of his execrable tobacco, getting the daily benefit of my *Star* and *Telegraph* (I take the *Star* for wisdom and charity, and the *Telegraph* for taste and style), and keeping me up yawning till two o'clock every morning to listen to his rubbishy transcendentalism, and yet be too fine a gentleman to make me the depositary of his ideas for transmission to the English public. But Arminius has the ridiculous pride of his grandfather, who, though the family estate had all gone to the dogs, and he was ruined and turned priest, chose to set his stiff German face against Candide's marriage with his sister. He got shipped off to the Jesuits at Rome, as every one knows ; but what is not so well known is,[1] that when the French Revolution came, this precious priest, like Talleyrand, married, and my Arminius is his grandson. Arminius came over here to make acquaintance with Mr. Lowe, who he has found out is in some odd way descended from the philosopher Pangloss,[2] a great friend of the Von Thunder-ten-Tronckh family ; but ever since the sack of their château by the Bulgarians, the

[1] It was necessarily unknown to Voltaire, who wrote the history of the Von T. family.—Ed.

[2] It is my firm belief that this relationship, which had become a fixed idea with Arminius, never really existed. The optimism of Mr. Lowe's estimate of the British middle class and its House of Commons, in his celebrated speech on Reform, had, in my opinion, struck Arminius's fancy, and made him imagine a kinship in the flesh where there was in truth only a kinship in the spirit.—Ed.

Von Thunder-ten-Tronckhs have not had a sixpence in the world except what they could get by their 'Geist,' and what Arminius gets by his is such beggar's allowance that he is hardly presentable ; well enough for Grub Street, but, as I told him, not at all the sort of company Mr. Lowe keeps.

I don't think Arminius has gained much by being his own expounder, for more vague declamatory trash than his letter I never read. The truth is, he cannot rise to an Englishman's conception of liberty, and understand how liberty, like virtue, is its own reward. 'We go for self-government,' I am always saying to him. 'All right,' he says, 'if it is government by your better self.' 'Fiddlesticks about our better self!' answer I. 'Who is to be the judge? No, the self every man chooses.' 'And what is the self the mass of mankind will choose,' cries he, 'when they are not told there is a better and a worse self, and shown what the better is like?' 'They will choose the worse, very likely,' say I, 'but that is just liberty.' 'And what is to bring good out of such liberty as that?' he asks. 'The glorious and sanative qualities of our matchless Constitution,' I reply ; and that is always a stopper for him.

But what I grieve most to observe in Arminius's letter, and what will lead to my breaking with him in the long run, in spite of my love for intellect, is the bad revolutionary leaven which I see works stronger and stronger in him, and which he no doubt got from the worthless French company his grandfather kept.[1] I noticed an instance of it while he was over here, and I have had another instance, besides his letter to you, since he went away. The instance while he was over here was this. I had taken him down to Wimbledon to see the shooting; and there, walking up and down before the grand tent, was Lord Elcho. Everybody knows Lord Elcho's appearance, and how admirably he looks the part of our governing classes; to my mind, indeed, the mere cock of his lordship's hat is one of the finest and most aristocratic things we have. So of course I pointed Lord Elcho out to Arminius. Arminius eyed him with a jacobinical sort of a smile, and then: 'Cedar of Lebanon which God has not yet broken!' sneered he. I was pleased at Arminius knowing his St. Augustine, for the Prussians are in general thought to be much tainted with irreligion; but I felt at the time, and I feel still, that this was not by any means the proper way of speaking of a dashing nobleman like Lord Elcho.

The other instance is worse still. Besides writing Arminius long letters, I keep him regularly supplied with the *Star*, sending him

[1] This partially explains, no doubt, though it cannot altogether excuse, the weak indulgence always cropping out in Arminius for France and its immoral people.—Ed.

my own copy after I have read it through twice. I particularly begged him to study the number for last Wednesday week, in which there was the most beautiful account of 'An Aristocratic Reformer.' The other papers had not got it. It related how the Honourable Charles Clifford, a gentleman of strikingly handsome appearance, addressed the crowd in Hyde Park from the foot-board of a hansom. He told them he cared nothing for the Walpoles or Pakingtons, who were for putting down the voice of the people, for, said he, he was higher in social position than they. He was the son of a peer, his son-in-law was a peer, and all his family belonged to the aristocratic classes. This announcement was received with enthusiastic applause by the street-Hampdens present. 'May I ask you, right honourable sir,' cried one of them, 'why, as you are such a big man, you do not open the Park gates to us poor people?' Mr. C. said he wished he had the keys of the Park in his pocket. But he delivered himself of the great principle that it is the duty of the aristocratic classes to protect and promote the interests of the working men, and then he drove off in his hansom amidst redoubled applause.

Now nothing, Sir, gives me such pride and pleasure as traits of this kind, which show that we have, as Lord Macaulay finely says, the most popular aristocracy and the most aristocratic people in the world. I thought it would do

Arminius good to study the incident, and I wrote him word to that effect. Would you believe it, Sir? Mr. 'Geist' cannot condescend to write me a letter, but he sends me back my *Star* with a vile sketch, or rather caricature, of this touching incident; and opposite Mr. C.'s gentlemanly figure he has written 'Esel,' and opposite the crowd 'Lumpenpack,' which a friend who knows German better than I do tells me are words of disrespect, and even contempt. This is a spirit which I hate and abhor, and I tell Arminius plainly through your columns (since he chooses to adopt this way of corresponding) that unless he can break himself of it all is ended between him and me, and when next he comes to England he will find the garret-door in Grub Street bolted against him.

Your obedient servant,

MATTHEW ARNOLD.

To the EDITOR *of the* PALL MALL GAZETTE.

LETTER IV

ARMINIUS ASSAILS THE BRITISH PRESS FOR ITS FREE AND INDEPENDENT COMMENTS ON FOREIGN POLITICS.

SIR, BERLIN, *August* 11, 1866.

FOR Heaven's sake try and prevail upon your countrymen, who are so very anxious for peace for themselves, not to go on biting first the French Emperor's tail and then ours, merely for the fun of the thing apparently, and to have the pleasure of at least seeing a fight between other people, if they cannot have one of their own. You know that Michelet, the French historian, all through his history, familiarly talks of your people as *ce dogue*; 'upon this, *ce dogue mordit* such a one'; 'upon that *ce dogue déchira* such another.' According to him, you must always be *mordre*-ing or *déchirer*-ing some one, at home or abroad, such is your instinct of savageness; and you have,—undoubtedly you have,—a strong share of pugnacity. When I was over in England the other day, my poor friend Mr.

Matthew Arnold insisted, with his usual blind adoration of everything English, on taking me down to admire one of your great public schools; precious institutions, where, as I tell him, for £250 sterling a year your boys learn gentlemanly deportment and cricket. Well, down we went, and in the playing-fields (which with you are the school): 'I declare,' says Mr. Matthew Arnold, 'if there isn't the son of that man you quarrelled with in the Reigate train! And there, close by him, is a son of one of our greatest families, a Plantagenet! It is only in England, Arminius, that this beautiful salutary intermixture of classes takes place. Look at the bottle-merchant's son and the Plantagenet being brought up side by side; none of your absurd separations and seventy-two quarterings here. Very likely young Bottles will end by being a lord himself.' I was going to point out to Mr. Matthew Arnold that what a middle class wants is ideas, and ideas an aristocracy has nothing to do with; so that that vulgar dog, Bottles the father, in sending his son to learn only cricket and a gentlemanly deportment, like the aristocracy, had done quite the wrong thing with him. But just at this moment our attention was attracted by what was passing between the boys themselves. First, a boy goes up to Bottles, and says: 'Bottles, Plantagenet says he could lick you with one hand; you are as big as he is,—you wouldn't take a licking from him, would you?' 'No!' answered poor Bottles, rather hesitatingly. Upon this another boy rushes to Plantagenet. 'Plantagenet,' cries he, 'that brute Bottles says he wouldn't take a licking from you.' 'Does he, the beast!' thunders Plantagenet, and, flying at Bottles, hits him full on the nose; and as Bottles's blood streamed out, and I turned away in disgust, I heard the exulting cries of your young 'dogues' making the arrangements for a systematic encounter.

Now really, Sir, since I have been back in Germany your newspapers are perpetually bringing to my mind Michelet's 'dogue' and what I saw in your playing-fields. First you go to the French Emperor, and say: 'Ha, tyrant, we hope humble-pie agrees with you! We hope your tail between your legs is not productive of much inconvenience. Just as the intellectual Emperor was overmatched by an Italian statesman, he now finds himself outdone by a German statesman; a most agreeable thing for an intellectual Emperor—ha! ha! The intellectual Emperor distinctly intimated there must be no disturbing the European equilibrium, else he should interpose. Now the map has been altered enormously to the profit of Prussia, so what is the intellectual Emperor to do? Acknowledge himself outwitted by Count Bismarck, just as he was outwitted by Count Cavour?—ha, ha! Humble-pie! Humble-pie!'

—With the greatest alacrity the malcontents in France, the old Constitutional party, take up your parable : 'France is eating humble-pie !' they scream out ; 'the tyrant is making France eat humble-pie ! France is humiliated ! France is suffocating !' France is not difficult to stir up, and the French Emperor has already had to ask for the frontier of 1814. If you go on at this rate I expect he will have to ask for the Mark of Brandenburg next week. Then you will come to Bismarck and say : 'Bismarck, the tyrant is stretching his greedy fist over German soil. Will you let him have it ? Think of the prodigious strength you have just shown, of the glory you have just won. Think of French insolence, think of 1813, think of German honour, think of *sauer-kraut*, think of the moral support of England. Not an inch of German soil for the French tyrant !' And so, while you yourselves,—the new man in you, that is,—teach the nations, as Lord Stanley says, how to live, by peacefully developing your bottle-man in the Reigate train, your half-naked starvelings selling matches in St. James's Park, your truss manufactories in Trafalgar Square, and your *Daily Telegraph* saying in spite of all powers human and divine what it likes, you at the same time want to throw a bone to the old 'dogue' in you, in the shape of a very pretty quarrel of your getting up between other people.

Do, Sir, let other people also have a chance of

teaching the nations how to live, and emulating your bottle-man and your *Daily Telegraph*. For my part, I have the greatest aversion, and so have all the clearest-headed Germans of my acquaintance, to a quarrel with France. We, as genuine Liberals, know that French democracy is our natural ally. You will observe it is the Constitutionalists in France who are crying out so loudly for more territory to make their strength keep pace with ours. And then think of our poor delicate constitutionalism at home, and of the cruelty of leaving it with its work to do in the face of a war with France, and Bismarck made stronger than ever by such a war! I know our German constitutionalism pretty well. It comes up to the throne, 'With fullest heart-devotion we approach Prussia's King, reverently beseeching him to turn away his unconstitutional ministers.' Prussia's gracious King gives a grunt, and administers a sound kick to his petitioner's behind, who then departs, singing in fervent tones: '*Hoch* for King and fatherland!'

No, Sir; peace, the growth of a republican spirit all through Europe, and a mutual support between all those who share this spirit, are what I wish for. The French are vain; they have been spoilt; we have been going very fast; and you and the Orleanists keep telling them they are humiliated if they do not get something. No doubt people have a right to go to war for the balance of power if they believe in it; you have gone to war for it often enough when it suited your turn. So the Emperor of the French, as you will not let him have a chance of being wise and of seeing that here is a new spiritual force he had not reckoned on, which yet he may perfectly make friends of and live happily with, thinks he must do something for the balance of power, must ask for some rectification or other of frontier. I only hope he will ask for something moderate, and that we shall be moderate when he asks for it. Pray, Sir, pray do not you play the 'dogue' and make moderation harder both for the Emperor and for us.

I assure you a war with France would be a curse to us which even the blessing of your moral support would hardly compensate. And supposing (for certainly you do hate the French pretty strongly) in a year or two you determined to give us your active support,[1] and to send, with infinite crying out, an expedition of fifteen thousand men to the coast of Gothland or some such place, I am afraid, Sir, with the vast

[1] This is puerile. War between France and Prussia has since happened. We have not been able to give our undivided moral support to either combatant; of our active support, therefore, there could be no question. But it may be fearlessly asserted, that the well-balanced alternations of our moral support, the wise and steady advice given by our newspapers, and, in fact, our attitude generally in regard to this war, have raised Great Britain to a height even more conspicuous than she has ever yet occupied, in the esteem and admiration of foreign countries.—Ed.

armaments and rapid operations of modern warfare, even this active support of yours would not do us any great good.

Your humble servant,

VON THUNDER-TEN-TRONCKH.

To the EDITOR *of the* PALL MALL GAZETTE.

P.S.—By the way, I read poor Mr. Matthew Arnold's letter to you the other day. You see just what he is ; the discursiveness, the incapacity for arguing, the artlessness, the not very delicate allusions to my private circumstances and his own. It is impossible to enter into any serious discussion with him. But on one point of fact I will set him right. I saw Mr. Lowe and found him very affable ; even more like his ancestor Pangloss than I should have thought possible. 'The best of all possible worlds' was always on his lips ; 'a system of such tried and tested efficiency' ; 'what can we want more ?' 'the grumbler fails to suggest even one grievance.' I told him of that bottle barbarian in the Reigate train, and he said that on men of this kind rested 'the mighty fabric of English prosperity.' I could not help saying that in my opinion no country could long stand being ruled by the spirit (or rather matter) of men like that ; that a discontent with the present state of things was growing up, and that to-morrow even, or next day, we might see a change. Upon this, Mr. Lowe threw himself into a theatrical attitude, and with the most enthusiastic vehemence exclaimed :—

To-morrow ?
Oh, spare it, spare it !
It ought not so to die. [1]

In a man like poor Mr. Matthew Arnold, this infatuation about everything English is conceivable enough, but in a man of Mr. Lowe's parts I own I cannot quite make it out, notwithstanding his descent from Pangloss.

Von T.

[1] As the sentiments here attributed to Mr. Lowe, together with this very remarkable and splendid passage of poetry with which he concludes, are all taken from Mr. Lowe's printed speeches, and may have been read by Arminius in the *Times*, I still retain my doubts whether his interview with Mr. Lowe had ever any existence except in his own fertile imagination.—Ed.

LETTER V

I COMMUNICATE A VALUABLE EXPOSITION, BY ARMINIUS, OF THE SYSTEM OF TENANT-RIGHT IN PRUSSIA.

SIR, GRUB STREET, *November* 8, 1866.

MY love for intellect has made me seek a reconciliation with Arminius, in spite of all I had to complain of in him, and any one who had looked in here to-night might have seen him puffing away at his pipe, and laying down the law just in his old style. He was so immensely tickled at the *Daily Telegraph* calling his poor friend,—artless and obscure garretteer that he knows him to be,—'a high priest of the kid-glove persuasion,'[1] that he has been in a good humour ever since, and to-night he has been giving me some information which I do think, notwithstanding the horrid *animus* he betrays in delivering it, is highly curious and

[1] Besides all I had to endure from Arminius himself, our leading newspapers persisted in holding me answerable for every paradox uttered by him.—ED.

interesting, and therefore I hasten to communicate it to you.

It is about the Prussian land reforms, and this is how I got it out of him. 'You made me look rather a fool, Arminius,' I began, 'by what you primed me with in Germany last year about Stein settling your land question.' 'I dare say you looked a fool,' says my Prussian boor, 'but what did I tell you?' 'Why,' says I, 'you told me Stein had settled a land question like the Irish land question, and I said so in the *Cornhill Magazine*, and now the matter has come up again by Mr. Bright talking at Dublin of what Stein did, and it turns out he settled nothing like the Irish land question at all, but only a sort of tithe-commutation affair.' 'Who says that?' asked Arminius. 'A very able writer in the *Times*,' I replied.

I don't know that I have ever described Arminius's personal appearance. He has the true square Teutonic head, a blond and disorderly mass of tow-like hair, a podgy and sanguine countenance, shaven cheeks, and a whity-brown moustache. He wears a rough pilot-coat, and generally smokes away with his hands in the pockets of it, and his light blue eyes fixed on his interlocutor's face. When he takes his hands out of his pockets, his pipe out of his mouth, and his eyes off his friend's face, it is a sign that he is deeply moved. He did all this on the present occasion, and passing his short thick fingers two or three times through his blond hair: 'That astonishing paper!' muttered he.

Then he began as solemn as if he was in a pulpit. 'My dear friend,' says he, 'of the British species of the great genus Philistine there are three main varieties. There is the religious Philistine, the well-to-do Philistine, and the rowdy Philistine. The religious Philistine is represented by——' 'Stop, Arminius,' said I, 'you will oblige me by letting religion alone!' 'As you please,' answered he; 'well, then, the rowdy Philistine is represented by the *Daily Telegraph*, and the well-to-do Philistine by the *Times*. The well-to-do Philistine looks to get his own view of the British world,—that it is the best of all possible worlds as it is, because he has prospered in it,—preached back to him *ore rotundo* in the columns of the *Times*. There must be no uncertain sound in his oracle, no faltering, nothing to excite misgivings or doubts; like his own bosom, everything his oracle utters must be positive, pleasant, and comfortable. So of course about the great first article of his creed, the sacro-sanctity of property, there must in the *Times* be no trifling. But what amuses me is that his oracle must not even admit, if these matters come to be talked of, that Stein trifled with it in another country. The ark is so sacred, the example so abominable, and the devotee so sensitive. And therefore

Stein's reforms become in the *Times*, for the reassurance of the well-to-do British Philistine, a sort of tithe-commutation affair,—nothing in the world more! nothing in the world more!'

'Don't go on in that absurd way, Arminius,' said I; 'I don't tell you it was a tithe-commutation, but a commutation like the tithe-commutation. It was simply, the *Times* says, the conversion of serf-tenures into produce-rents. I hope that gives you a perfectly clear notion of what the whole thing was, for it doesn't me. But I make out from the *Times* that the *leibeigener*——' 'Rubbish about the *leibeigener*,' cries Arminius, in a rage, 'and all this jargon to keep your stupid mind in a mist; do you want to know what really happened?' 'Yes, I do,' said I, quietly, my love for knowledge making me take no notice of his impertinence. 'Yes, I do, and particularly this: In the first place, was the land, before Stein's reforms, the landlord's or the tenant's?' 'The landlord's,' says Arminius. 'You mean,' said I, 'that the landlord could and did really eject his tenant from it if he chose.' 'Yes, I do,' says Arminius. 'Well, then, what did Stein do?' asked I. 'He did this,' Arminius answered. 'In these estates, where the landlord had his property-right on the one hand, and the tenant his tenant-right on the other, he made a compromise. In the first place he assigned, say, two-fifths of the estate to the landlord in absolute property, without any further claim of tenant-right upon it thenceforth for ever. But the remaining three-fifths he compelled the landlord to sell to the tenant at eighteen years' purchase, so that this part should become the tenant's absolute property thenceforth for ever. You will ask, where could the tenant find money to buy? Stein opened rent-banks in all the provincial chief towns, to lend the tenant the purchase-money required, for which the State thus became his creditor, not the landlord. He had to repay this loan in a certain number of years. To free his land from this State mortgage on it and make it his own clear property, he had every inducement to work hard, and he did work hard; and this was the grand source of the frugality, industry, and thrivingness of the Prussian peasant. It was the grand source, too, of his attachment to the State.'

'It was rotten bad political economy, though,' exclaimed I. 'Now I see what the *Times* meant by saying in its leading article yesterday that Ireland is incomparably better governed than the United States, France, Germany, or Italy, because the excellence of government consists in keeping obstacles out of the way of individual energy, and you throw obstacles in the way of your great proprietors' energy, and we throw none in the way of ours. Talk of a commutation like the tithe-commutation, indeed! Why it was downright spoliation; it was just what Lord Clanricarde says some people are driving at in

Ireland, a system of confiscation.' 'Well,' says Arminius, calmly, 'that is exactly what the Prussian junkers called it. They did not call it commutation, they called it confiscation. They will tell you to this day that Stein confiscated their estates. But you will be shocked to hear that the Prussian Government had, even before Stein's time, this sad habit of playing tricks with political economy. To prevent the absorption of small proprietors by a great landed aristocracy, the Prussian Government made a rule that a *bauer-gut*,—a peasant property,—could not, even if the owner sold it, be bought up by the Lord Clanricarde of the neighbourhood ; it must remain a *bauer-gut* still. I believe you in England are for improving small proprietors off the face of the earth, but I assure you in Prussia we are very proud of ours, and think them the strength of the nation. Of late years the Hohenzollerns have taken up with the junkers, but for a long time their policy was to uphold the *bauer* class against the *junker* class ; and, if you want to know the secret of the hold which the house of Hohenzollern has upon the heart of the Prussian people, it is not in Frederick the Great's victories that you will find it, it is in this policy of their domestic government.' 'My dear Arminius,' said I, 'you make me perfectly sick. Government here, government there ! We English are for self-government. What business has any Mr. Stein to settle that this or that estate is too large for Lord Clanricarde's virtues to expand in? Let each class settle its own affairs, and don't let us have Governments and Hohenzollerns pretending to be more enlightened than other people, and cutting and carving for what they call the general interest, and God knows what nonsense of that kind. If the landed class with us has got the magistracy and settled estates and game laws, has not the middle class got the vestries, and business, and civil and religious liberty? I remember when the late Sir George Cornewall Lewis wanted to get some statistics about the religious denominations, your friend Bottles, who is now a millionaire and a Churchman, was then a Particular Baptist. "No," says Bottles, "here I put down my foot. No Government on earth shall ask me whether I am a Particular Baptist or a Muggletonian." And Bottles beat the Government, because of the thorough understanding the upper and middle classes in this country have with one another that each is to go its own way, and Government is not to be thrusting its nose into the concerns of either. There is a cordial alliance between them on this basis.' 'Yes, yes, I know,' Arminius sneeringly answered; 'Herod and Pontius Pilate have shaken hands.'

'But I will show you, Arminius,' I pursued, 'on plain grounds of political economy——' 'Not to-night,' interrupted Arminius, yawning;

'I am going home to bed.' And off he went, descending the garret stairs three at a time, and leaving me to burn the midnight oil in order to send you, Sir, what is really, I flatter myself, an interesting, and I may even say a valuable communication.

Your humble servant,

MATTHEW ARNOLD.

To the EDITOR *of the* PALL MALL GAZETTE.

LETTER VI

I BECOME ENTRUSTED WITH THE VIEWS OF ARMINIUS ON COMPULSORY EDUCATION

SIR, GRUB STREET, *April* 20, 1867.

IT is a long while since you have heard anything of Arminius and me, though I do hope you have sometimes given a thought to us both. The truth is we have been in the country. You may imagine how horribly disagreeable Arminius made himself during the famous snow in London at the beginning of this year. About the state of the streets he was bad enough, but about the poor frozen-out working men who went singing without let or hindrance before our houses, he quite made my blood creep. 'The dirge of a society *qui s'en va*,' he used to call their pathetic songs. It is true I had always an answer for him—'Thank God, we are not Haussmannised yet!' and if that was not enough, and he wanted the philosophy of the thing, why I turned to a sort of constitutional commonplace book, or true Englishman's *vade mecum*, which I have been these many years forming for my own use by potting extracts from the *Times*, and which I hope one day to give to the world, and I read him this golden aphorism: 'Administrative, military, and clerical tyranny are unknown in this country, because the educated class discharges all the corresponding functions through committees of its own body.' 'Well, then,' Arminius would answer, 'show me your administrative committee for ridding us of these cursed frozen-out impostors.' 'My dear Arminius,' was my quiet reply, 'voluntary organisations are not to be dealt with in this peremptory manner. The administrative committee you ask for will develop itself in good time; its future members are probably now at nurse. In England we like our improvements to *grow*, not to be manufactured.'

However the mental strain, day after day, of this line of high constitutional argument was so wearing, that I gladly acceded to a proposal made by Arminius in one of his fits of grumbling to go with him for a little while into the country. So into the country we went, and there, under his able guidance, I have been assiduously pursuing the study of German philosophy. As a rule, I attend to nothing else just now; but when we were taking one of our walks abroad the other morning, an incident happened which led us to discuss the subject of compulsory education, and, as this subject is beginning to awaken deep interest in the public mind, I think you may be glad to have an account of the incident, and of the valuable remarks on compulsory education which were drawn from Arminius by it.

We were going out the other morning on one of our walks, as I said, when we saw a crowd before the inn of the country town where we have been staying. It was the magistrates' day for sitting, and I was glad of an opportunity to show off our local self-government to a bureaucracy-ridden Prussian like Arminius. So I stopped in the crowd, and there we saw an old fellow in a smock-frock, with a white head, a low forehead, a red nose, and a foxy expression of countenance, being taken along to the justice-room. Seeing among the bystanders a contributor to the *Daily Telegraph*,[1] whom I formerly knew well enough,—for he had the drawing-room floor underneath me in Grub Street, but the magnificent circulation of that journal has long since carried him, like the course of empire, westward,—I asked him if he could tell me what the prisoner was charged with. I found it was a hardened old poacher, called Diggs,—Zephaniah Diggs,—and that he was had up for snaring a hare,—probably his ten-thousandth. The worst of the story, to

[1] Do you recognise yourself, Leo? Is it presumptuous in me, upon giving this volume to the world, to bid you too, my friend, say with the poet: *Non omnis moriar?*—Ed.

my mind, was that the old rogue had a heap of young children by a second wife whom he had married late in life, and that not one of these children would he send to school, but persisted in letting them all run wild, and grow up in utter barbarism.

I hastened to tell Arminius that it was a poaching case; and I added that it was not always, perhaps, in poaching cases that our local self-government appeared to the best advantage. 'In the present case, however, there is,' said I, 'no danger; for a representative of the *Daily Telegraph* is down here, to be on the look-out for justices' justice, and to prevent oppression.' Immediately afterwards I was sorry I had said this, for there are unfortunately several things which operate on Arminius like scarlet on a bull, making him vicious the moment he comes across them; and the *Daily Telegraph* is one of these things. He declares it foments our worst faults; and he is fond of applying to it Dryden's dictum on Elkanah Settle, that its style is boisterous and its prose incorrigibly lewd. Though I do certainly think its prose a little full-bodied, yet I cannot bear to hear Arminius apply such a term to it as 'incorrigibly lewd'; and I always remonstrate with him. 'No, Arminius,' I always say, 'I hope not *incorrigibly;* I should be sorry to think that of a publication which is forming the imagination and taste of millions of Englishmen.' 'Pleasant news,' was Arminius's answer, the last time I urged this to him, 'pleasant news; the next batch of you, then, will be even more charming than the present!'

I trouble you with all this, Sir, to account for the acerbity of tone in some of Arminius's subsequent conversation; an acerbity he too often manifests, and which tends, as I tell him, to detract from the influence which his talents and acquirements would otherwise give him. On the present occasion he took no direct notice of my mention of the *Daily Telegraph*, but seemed quite taken up with scrutinising old Diggs. 'Such a peasant as that wretched old creature,' he said at last, 'is peculiar, my dear friend, to your country. Only look at that countenance! Centuries of feudalism have effaced in it every gleam of humane life.' . . . 'Centuries of fiddlesticks!' interrupted I (for I assure you, Sir, I can stand up to Arminius well enough on a proper occasion). 'My dear Arminius, how can you allow yourself to talk such rubbish? Gleam of humane life, indeed! do but look at the twinkle in the old rogue's eye. He has plenty of life and wits about him, has old Diggs, I can assure you; you just try and come round him about a pot of beer!' 'The mere cunning of an animal!' retorted Arminius. 'For my part,' pursued I, 'it is his children I think most about; I am told not one of them has ever seen the inside of a school. Do you know, Arminius, I begin to think, and many people in this country begin to think, that the time has almost come for taking a leaf out of your Prussian book, and applying, in the education of children of this class, what the great Kant calls the categorical imperative. The gap between them and our educated and intelligent classes is really too frightful.' 'Your educated and intelligent classes!' sneered Arminius, in his very most offensive manner; 'where are they? I should like to see them.'

I was not going to stand and hear our aristocracy and middle class set down in this way; so, treating Arminius's ebullition of spite as beneath my notice, I pushed my way through the crowd to the inn-door. I asked the policeman there what magistrates were on the bench to-day. 'Viscount Lumpington,' says the man, 'Reverend Esau Hittall, and Bottles, Esquire.' 'Good heavens!' I exclaimed, turning round to Arminius, who had followed me, and forgetting, in my excitement, my just cause of offence with him,—'Good heavens, Arminius, if Bottles hasn't got himself made a county magistrate! *Sic itur ad astra.*' 'Yes,' says Arminius, with a smile, 'one of your educated and intelligent classes, I suppose. And I dare say the other two are to match. Your magistrates are a sort of judges, I know; just the people who are drawn from the educated and intelligent classes.

Now, what's sauce for the goose is sauce for the gander; if you put a pressure on one class to make it train itself properly, you must put a pressure on others to the same end. That is what we do in Prussia, if you are going to take a leaf out of our book. I want to hear what steps you take to put this pressure on people above old Diggs there, and then I will talk to you about putting it on old Diggs. Take his judges who are going to try him to-day; how about them? What training have you made them give themselves, and what are their qualifications?'

I luckily happen to know Lord Lumpington and Hittall pretty well, having been at college with them in former days, when I little thought the Philistines would have brought my gray hairs to a garret in Grub Street; and I have made the acquaintance of Mr. Bottles since, and know all about him. So I was able to satisfy Arminius's curiosity, and I had great pleasure in making him remark, as I did so, the rich diversity of our English life, the healthy natural play of our free institutions, and the happy blending of classes and characters which this promotes. 'The three magistrates in that inn,' said I, 'are not three Government functionaries all cut out of one block; they embody our whole national life;—the land, religion, commerce, are all represented by them. Lord Lumpington is a peer of old family and great estate; Esau Hittall is a clergyman ; Mr. Bottles is one of our self-made middle-class men. Their politics are not all of one colour, and that colour the Government's. Lumpington is a Constitutional Whig ; Hittall is a benighted old Tory. As for Mr. Bottles, he is a Radical of the purest water ; quite one of the Manchester school. He was one of the earliest free-traders ; he has always gone as straight as an arrow about Reform ; he is an ardent voluntary in every possible line, opposed the Ten Hours' Bill, was one of the leaders of the Dissenting opposition out of Parliament which smashed up the education clauses of Sir James Graham's Factory Act ; and he paid the whole expenses of a most important church-rate contest out of his own pocket. And, finally, he looks forward to marrying his deceased wife's sister. Table, as my friend Mr. Grant Duff says, the whole Liberal creed, and in not a single point of it will you find Bottles tripping !'

'That is all very well as to their politics,' said Arminius, 'but I want to hear about their education and intelligence.' 'There, too, I can satisfy you,' I answered. 'Lumpington was at Eton. Hittall was on the foundation at Charterhouse, placed there by his uncle, a distinguished prelate, who was one of the trustees. You know we English have no notion of your bureaucratic tyranny of treating the appointments to these great foundations as public patronage, and vesting them in a responsible minister; we vest them in independent magnates, who relieve the State of all work and responsibility, and never take a shilling of salary for their trouble. Hittall was the last of six nephews nominated to the Charterhouse by his uncle, this good prelate, who had thoroughly learnt the divine lesson that charity begins at home.' 'But I want to know what his nephew learnt,' interrupted Arminius, 'and what Lord Lumpington learnt at Eton. 'They followed,' said I, 'the grand, old, fortifying, classical curriculum.' 'Did they know anything when they left?' asked Arminius. 'I have seen some longs and shorts of Hittall's,' said I, 'about the Calydonian Boar, which were not bad. But you surely don't need me to tell you, Arminius, that it is rather in training and bracing the mind for future acquisition,—a course of mental gymnastics, we call it,—than in teaching any set thing, that the classical curriculum is so valuable.' 'Were the minds of Lord Lumpington and Mr. Hittall much braced by their mental gymnastics?' inquired Arminius. 'Well,' I answered, 'during their three years at Oxford they were so much occupied with Bullingdon and hunting that there was no great opportunity to judge. But for my part I have always thought that their both getting their degree at last with flying colours, after three weeks of a famous coach for fast men, four nights without going to bed, and an incredible consumption of wet towels, strong cigars, and brandy-and-water, was one of the most astonishing feats of mental gymnastics I ever heard of.'

'That will do for the land and the Church,' said Arminius. 'And now let us hear about commerce.' 'You mean how was Bottles educated?' answered I. 'Here we get into another line altogether, but a very good line in its way, too. Mr. Bottles was brought up at the Lycurgus House Academy, Peckham. You are not to suppose from the name of Lycurgus that any Latin and Greek was taught in the establishment; the name only indicates the moral discipline, and the strenuous earnest character, imparted there. As to the instruction, the thoughtful educator who was principal of the Lycurgus House Academy,—Archimedes Silverpump, Ph.D., you must have heard of him in Germany?—had modern views. "We must be men of our age," he used to say. "Useful knowledge, living languages, and the forming of the mind through observation and experiment, these are the fundamental articles of my educational creed." Or, as I have heard his pupil Bottles put it in his expansive moments after dinner (Bottles used to ask me to dinner till that affair of yours with him in the Reigate train): "Original man, Silverpump! fine mind! fine system! None of your antiquated rubbish—all practical work—latest discoveries in science—mind constantly kept excited—lots of interesting experiments—lights of all colours—fizz! fizz! bang! bang! That's what I call forming a man."'

'And pray,' cried Arminius, impatiently, 'what sort of man do you suppose this infernal quack really formed in your precious friend Mr. Bottles?' 'Well,' I replied, 'I hardly know how to answer that question. Bottles has certainly made an immense fortune; but as to Silverpump's effect on his mind, whether it was from any fault in the Lycurgus House system, whether it was that with a sturdy self-reliance thoroughly English, Bottles, ever since he quitted Silverpump, left his mind wholly to itself, his daily newspaper, and the Particular Baptist minister under whom he sate, or from whatever cause it was, certainly his mind, *quâ* mind——' 'You need not go on,' interrupted Arminius, with a magnificent wave of his hand, 'I know what that man's mind, *quâ* mind, is, well enough.'

But, Sir, the midnight oil is beginning to run very low; I hope, therefore, you will permit me to postpone the rest of Arminius's discourse till to-morrow. And meanwhile, Sir, I am, with all respect,

Your humble servant,

MATTHEW ARNOLD.

To the EDITOR *of the* PALL MALL GAZETTE.

LETTER VII

MORE ABOUT COMPULSORY EDUCATION

SIR, GRUB STREET, *April* 21, 1867.

I TAKE up the thread of the interesting and important discussion on compulsory education between Arminius and me where I left it last night.

'But,' continued Arminius, 'you were talking of compulsory education, and your common people's want of it. Now, my dear friend, I want you to understand what this principle of compulsory education really means. It means that to ensure, as far as you can, every man's being fit for his business in life, you put education as a bar, or condition, between him and what he aims at. The principle is just as good for one class as another, and it is only by applying it impartially that you save its application from being insolent and invidious. Our Prussian peasant stands our compelling him to instruct himself before he may go about his calling, because he sees we believe in instruction, and compel our own class, too, in a way to make it really feel the pressure, to instruct itself before it may go about its calling. Now, you propose to make old Diggs's boys instruct themselves before they may go bird-scaring or sheep-tending. I want to know what you do to make those three worthies in that justice-room instruct themselves before they may go acting as magistrates and judges.' 'Do?' said I; 'why, just look what they have done all of themselves. Lumpington and Hittall have had a public-school and university education; Bottles has had Dr. Silverpump's, and the practical training of business. What on earth would you have us make them do more?' 'Qualify themselves for administrative or judicial functions, if they exercise them,' said Arminius. 'That is what really answers, in their case, to the compulsion you propose to apply to Diggs's boys. Sending Lord Lumpington and Mr. Hittall to school is nothing; the natural course of things takes them there. Don't suppose that, by doing this, you are applying the principle of compulsory education fairly, and as you apply it to Diggs's boys. You are not interposing, for the rich, education as a bar or condition between them and that which they aim at. But interpose it, as we do, between the rich and things they aim at, and I will say something to you. I should like to know what has made Lord Lumpington a magistrate?' 'Made Lord Lumpington a magistrate?' said I; 'why, the Lumpington estate, to be sure.' 'And the Reverend Esau Hittall?' continued Arminius. 'Why, the Lumpington living, of course,' said I. 'And that man Bottles?' he went on. 'His English energy and self-reliance,' I answered very stiffly, for Arminius's incessant carping began to put me in a huff; 'those same incomparable and truly British qualities which have just triumphed over every obstacle and given us the Atlantic telegraph!—and let me tell you, Von T., in my opinion it will be a long time before the "Geist" of any pedant of a Prussian professor gives us anything half so valuable as that.' 'Pshaw!' replied Arminius, contemptuously; 'that great rope, with a Philistine at each end of it talking inutilities!

'But in my country,' he went on, 'we should have begun to put a pressure on these future magistrates at school. Before we allowed Lord Lumpington and Mr. Hittall to go to the university at all, we should have examined them, and we should not have trusted the keepers of that absurd cockpit you took me down to see, to examine them as they chose, and send them jogging comfortably off to the university on their lame longs and shorts. No; there would have been some Mr. Grote as School Board Commissary, pitching into them questions about history, and some Mr. Lowe, as Crown Patronage Commissary, pitching into them questions about English literature; and these young men would have been kept from the university, as Diggs's boys are kept from their bird-scaring, till they instructed themselves. Then, if, after three years of their university, they wanted to be magistrates, another pressure!—a great Civil Service examination before a board of experts, an examination in English law, Roman law, English history, history of jurisprudence——' 'A most abominable liberty to take with Lumpington and Hittall!' exclaimed I. 'Then your compulsory education is a most abominable liberty to take with Diggs's boys,' retorted Arminius. 'But, good gracious! my dear Arminius,' expostulated I, 'do you really mean to maintain that a man can't put old Diggs in quod for snaring a hare without all this elaborate apparatus of Roman law and history of jurisprudence?' 'And do you really mean to maintain,' returned Arminius, 'that a man can't go bird-scaring or sheep-tending without all this elaborate apparatus of a compulsory school?' 'Oh, but,' I answered, 'to live at all, even at the lowest stage of human life, a man needs instruction.' 'Well,' returned Arminius, 'and to administer at all, even at the lowest stage of public administration, a man needs instruction.' 'We have never found it so,' said I.

Arminius shrugged his shoulders and was silent. By this time the proceedings in the justice-room were drawn to an end, the majesty of the law had been vindicated against old

Diggs, and the magistrates were coming out. I never saw a finer spectacle than my friend Arminius presented, as he stood by to gaze on the august trio as they passed. His pilot-coat was tightly buttoned round his stout form, his light blue eye shone, his sanguine cheeks were ruddier than ever with the cold morning and the excitement of discourse, his fell of tow was blown about by the March wind, and volumes of tobacco-smoke issued from his lips. So in old days stood, I imagine, his great namesake by the banks of the Lippe, glaring on the Roman legions before their destruction.

Lord Lumpington was the first who came out. His lordship good-naturedly recognised me with a nod, and then eyeing Arminius with surprise and curiosity: 'Whom on earth have you got there?' he whispered. 'A very distinguished young Prussian *savant*,' replied I; and then dropping my voice, in my most impressive undertones I added: 'And a young man of very good family, besides, my lord.' Lord Lumpington looked at Arminius again; smiled, shook his head, and then, turning away, and half aloud: 'Can't compliment you on your friend,' says he.

As for that centaur Hittall, who thinks on nothing on earth but field-sports, and in the performance of his sacred duties never warms up except when he lights on some passage about hunting or fowling, he always, whenever he meets me, remembers that in my unregenerate days, before Arminius inoculated me with a passion for intellect, I was rather fond of shooting, and not quite such a successful shot as Hittall himself. So, the moment he catches sight of me: 'How d'ye do, old fellow?' he blurts out; 'well, been shooting any straighter this year than you used to, eh?'

I turned from him in pity, and then I noticed Arminius, who had unluckily heard Lord Lumpington's unfavourable comment on him, absolutely purple with rage and blowing like a turkey-cock. 'Never mind, Arminius,' said I soothingly; 'run after Lumpington, and ask him the square root of thirty-six.' But now it was my turn to be a little annoyed, for at the same instant Mr. Bottles stepped into his brougham, which was waiting for him, and observing Arminius, his old enemy of the Reigate train, he took no notice whatever of me who stood there, with my hat in my hand, practising all the airs and graces I have learnt on the Continent; but, with that want of amenity I so often have to deplore in my countrymen, he pulled up the glass on our side with a grunt and a jerk, and drove off like the wind, leaving Arminius in a very bad temper indeed, and me, I confess, a good deal shocked and mortified.

However, both Arminius and I got over it, and have now returned to London, where I hope we shall before long have another good talk about educational matters. Whatever Arminius may say, I am still for going straight, with all our heart and soul, at compulsory education for the lower orders. Why, good heavens! Sir, with our present squeezable Ministry, we are evidently drifting fast to household suffrage, pure and simple; and I observe, moreover, a Jacobinical spirit growing up in some quarters which gives me more alarm than even household suffrage. My elevated position in Grub Street, Sir, where I sit commercing with the stars, commands a view of a certain spacious and secluded back yard; and in that back yard, Sir, I tell you confidentially that I saw the other day with my own eyes that powerful young publicist, Mr. Frederic Harrison, in full evening costume, furbishing up a guillotine. These things are very serious; and I say, if the masses are to have power, let them be instructed, and don't swamp with ignorance and unreason the education and intelligence which now bear rule amongst us. For my part, when I think of Lumpington's estate, family, and connections, when I think of Hittall's shooting, and of the energy and self-reliance of Bottles, and when I see the unexampled pitch of splendour and security to which these have conducted us, I am bent, I own, on trying to make the new elements of our political system worthy of the old; and I say kindly, but firmly, to the compound householder in the French poet's beautiful words,[1] slightly altered: 'Be great, O working class, for the middle and upper class are great!'

I am, Sir,

Your humble servant,

MATTHEW ARNOLD.

To the EDITOR *of the* PALL MALL GAZETTE.

(From the autumn of this year (1867) dates one of the most painful memories of my life. I have mentioned in the last letter but one how in the spring I was commencing the study of German philosophy with Arminius. In the autumn of that year the celebrated young Comtist, Mr. Frederic Harrison, resenting some supposed irreverence of mine towards his master, permitted himself, in a squib, brilliant indeed, but unjustifiably severe, to make game of my inaptitude for philosophical pursuits. It was on this occasion he launched the damning sentence: 'We seek vainly in Mr. A. a system of philosophy with principles coherent, interdependent, subordinate, and derivative.' The blow came at an unlucky moment for me. I was studying, as I have said, German philosophy with Arminius; we were then engaged on Hegel's 'Phenomenology of *Geist*,'

[1] 'Et tâchez d'être grand, car le peuple grandit.'

and it was my habit to develop to Arminius, at great length, my views of the meaning of his great but difficult countryman. One morning I had, perhaps, been a little fuller than usual over a very profound chapter. Arminius was suffering from dyspepsia (brought on, as I believe, by incessant smoking) ; his temper, always irritable, seemed suddenly to burst from all control,—he flung the *Phänomenologie* to the other end of the room, exclaiming : 'That smart young fellow is quite right ! it is impossible to make a silk purse out of a sow's ear !' This led to a rupture, in which I think I may fairly say that the chief blame was not on my side. But two invaluable years were thus lost ; Arminius abandoned me for Mr. Frederic Harrison, who must certainly have many memoranda of his later conversations, but has never given them, as I always did mine of his earlier ones, to the world. A melancholy occasion brought Arminius and me together again in 1869 ; the sparkling pen of my friend Leo has luckily preserved the record of what then passed.)—Ed.

LETTER VIII

UNDER A PLAYFUL SIGNATURE, MY FRIEND LEO, OF THE 'DAILY TELEGRAPH,' ADVOCATES AN IMPORTANT LIBERAL MEASURE, AND, IN SO DOING, GIVES NEWS OF ARMINIUS.

SIR, ST. JAMES'S PLACE, *June* 8, 1869.

FOR the sake of my health it is my custom at this full-blooded time of the year to submit myself to a lowering course of medical treatment, which causes me for a few days to be voted below par for Fleet Street; so I have bethought myself of utilising my leisure, while universal humanity does not claim me, and while my style is reduced nearer the pitch of the *Pall Mall Gazette*, by writing to you on a subject in which I am strongly interested, and on which your ideas are, I am sorry to see, far from sound. I mean that great subject of which a fragment will be brought under discussion to-night, by the House of Commons going into Committee on Mr. Chambers's admirable bill for enabling a woman to marry her sister's husband.

My ideas on this subject have been stirred into lively activity by a visit I have just been making. I believe my name has been once or twice mentioned in your columns in connection with the Bottles family near Reigate, and with a group of friends gathered round them. Poor Mrs. Bottles, I grieve to say, is not long for this world. She and her family showed an interest in me while I was rising to name and fame, and I trust I have never forgotten it. She sate, as Curran says, by my cradle, and I intend to follow her hearse. Meanwhile, with our Paris correspondent, who happens to be over here for a few days, I have been down to Reigate to inquire after her. The accounts were unhappily as bad as possible ; but what I saw awakened a train of ideas and suggestions which I am going to communicate to you.

I found a good many people assembled, of whom several had come on the same errand as I. There was that broken-down acquaintance of my early youth, Mr. Matthew Arnold, who has had many a dinner from Mrs. Bottles (for she was kind to literature even in its humblest manifestations), snivelling and crying in a corner. There was that offensive young Prussian of his, who seems to have dropped him entirely, and to have taken up with a much younger man than my poor old acquaintance, and a much better-dressed man, with whom he is pursuing researches concerning labour and capital, which are hardly, as our Paris correspondent says, palpitating with actuality. There was a Baptist minister who had been the shepherd of the Bottles family in the old days when they were Dissenters, and who has never quite lost his hold upon Mrs. Bottles. There was her sister Hannah, just about the same age as poor Sarah who married Bottles, and the very image of her. There was Job Bottles, Bottles's brother, who is on the Stock Exchange; a man with black hair at the sides of his head, a bald crown, dark eyes, and a fleshy nose, and a camellia in his button-hole. Finally, there was that handsome niece of Mr. and Mrs. Bottles, Mary Jane. *Mary Jane!* I never pronounce the name without emotion; in season and out of season it keeps rising to my lips.[1] But the life we live in Fleet Street is devouring, and I have sacrificed to it all thought of marriage. Our Paris correspondent comforts me by saying that, even with the domestic affections suppressed, existence turns out to be a much more tolerable affair than humdrum people fancy.

Presently the members of the family left the room, and as the Baptist minister took the *Nonconformist* out of his pocket and began to read it, as the Prussian *savant* was quite absorbed with his new young man, and as Mr.

[1] Leo here alludes, I imagine, to what the world has doubtless noticed,—the frequent introduction of *Mary Jane* into his articles for the *D.T.*—ED.

Matthew Arnold counts for nothing, I was left to the conversation of our Paris correspondent, whom we call Nick because of the diabolical salt which sparkles in his deliverances. 'They say,' I began, 'that if Mr. T. Chambers's excellent bill, which the Liberal party are carrying with such decisive majorities, becomes law, the place of poor Mrs. Bottles will be taken by her sister Hannah, whom you have just seen. Nothing could be more proper; Mrs. Bottles wishes it, Miss Hannah wishes it, this reverend friend of the family, who has himself made a marriage of the same kind, wishes it, everybody wishes it.' 'Everybody but old Bottles himself, I should think,' retorted my friend: 'don't envy him at all!—shouldn't so much mind if it were the younger one, though.'

These light words of my friend, Sir, seemed to touch a spring in me. Instantly I felt myself visited by a shower of ideas, full of import for the Liberal party and for the future, and which impel me to address to you the present letter. 'And why not the younger one, Nick?' said I, gently: 'why not? Either as a successor to Miss Hannah or in lieu of Miss Hannah, why not? Let us apply John Bright's crucial tests. Is she his first cousin? Could there be a more natural companion for Selina and the other Bottles girls? Or,—to take the moral ground so touchingly and irresistibly chosen by our great popular tribune,—if legislation on this subject were impeded by the party of bigotry, if they chose not to wait for it, if they got married without it, and if you were to meet them on the boulevard at Paris during their wedding tour, should you go up to Bottles and say: Mr. Bottles, you are a profligate man?' 'Oh dear, no,' said Nick; 'I should never dream of it.' 'And if you met them a year later on the same spot,' I continued, 'with a Normandy nurse behind them carrying a baby, should you cry out to the poor little thing: Bastard?' 'Nothing of the kind,' he answered.

I noticed that my friend accompanied each of these assurances with a slight rapid droop of one eyelid. 'Let us have no flippancy, Nick,' I said. 'You mean that you hardly feel yourself in a position to take high moral ground of this kind.' 'Well,' said he, 'I suppose that even our great tribune, John Bright himself, does not very often address people as bastards and profligates, whatever he thinks of them. At least, I should imagine the offender must almost be a bishop or some other high-placed Anglican ecclesiastic to provoke him to do so.' 'A fig for your fine distinctions,' cried I. 'Secretly or openly, will any one dare call Bottles, if he contracts a marriage of this kind, a profligate man?'

Poor Mr. Matthew Arnold, upon this, emerged suddenly from his corner, and asked hesitatingly : 'But will any one dare call him a man of delicacy ?' The question was so utterly unpractical that I took no notice of it whatever, and should not have mentioned it if it had not led, by its extraordinary effect upon our Paris correspondent, to the introduction and criticism of a literary star of the first magnitude. My friend Nick, who has all the sensitive temperament of genius, seemed inexplicably struck by this word delicacy, which he kept repeating to himself. 'Delicacy,' said he, 'delicacy,—surely I have heard that word before! Yes, in other days,' he went on dreamily, 'in my fresh, enthusiastic youth; before I knew Sala, before I wrote for that infernal paper, before I called Dixon's style lithe and sinewy——'

'Collect yourself, my friend,' said I, laying my hand on his shoulder; 'you are unmanned. But in mentioning Dixon you redouble my strength; for you bring to my mind the great sexual insurrection of the Anglo-Teutonic race, and the master-spirit which guides it. This illustrious man who has invented a new style——'

'He has, indeed,' says Mr. Arminius the Prussian, turning towards us for the first time; 'he has, indeed, and its right name is middle-class Macaulayese.'

Now, I detest this German lecturer and his oracles, but as I am, above everything, a man of letters myself, I never refuse to listen to a remark upon style. 'Explain yourself,' said I; 'why do you call Mr. Hepworth Dixon's style middle-class Macaulayese?' 'I call it Macaulayese,' says the pedant, 'because it has the same internal and external characteristics as Macaulay's style; the external characteristic being a hard metallic movement with nothing of the soft play of life, and the internal characteristic being a perpetual semblance of hitting the right nail on the head without the reality. And I call it middle-class Macaulayese, because it has these faults without the compensation of great studies and of conversance with great affairs, by which Macaulay partly redeemed them.'

I turned away in pity. 'Let us leave the envious,' said I to Nick, 'to break their teeth on this magnificent file, the countlessness of whose editions has something analogous to the world-wide circulation of the *Daily Telegraph*. Let us pursue his fine regenerating idea of sexual insurrection. Let us deal with this question as a whole. Why, after Mr. Chambers has succeeded at his one single point to-night, are we to have to begin afresh at other points to-morrow? We have established, I hope, that no man may presume to call Bottles profligate for marrying either his sister-in-law Hannah or his niece Mary Jane. But this is not enough. A complication, like the complications of Greek tragedy, suggests itself to my mind.

You noticed Mr. Job Bottles. You must have seen his gaze resting on Mary Jane. But what with his cigars, his claret, his camellias, and the state of the money-market, Mr. Job Bottles is not a marrying man just at this moment. His brother is; but his brother cannot last for ever. Job, on the other hand, is full of vigour and vitality. We have heard of the patience of Job; how natural, if his brother marries Mary Jane now, that Job, with his habits tempered, his view of life calmed, and the state of the money-market different, may wish, when she is a widow some five years hence, to marry her himself. And we have arrangements which make this illegal! At such arrangements I hurl, with scorn and disgust, the burning words of our great leader :—Ecclesiastical rubbish!

I thank thee, Friend! for teaching me that word.

Why, I ask, is Mr. Job Bottles's liberty, his Christian liberty, as my reverend friend yonder would say, to be abridged in this manner? And why is Protestant Dissent to be diverted from its great task of abolishing State Churches for the purpose of removing obstacles to the sexual insurrection of our race? Why are its more devoted ministers to be driven to contract, in the interests of Christian liberty, illegal unions of this kind themselves, *pour encourager les autres?* Why is the earnest liberalism and nonconformity of Lancashire and Yorkshire to be agitated on this question by hope deferred? Why is it to be put incessantly to the inconvenience of going to be married in Germany or in the United States, that greater and better Britain

> Which gives us manners, freedom, virtue, power.

Why must ideas on this topic have to be incubated for years in that nest of spicery, as the divine Shakspeare says, the mind of Mr. T. Chambers, before they can rule the world? For my part, my resolve is formed. This great question shall henceforth be seriously taken up in Fleet Street. As a sop to those toothless old Cerberuses, the bishops, who impotently exhibit still the passions, as Nick's French friends say, of another age, we will accord the continuance of the prohibition which forbids a man to marry his grandmother. But in other directions there shall be freedom. Mr. Chambers's admirable bill for enabling a woman to marry her sister's husband will doubtless pass triumphantly through Committee to-night, amidst the cheers of the ladies' gallery. The Liberal party must supplement that bill by two others: one enabling people to marry their brothers' and sisters' children, the other enabling a man to marry his brother's wife.

But this glorious prospect fills me with an *afflatus* which can find its fit employment only in Fleet Street, and I am forced to subscribe myself,

Yours in haste,

A Young Lion.

(After our meeting at Laburnum House,—have I ever mentioned that the mansion of Mr. Bottles at Reigate is called Laburnum House?—intercourse was renewed between Arminius and me, but alas! not the close intimacy of old days. Perhaps, had I foreseen his approaching end, I should have made more strenuous efforts to regain his confidence. But it was not to be; and the following letter will show the cruel injustice with which Arminius, misled, I am sure, by Mr. Frederic Harrison and the party with whom that gentleman generally acts, could bring himself to speak of the man who has done so much to popularise his name and ideas.)

LETTER IX

ARMINIUS, STARTING FOR THE CONTINENT TO TAKE PART IN THE WAR BETWEEN FRANCE AND PRUSSIA, ADDRESSES A DISRESPECTFUL FAREWELL TO OUR PEOPLE AND INSTITUTIONS.

SIR, CHEQUER ALLEY,[1] *August* 9, 1870.

I AM off to-night for the Continent to join the Prussian army; if it had not been for an accidental circumstance with which I need not trouble you,[2] I should have been off a fortnight ago. I have no love for the preaching old drill-sergeant who is called King of Prussia, or for the audacious conspirator who pulls his wires; this conspirator and his rival conspirator, Louis Bonaparte, stand in my affections pretty much on a par. Both play their own game, and are obstacles to better things. I am a republican, I desire a republic for every country in Europe.

[1] After our rupture, Arminius removed from my immediate neighbourhood in Grub Street and established himself in Chequer Alley. I love to think that pilgrims will one day seek out his lodging there!—ED.

[2] His debts, alas!—ED.

I believe no country of Europe is so fitted to be a republic as Germany; I believe her difficulties are from her Hohenzollerns and Hapsburgs, and nothing else. I believe she will end by getting rid of these gentry; and that till that time comes the world will never know of what real greatness she is capable. But the present war, though we are led by the old drill-sergeant and his wire-puller, is a war of Germany against France. I must go and take part in it.

Before I go, I am moved to send you a few farewell remarks on your country and its position, about which you seem (and I am sure I do not wonder at it) to be much concerned and embarrassed just now. I have a great esteem for your nation, its genius, and its past history; and your present stage of development has been a subject of constant study and thought with me during the years I have lived here. Formerly I have more than once communicated my ideas to you, as occasion arose, through Mr. Matthew Arnold. But experience has shown me that, though willing and inquisitive, he has hardly brain enough for my purpose; besides, he has of late been plunged over head and ears in some dispute of Greeks of the Lower Empire with your foolish and impracticable Dissenters.[1]

[1] I make no comment on the tone and spirit of this; but I cannot forbear remarking that with the removal of Arminius and his influence the main obstacle to my reconciliation with the Dissenters is withdrawn.—Ed.

Finding him unserviceable, therefore, I address you myself; but I shall use some of the phrases with which he has familiarised you, because they save circumlocution; and as he learnt them all from me in the first instance, I see no reason why I should not take back my own property when I want it.

You are horrified and astounded at this war; horrified and astounded at the projects for altering the face of Europe which have been going on under your nose without your knowledge; horrified and astounded at the coolness with which foreign nations seem to leave you out of their account, or to estimate the chances and character of your intervention. They put you aside as if you were of no consequence; and this to you, who won the last great European war, and made the treaties of Vienna! The time, you think, has clearly come when you must make a demonstration. Your popular veteran, Lord Russell, declares amid universal applause that 'it is only the doubt that has long prevailed as to the course which England would take, which has encouraged and fostered all these projects of treaty, these combinations and intrigues.' You have but to speak plainly, and all will be well. Your great organ, the *Times*, not satisfied with itself conveying to other Powers in the most magnificent manner (a duty, to say the truth, it always fulfils) 'what

England believes to be due from and to her,' keeps exhorting your Government to do the same, to speak some brave words, and to speak them 'with promptitude and energy.'

I suppose your Government will do so. But forgive me if I tell you that to us disrespectful foreigners it makes very little difference in our estimate of you and of the future whether your Government does so or not. What gives the sense and significance to a Government's declarations is the power which is behind the Government. And what is the power which is behind the Government of England at the present epoch? The Philistines.

Simply and solely the Philistines, my dear friend, take my word for it! No, you will say, it is the nation. Pardon me, you have no nation. France is fused into one nation by the military spirit, and by her democracy, the great legacy of 1789, and subsisting even amidst her present corruption. Germany is fused into one nation by her idea of union and of the elevation of her whole people through culture. You are made up, as I have often told you through my poor disciple whom you so well know, of three distinct and unfused bodies,—Barbarians, Philistines, Populace. You call them aristocracy, middle, and lower class. One of these three must be predominant and lead. Your lower class counts as yet for little or nothing. There is among them a small body of workmen with modern ideas, ideas of organisation, who may be a nucleus for the future; there are more of them Philistines in a small way, Philistines in embryo; but most of them are mere populace, or, to use your own kindly term, *residuum.* Such a class does not lead. Formerly your aristocracy led; it commanded the politics of the country; it had an aristocracy's ideas,—limited enough, but the idea of the country's grandeur and dignity was among them;—it took your middle and lower class along with it, and used them in its own way, and it made the great war which the battle of Waterloo crowned. But countries must outgrow a feudal organisation, and the political command of an aristocracy; your country has outgrown it. Your aristocracy tells upon England socially; by all the power of example of a class high-placed, rich, idle, self-indulgent, without mental life, it teaches your Philistines how to live fast. But it no longer rules; at most it but administers; the Philistines rule. That makes the difference between Lord Grenville and Lord Granville. When Lord Grenville had to speak to Europe in 1793, he had behind him your aristocracy, not, indeed, fused with your middle and lower class, but wielding them and using their force; and all the world knew what your aristocracy meant, for they knew it themselves. But Lord Granville has behind him, when he speaks to Europe in 1870, your Philistines or middle class;

and how should the world know, or much care, what your middle class mean? for they do not know it themselves.

You may be mortified, but such is the truth. To be consequent and powerful, men must be bottomed on some vital idea or sentiment, which lends strength and certainty to their action. Your aristocracy of seventy years ago had the sentiment of the greatness of the old aristocratical England, and that sentiment gave them force to endure labours, anxiety, danger, disappointment, loss, restrictions of liberty. Your ruling middle class has no such foundation; hence its imbecility. It would tell you it believes in industrial development and liberty. Examine what it means by these, and you find it means getting rich and not being meddled with. And these it imagines to be self-acting powers for good, and agents of greatness; so that if more trade is done in England than anywhere else, if your personal independence is without a check, and your newspaper publicity unbounded, your Philistines think they are by the nature of things great, powerful, and admirable, and that their England has only to speak 'with promptitude and energy' in order to prevail.

My dear friend, do not hold your notions in this mechanical fashion, and do not be misled by that magnificent *Times* of yours; it is not the failing to speak 'with promptitude and energy' which injures you, it is the having nothing wise or consistent to say. Your ruling middle class have no great, seriously and truly conceived end; —therefore no greatness of soul or mind;—therefore no steadfastness and power in great affairs. While you are thus, in great affairs you do and must fumble. You imagine that your words must have weight with us because you are very rich and have unbounded liberty and publicity; you will find yourselves mistaken, and you will be bewildered. Then you may get involved in war, and you imagine that you cannot but make war well by dint of being so very rich; that you will just add a penny or two to your income-tax, change none of your ways, have clap-trap everywhere, as at present, unrestricted independence, legions of newspaper correspondents, boundless publicity; and thus, at a grand high pressure of expenditure, bustle, and excitement, arrive at a happy and triumphant result. But authority and victory over people who are in earnest means being in earnest oneself, and your Philistines are not in earnest; they have no idea great enough to make them so. They want to be important and authoritative; they want to enforce peace and curb the ambitious; they want to drive a roaring trade; they want to know and criticise all that is being done; they want no restrictions on their personal liberty, no interference with their usual way of going on; they want all these incompatible things equally and at once, because they have no idea deep and strong enough to subordinate everything else to itself. A correspondent of your own *Times* wrote from Berlin the other day, 'The complete control of this people by the State is most striking.' How would your Philistines like that? Not at all. But it is by sacrifices of this kind that success in great affairs is achieved; and when your Philistines find this out, or find that a raised income-tax, torrents of clap-trap, everybody saying what he likes and doing what he likes, newspaper correspondents everywhere, and a generally animated state of the public mind, are not enough to command success, they will be still more bewildered.

And this is the power which Lord Granville has behind him, and which is to give the force and meaning to his words. Poor Lord Granville! I imagine he is under no illusions. He knows the British Philistine, with his likes and dislikes, his effusion and confusion, his hot and cold fits, his want of dignity and of the steadfastness which comes from dignity, his want of ideas and of the steadfastness which comes from ideas;—he has seen him at work already. He has seen the Russian war and the Russian peace; a war and peace your aristocracy did not make and never would have made,—the British Philistine and his newspapers have the whole merit of it. In your social gatherings I know you have the habit of assuring one another that in some mysterious way the Russian war did you good in the eyes of Europe. Undeceive yourselves ; it did you nothing but harm, and Lord Granville is far too clever a man not to know it. Then, in the Denmark quarrel, your Philistines did not make war, indeed, but they threatened it. Surely in the Denmark case there was no want of brave words ; no failure to speak out 'with promptitude and energy.' And we all know what came of it. Unique British Philistine ! Is he most to be revered when he makes his wars or when he threatens them ? And at the prompting of this great backer Lord Granville is now to speak ! Probably he will have, as the French say, to execute himself ; only do not suppose that we are under any delusion as to the sort of force he has behind him.

My dear friend, I think I am perhaps writing to you for the last time, and by the love I bear to the England of your past literature and history, I do exhort your Philistine middle class, which is now England, to get, as I say, 'Geist' ; to search and not rest till it sees things more as they really are, and how little of a power over things as they really are is its money-making, or its unrestricted independence, or its newspaper publicity, or its Dissent, or any of the things with which it is now most taken ; and how its newspapers deceive it when they tell it night and day that, being what it is, and having the objects it has, it commands the envy and deference of the world, and is on the sure road to greatness and happiness, if indeed it be not already arrived there. My dear friend, I have told you our German programme,—*the elevation of a whole people through culture*. That need not be your English programme, but surely you may have some better programme than this your present one,—*the beatification of a whole people through clap-trap.*

And now, my dear friend, it is time for me to go, and to what fate I go I know not; but this I know, that your country, where I have lived so long and seen so much, is on its way either to a great transformation or to a great disaster.

Your sincere well-wisher,

VON THUNDER-TEN-TRONCKH.

To the EDITOR *of the* PALL MALL GAZETTE.

LETTER X

ARMINIUS, WRITING FROM THE GERMAN CAMP BEFORE PARIS, COMMENTS, IN HIS OLD UN-APPRECIATIVE SPIRIT, ON THE ATTITUDE OF OUR BELOVED COUNTRY IN THE BLACK SEA QUESTION.

SIR, BEFORE PARIS, *November* 21, 1870.

ANOTHER call 'to speak with promptitude and energy'! We had all been full of the Russian note, and here is your magnificent *Times* to tell me what the great heart of my dear English friends is thinking of it. You have not forgotten, of course, that sentence of Mr. Lowe (a descendant of Pangloss, and a sort of hereditary connection of my family, though he took scant notice of me when I was in England): 'The destiny of England is in the great heart of England.' So, having a sincere regard for you, I always listen when your great heart speaks, that I may see what sort of a destiny it is about to create for you. And I find that it is now speaking very loud indeed, even louder than when I wrote to you in August last, and that it is bent on telling Russia 'with promptitude and energy,' in your own fine, full-mouthed fashion, 'what England believes to be due from and to her.' But even at such a crisis you do not forget to improve the occasion, and to indulge in the peculiar strain of moral reflection whence you get, your oracles tell us, 'that moral weight which your action, if conducted with tolerable judgment, is sure to command' (see, in the last *Edinburgh Review*, 'Germany, France, and England,' p. 591). It is not so much the matter of the Russian incident as its manner that pains you. 'We protest,' says your magnificent *Times*, 'that our sharpest feeling at the moment is pain at the apparent faithlessness of the Czar, and at the rudeness with which he has denounced the treaty.'

My dear friend, the weather is abominable, and the supply of tobacco, to me at any rate, short and bad; but I cannot resist sitting down without a pipe, in the mud, to write to you, when I see your great heart beating in this manner.

How like you,—how like the British Philistine in one of his hot fits, when he is moved to speak to Europe 'with promptitude and energy'! Of history, the future, the inevitable drive of events, not an inkling! A moral criticism of Russia and a wounded self-consequence,—that is all you are full of. The British Philistine all over!

At your present stage of development, as I

have often remarked to you, this beneficent being is the depositary of your force, the mover of your policy. Your Government is, in and by itself, nothing. You are a self-governing people, you are represented by your 'strong middle part,' your Philistine: and this is what your Government must watch; this is what it must take its cue from.

Here, then, is your situation, that your Government does not and cannot really govern, but at present is and must be the mouthpiece of your Philistines; and that foreign Governments know this very well, know it to their cost. Nothing the best of them would like better than to deal with England seriously and respectfully,—the England of their traditions, the England of history; nothing, even, they would like better than to deal with the English Government,—as at any time it may happen to stand, composed of a dozen men more or less eminent,—seriously and respectfully. But, good God! it is not with these dozen men in their natural state that a foreign Government finds it has to deal; it is with these dozen men sitting in devout expectation to see how the cat will jump,—and that cat the British Philistine!

What statesman can deal seriously and respectfully when he finds that he is not dealing mind to mind with an intelligent equal, but that he is dealing with a tumult of likes and dislikes, hopes, panics, intrigues, stock-jobbing, quidnuncs, newspapers,—dealing with *ignorance* in short, for that one word contains it all,—behind his intelligent equal? Whatever he says to a British Minister, however convincing he may be, a foreign statesman knows that he has only half his hearer's attention, that only one of the British Minister's eyes is turned his way; the other eye is turned anxiously back on the home Philistines and the home press, and according as these finally go the British Minister must go too. This sort of thing demoralises your Ministers themselves in the end, even your able and honest ones, and makes them impossible to deal with. God forgive me if I do him wrong!—but I always suspect that your sly old Sir Hamilton Seymour, in his conversations with the Emperor Nicholas before the Crimean war, had at last your Philistines and your press, and their unmistakable bent, in his eye, and did not lead the poor Czar quite straight. If ever there was a man who respected England, and would have gone cordially and easily with a capable British minister, that man was Nicholas. England, Russia, and Austria are the Powers with a real interest in the Eastern question, and it ought to be settled fairly between them. Nicholas wished nothing better. Even if you would not thus settle the question, he would have forborne to any extent sooner than go to war with you, if he could only have known what you were really at. To be sure, as you did not know this yourselves, you could not possibly tell *him*, poor man! Louis Napoleon, meanwhile, had his prestige to make. France pulled the wires right and left; your Philistines had a passion for that old acrobat Lord Palmerston, who, clever as he was, had an aristocrat's inaptitude for ideas, and believed in upholding and renovating the Grand Turk; Lord Aberdeen knew better, but his eye was nervously fixed on the British Philistine and the British press. The British Philistine learnt that he was being treated with rudeness and must make his voice heard 'with promptitude and energy.' There was the usual explosion of passions, prejudices, stock-jobbing, newspaper articles, chatter, and general ignorance, and the Czar found he must either submit to have capital made out of him by French vanity and Bonapartist necessities, or enter into the Crimean war. He entered into the Crimean war, and it broke his heart. France came out of the Crimean war the first Power in Europe, with French vanity and Bonapartist necessities fully served. You came out of it with the British Philistine's *rôle* in European affairs for the first time thoroughly recognised and appreciated.

Now for the 'faithlessness' and 'rudeness' of Russia's present proceeding. It has been known for the last half-dozen years in every chancery of Europe that Russia declared her position in the Black Sea to be intolerable, and was resolved to get it altered. France and Bonaparte, driven by the French *fat* as you are driven by the British Philistine,—and the French *fat* has proved a yet more fatal driver than yours, being debauched and immoral, as well as ignorant,—came to grief. I suppose Russia was not bound to wait till they were in a position to make capital out of her again. 'But with us, at any rate,' you will say, 'she might have dealt seriously and respectfully, instead of being faithless and rude.' Again, I believe Russia would have wished nothing better than to deal seriously with you, and to settle with you, not only the question of the Black Sea, but the whole Eastern question, which begins to press for settlement;—but it was impossible. It was impossible, because you offer nobody with whom a serious statesman can deal seriously. You offer a Government, with men in it eminent and able no doubt, but they do not make your policy; and their eye is always turning back to the power behind them which *does* make it. That power is the British Philistine. Was Russia, at a critical moment, to lose precious time waiting for the chance medley of accidents, intrigues, hot and cold fits, stock-jobbing, newspaper-articles, conversations on the railway, conversations on the omnibus, out of which grows the foreign policy of a self-governing people, when that self is the British Philistine? Russia thought not, and passed on to its object.

For my part, I cannot call this faithless, though I admit it may be called rude. But it was a rudeness which Governments with a serious object before them cannot well help committing when they are dealing with you. The question is: Will you at all better yourselves by having now one of your hot fits, speaking 'with promptitude and energy,' and, in fact, going to war with Russia for what she has done? Alas, my dear friend, this would be throwing the handle after the blade with a vengeance! Because your governing part, your Philistine middle class, is ignorant and impracticable, Russia has unceremoniously taken a step in the Eastern question without you. And what does your going to war with Russia in the present posture of affairs mean? It means backing up the Porte to show fight; going in, in Lord Palmerston's old line, for upholding and renovating the Grand Turk;—it means fighting against nature. This is how the ignorant and impracticable get punished; they are made to smart for being ignorant and impracticable, and they can only resent being made to smart by showing themselves more ignorant and impracticable still. Do not do so, my dear friend! Russia has no wish to quarrel with you; she had a serious object to gain, and, as time pressed, she did what she had to do without entering into an interminable and possibly fruitless conversation with your 'young man from the country.' But she does not mean more than her avowed object, which was really indispensable to her ; she will try to make things now as pleasant as she can (consistently with getting her object) for your young man from the country ; and the moment the young man has clear ideas she will ask nothing better than to deal with him seriously and respectfully.

All turns upon that, my dear friend !—the improving your young man and giving him clear ideas. At present he is vulgar, ignorant, and consequential ; and because he is vulgar, he is ignoble ; because he is ignorant, he is unstable ; because he is consequential, he is on the look-out for affronts and apt to fly into a heat. With these qualities he cannot but bring mortifications upon you and himself, so long as he governs or tries to govern. All nations have their young man of this sort, but with you alone he governs, and hence the European importance of him and his failings. You know how I dislike the Junkerism and militarism of my own Prussian country and its government ; all I say is, that the self-government of your Philistines is as bad, or even worse. There is nothing like it anywhere ; for America, which in some respects resembles you, has not your necessary relations with Europe ; and besides, her Philistines, if they govern, administer also, and get the training which great affairs give. With you the Barbarians administer, the Philistines govern ; between them your policy is made. One class contributes its want of ideas, the other its want of dignity ;—an unlucky mixture for you, my dear friend, it must be confessed.

The worst of it is, I do not see how things are to get better with you at present. The Philistines rule and rule abominably, but for the moment there is no remedy. Bismarck would say, 'Muzzle them'; but I know well this cannot, nay, should not be. I say, 'Improve them'; but for this time is needed. Your Government might, no doubt, do something to speed the improvement, if it cared a little more, in serving the Philistines, for what might do them good, and a little less for what might please them ; but perhaps this is too much to expect from your Government. So you must needs have, my dear friend, I am afraid, what these poor wretched people here call a *mauvais quart d'heure*, in which you will be peculiarly liable to mistakes, mortifications, and troubles. While this period lasts, *your strength*, forgive me for saying so, *is to sit still*. What your friends (of whom I am one) must wish for you is that you may keep as quiet as possible ; that the British Philistine may not be moved much to speak to Europe 'with promptitude and energy'; that he may get out of his hot fits always as soon as possible. And perhaps you *are* getting out of your recent hot fit already ; perhaps, even while I write, you have got into one of your cold fits, and are all for pacific solutions and moral suasion. I say, Heaven grant it ! with all my heart.

And, meanwhile, how are my friends in England? I think I see Bottles by the Royal Exchange at this moment, holding forth, with the *Times* in his hand, on 'the perfect unanimity of opinion among the mercantile community of the City of London!' I think I hear poor Mr. Matthew Arnold's platitudes about 'the two great conquests of English energy,—*liberty and publicity!*' Liberty, my dear friend, to make fools of yourselves, and publicity to tell all the world you are doing so.

Forgive my *ur-deutsch* frankness, and believe me, your sincere friend,

VON THUNDER-TEN-TRONCKH.

To the EDITOR *of the* PALL MALL GAZETTE.

LETTER XI

I TAKE UP THE CUDGELS FOR OUR BELOVED COUNTRY

SIR, GRUB STREET, *November* 25, 1870.

I KNOW by experience how hard it is to get my bald, disjointed chat, as Arminius calls it, into the newspapers in these stirring times, and that was why I did not attempt to complain of that extraordinary effusion of his which you published in August last. He must have written that letter, with its unhandsome remarks at my expense, just after I had parted with him at his lodgings in Chequer Alley, with expressions of the tenderest concern, before he went off to the war. Since then, I have discovered that he had referred nearly all his tradespeople to me for payment; I am daily besieged in my garret by his tobacconist, and when I get out, the street is made quite intolerable to me by the violence of his washerwoman, though I am sure Arminius, like all foreigners, always gave his washerwoman as little trouble as possible.

These things have nettled me a good deal; and now there comes this new letter of his from Paris, in which, besides totally uncalled-for sneers at Mr. Bottles and me, Arminius indulges in an outrageous attack on my country and her behaviour in this Russian business. I have kept silence for a few days to make sure of being perfectly cool; but now, Sir, I do hope you will give me space for a few lines in reply to him.

About the Russian note I disagree with Arminius *in toto*. I go thoroughly along with Lord Shaftesbury, whose admirable letter to the *Times* proves, what I have always thought, how unjust Arminius is in denying ideas to the British aristocracy. A treaty is a promise,—so I read Lord Shaftesbury's argument; men should keep their promises; if bad men will not, good men must compel them.

It is singular, Sir, but in my immediate neighbourhood here in Cripplegate we have lately had a case which exactly illustrates the Russian difficulty, and bears out Lord Shaftesbury's argument. We all do our marketing in Whitecross Street; and in Whitecross Street is a famous tripe-shop which I always visit before entertaining Arminius, who, like all North Germans, and like our own celebrated Dr. Johnson, is a very gross feeder. Two powerful labourers, who lodge like Arminius in Chequer Alley, and who never could abide one another, used to meet at this tripe-shop and quarrel till it became manifest that the shop could not stand two such customers together, and that one of the couple must give up going there. The fellows' names were Mike and Dennis; it was generally thought the chief blame in the quarrel lay with Mike, who was at any rate much the less plausible man of the two, besides being greatly the bigger. However that may be, the excellent City Missionary in this quarter, the Rev. *J-hn B-ll* (I forbear to write his name at length for fear of bringing a blush to his worthy cheek), took Dennis's part in the matter. He and Dennis set both together upon Mike, and got the best of him. It was Dennis who appeared to do the most in the set-to; at all events, he got the whole credit, although I have heard the Rev. *J-hn B-ll* (who was undoubtedly a formidable fellow in his old unregenerate days) describe at tea in the Mission Room how he got his stick between Mike's legs at all the critical moments; how he felt fresher and stronger when the fight ended than when it began; and how his behaviour had somehow the effect of leaving on the bystanders' minds an impression immensely to his advantage. What is quite certain is, that not only did our reverend friend take part in the engagement, but that also, before, during, and after the struggle, his exhortations and admonitions to Mike, Dennis, the bystanders, and himself, never ceased, and were most edifying. Mike finally, as I said, had to give in, and he was obliged to make a solemn promise to Dennis and the City Missionary that he would use the tripe-shop no more. On this condition a treaty was patched up, and peace reigned in Cripplegate.

And now, Sir, comes the startling point of resemblance to the present Russian difficulty. A great big hulking German, called Fritz, has been for some time taking a lead in our neighbourhood, and carrying his head a great deal higher in Whitecross Street Market than Dennis liked. At last Dennis could stand it no longer; he picked a quarrel with Fritz, and they had a battle-royal to prove which was master. In this encounter our City Missionary took no part, though he bestowed, as usual, on both sides good advice and beautiful sentiments in abundance. Dennis had no luck this time; he got horribly belaboured, and now lies confined to his bed at his lodgings, almost past praying for. But what do you think has been Mike's conduct at this juncture? Seeing Dennis disabled, he addressed to the City Missionary an indecent scrawl, couched in language with which I will not sully your pages, to the effect that the tripe-shop lay handy to his door (which is true enough); and that use it he needs must, and use it he would, in spite of all the Rev. *J-hn B-ll* might say or do to stop him.

The feelings, Sir, of the worthy Missionary at this communication may be easier imagined than described. He launched at Mike the most indignant moral rebuke; the brute put his thumb to his nose. To get Mike out of the tripe-shop there is nothing left but physical force. Yet how is our estimable friend to proceed? Years of outpouring, since he has been engaged in mission-work, have somewhat damaged his wind; the hospitalities of the more serious-minded citizens of Cripplegate to a man in his position have been, I hope, what they should be; there are apprehensions, if violent exercise is taken, of gout in the stomach. Dennis can do nothing; what is worse, Fritz has been seen to wink his eye at Mike in a way to beget grave suspicion that the ruffians have a secret compact together. The general feeling in Cripplegate is that nothing much can be done, and that Mike must be allowed to resort again to the tripe-shop.

But I ask you, Sir, is this morally defensible? Is it right? Is it honest? Has not Lord Shaftesbury's English heart (if it is not presumptuous in me to speak thus of a person in his lordship's position) guided him true in the precisely similar case of Russia? A treaty is a promise, and we have a moral right to demand that promises shall be kept. If Mike wanted to use the tripe-shop, he should have waited till Dennis was about again and could talk things over with the City Missionary, and then, perhaps, the two might have been found willing to absolve Mike from his promise. His present conduct is inexcusable ; the only comfort is that the Rev. *J-hn B-ll* has a faithful press still to back him, and that Mike is being subjected to a fearful daily castigation in the columns of the *Band of Hope Review*.

Therefore, Sir, as to Russia, I emphatically think Arminius wrong. His sneers at my zeal for the grand principles of liberty and publicity I have hardly left myself space to notice. But, Sir, I do believe, with Mr. Bright, that the great function committed by Providence to our English-speaking race is 'the assertion of personal liberty.' If this be an error, I would rather, I own, err with Mr. Bright than be right with Von Thunder-ten-Tronckh. I know Von T. maintains that we so intently pursue liberty and publicity as quite to neglect wisdom and virtue ; for which alone, he says, liberty and publicity are worth having. But I will ask him, Sir, have we ever given liberty and publicity a full trial ? Take liberty. The Lord Chancellor has, indeed, provided for Mr. Beales, and it is whispered that Colonel Dickson will have a high command in the approaching Russian war ;—*but why is Mr. Bradlaugh not yet a Dean ?* These, Sir, are the omissions, these the failures to carry into full effect our own great principles, which drive earnest Liberals to despair !

Again, take the principle of publicity. Arminius (who, as an observer of manners, attended the proceedings in the Mordaunt case, and again in the Park and Boulton case, with unflagging assiduity) has said to me scores of times : 'By shooting all this garbage on your public, you are preparing and assuring for your English people an immorality as deep and wide as that which destroys the Latin nations.' What is my reply ? That we have never yet given publicity a fair trial. It is true, when a member of Parliament wanted to abridge the publicity given to the Mordaunt case, the Government earnestly reminded him that it had been the solemn decision of the House of Commons that all the proceedings of the Divorce Court should be open as the day. It is true, when there was a suggestion to hear the Boulton and Park case in private, the upright magistrate who was appealed to said firmly that he could never trifle with the public mind in that manner. All this was as it should be ; so far, so good. But was the publicity thus secured for these cases perfectly full and entire ? Were there not some places which the details did not reach ? There were few, but there were some. And this while the Government has an organ of its own, the *London Gazette*, dull, high-priced, and of comparatively limited circulation. I say, make the price of the *London Gazette* a halfpenny ; change its name to the *London Gazette and Divorce Intelligencer* ;

let it include, besides divorce news, all cases whatever that have an interest of the same nature for the public mind; distribute it *gratis* to mechanics' institutes, workmen's halls, seminaries for the young (these latter more especially); and then you will be giving the principle of publicity a full trial. This is what I often say to Arminius; and, when he looks astounded, I reassure him with a sentence which, I know very well, the moment I make it public, will be stolen by all the Liberal newspapers. But it is getting near Christmas-time, and I do not mind making them a present of it. It is this:—*The spear of freedom, like that of Achilles, has the power to heal the wounds which itself makes!*

This Arminius can never answer; and, badly as he has treated me, my heart relents to think of the stupefied face I have often seen him with at hearing it. Poor Arminius! I wonder what he is doing now? If the Prussians keep sticking in the mud before Paris, how will he continue to bear the wet weather, the winter nights, the exposure? And may not his prolonged requisitions for tobacco and sausages (merciless I know they will be!) prove too much at last for the patience of even some down-trodden worm of a French *bourgeois?* Or, again, this is the hour for a *sortie*, and Arminius is as brave as a lion. I go to my garret-window; it is just midnight; how gloomy is Grub Street at this hour! I look towards the familiar regions of

Whitecross Street Market and Chequer Alley; the venerable pile of Cripplegate Church, which I could never get Arminius to enter, rises darkly and sadly before me. Dismal presentiments begin to crowd upon my soul, and I sign myself,

Sir, your uneasy servant,

MATTHEW ARNOLD.

To the EDITOR *of the* PALL MALL GAZETTE.

LETTER XII

'LIFE,' AS MR. G. A. SALA SAYS, 'A DREAM!'

MON CHER, VERSAILLES, *November* 26, 1870.

AN event has just happened which I confess frankly will afflict others more than it does me, but which you ought to be informed of.

Early this morning I was passing between Rueil and Bougival, opposite Mont Valérien. How came I in that place at that hour? *Mon cher*, forgive my folly! You have read *Romeo and Juliet*, you have seen me at Cremorne, and though Mars has just now this *belle France* in his gripe, yet you remember, I hope, enough of your classics to know that, where Mars is, Venus is never very far off. Early this morning, then, I was between Rueil and Bougival, with Mont Valérien in grim proximity. On a bank by a poplar-tree at the roadside I saw a knot of German soldiers, gathered evidently round a wounded man. I approached and frankly tendered my help, in the name of British humanity. What answer I may have got I do not know; for, petrified with astonishment, I recognised in the wounded man our familiar acquaintance, Arminius von Thunder-ten-Tronckh. A Prussian helmet was stuck on his head, but there was the old hassock of whity-brown hair,—there was the old square face,—there was the old blue pilot coat! He was shot through the chest, and evidently near his end. He had been on outpost duty;—the night had been quiet, but a few random shots had been fired. One of these had struck Arminius in the breast, and gone right through his body. By this stray bullet, without glory, without a battle, without even a foe in sight, had fallen the last of the Von Thunder-ten-Tronckhs!

He knew me, and with a nod, 'Ah,' said he, 'the rowdy Philistine!' You know his turn, *outré* in my opinion, for flinging nicknames right and left. The present, however, was not a moment for resentment. The Germans saw that their comrade was in friendly hands, and gladly left him with me. He had evidently but a few minutes to live. I sate down on the bank by him, and asked him if I could do anything to relieve him. He shook his head. Any message to his friends in England? He nodded. I ran over the most prominent names which occurred to me of the old set. First, our Amphitryon, Mr. Bottles. 'Say to Bottles from me,' said Arminius coldly, 'that I hope he will be comfortable with his dead wife's sister.' Next, Mr. Frederic Harrison. 'Tell him,' says Arminius, 'to do more in literature,—he has a talent for it; and to avoid Carlylese as he would the devil.' Then I mentioned a personage to whom Arminius had taken a great fancy last spring, and of whose witty writings some people had, absurdly enough, given Mr. Matthew Arnold the credit,—Azamat-Batuk. Both writers are simple; but Azamat's is the simplicity of shrewdness, the other's of helplessness. At hearing the clever Turk's name, 'Tell him only,' whispers Arminius, 'when he writes about the sex, not to show such a turn for sailing so very near the wind!' Lastly, I mentioned Mr. Matthew Arnold. I hope I rate this poor soul's feeble and rambling performances at their proper value; but I am bound to say that at the mention of his name Arminius showed signs of tenderness. 'Poor fellow!' sighed he; 'he had a soft head, but I valued his heart. Tell him I leave him my ideas,—the easier ones; and advise him from me,' he added, with a faint smile, 'to let his Dissenters go to the devil their own way!'

At this instant there was a movement on the road at a little distance from where we were,—some of the Prussian Princes, I believe, passing; at any rate, we heard the honest German soldiers *Hoch-ing*, hurrahing, and God-blessing, in their true-hearted but somewhat *rococo* manner. A flush passed over Von Thunder-ten-Tronckh's face. 'God bless *Germany*,' he murmured, 'and confound all her kings and princelings!' These were his last coherent words. His eyes closed and he seemed to become unconscious. I stooped over him and inquired if he had any wishes about his interment. 'Pangloss—Mr. Lowe—mausoleum—Caterham,' was all that, in broken words, I could gather from him. His breath came with more and more difficulty, his fingers felt instinctively for his tobacco-pouch, his lips twitched;—he was gone.

So died, *mon cher*, an arrant Republican, and, to speak my real mind, a most unpleasant companion. His great name and lineage imposed on the Bottles family, and authors who had never succeeded with the British public took pleasure in his disparaging criticisms on our free and noble country; but for my part I always thought him an overrated man.

Meanwhile I was alone with his remains. His notion of their being transported to Caterham was of course impracticable. Still, I did not like to leave an old acquaintance to the crows, and I looked round in perplexity. Fortune in the most unexpected manner befriended me. The grounds of a handsome villa came down to the road close to where I was; at the end of the grounds and overhanging the road was a summer-house. Its shutters had been closed when I first discovered Arminius; but while I was occupied with him they had been opened, and a gay trio was visible within the summer-house at breakfast. I could scarcely believe my eyes for satisfaction. Three English members of Parliament, celebrated for their ardent charity and advanced Liberalism, were sitting before me adorned with a red cross and eating a Strasburg pie! I approached them and requested their aid to bury Arminius. My request seemed to occasion them painful embarrassment; they muttered something about 'a breach of the understanding,' and went on with their breakfast. I insisted, however; and at length, having stipulated that what they were about to do should on no account be drawn into a precedent, they left their breakfast, and together we buried Arminius under the poplar-tree. It was a hurried business, for my friends had an engagement to lunch at Versailles at noon. Poor Von Thunder-ten-Tronckh, the earth lies light on him, indeed! I could see, as I left him, the blue of his pilot coat and the whity-brown of his hair through the mould we had scattered over him.

My benevolent helpers and I then made our way together to Versailles. As I parted from them at the Hôtel des Reservoirs I met Sala. Little as I liked Arminius, the melancholy scene I had just gone through had shaken me, and I needed sympathy. I told Sala what had happened. 'The old story,' says Sala; '*life a dream!* Take a glass of brandy.' He then inquired who my friends were. 'Three admirable members of Parliament,' I cried, 'who, donning the cross of charity——' 'I know,' interrupted Sala; 'the cleverest thing out!'

But the emotions of this agitating day were not yet over. While Sala was speaking, a group had formed before the hotel near us, and our attention was drawn to its central figure. Dr. Russell, of the *Times*, was preparing to mount his war-horse. You know the sort of thing,—he has described it himself over and over again. Bismarck at his horse's head, the Crown Prince holding his stirrup, and the old King of Prussia hoisting Russell into the saddle. When he was there, the distinguished public servant waved his hand in acknowledgment, and rode slowly down the street, accompanied by the *gamins* of Versailles, who even in their present dejection could not forbear a few involuntary cries of '*Quel homme!*' Always unassuming, he alighted at the lodgings of the Grand Duke of Oldenburg, a potentate of the second or even the third order, who had beckoned to him from the window.

The agitation of this scene for me, however (may I not add, *mon cher*, for you also, and for the whole British press?), lay in a suggestion which it called forth from Sala. 'It is all very well,' said Sala, 'but old Russell's guns are getting a little honeycombed; anybody can perceive that. He will have to be pensioned off, and why should not you succeed him?' We passed the afternoon in talking the thing over, and I think I may assure you that a train has been laid of which you will see the effects shortly.

For my part, I can afford to wait till the pear is ripe ; yet I cannot, without a thrill of excitement, think of inoculating the respectable but somewhat ponderous *Times* and its readers with the divine madness of our new style,—the style we have formed upon Sala. The world, *mon cher*, knows that man but imperfectly. I do not class him with the great masters of human thought and human literature,—Plato, Shakspeare, Confucius, Charles Dickens. Sala, like us his disciples, has studied in the book of the world even more than in the world of books. But his career and genius have given him somehow the secret of a literary mixture novel and fascinating in the last degree : he blends the airy epicureanism of the *salons* of Augustus with the full-bodied gaiety of our English Cider-cellar. With our people and country, *mon cher*, this mixture, you may rely upon it, is now the very thing to go down ; there arises every day a larger public for it ; and we, Sala's disciples, may be trusted not willingly to let it die.—*Tout à vous*,

A YOUNG LION.[1]

To the EDITOR *of the* PALL MALL GAZETTE.

[1] I am bound to say that in attempting to verify Leo's graphic description of Dr. Russell's mounting on horseback, from the latter's

(I have thought that the memorial raised to Arminius would not be complete without the following essay, in which, though his name is not actually mentioned, he will be at once recognised as the leading spirit of the foreigners whose conversation is quoted.

Much as I owe to his intellect, I cannot help sometimes regretting that the spirit of youthful paradox which led me originally to question the perfections of my countrymen, should have been, as it were, prevented from dying out by my meeting, six years ago, with Arminius. The *Saturday Review*, in an article called 'Mr. Matthew Arnold and his Countrymen,' had taken my correction in hand, and I was in a fair way of amendment, when the intervention of Arminius stopped the cure, and turned me, as has been often said, into a mere mouthpiece of this dogmatic young Prussian. It was not that I did not often dislike his spirit and boldly stand up to him; but, on the whole, my intellect was (there is no use denying it)

own excellent correspondence, to which Leo refers us, I have been unsuccessful. Repeatedly I have seemed to be on the trace of what my friend meant, but the particular description he alludes to I have never been lucky enough to light upon.

I may add that, in spite of what Leo says of the train he and Mr. Sala have laid, of Dr. Russell's approaching retirement, of Leo's prospect of succeeding him, of the charm of the leonine style, and of the disposition of the public mind to be fascinated by it,—I cannot myself believe that either the public, or the proprietors of the *Times*, are yet ripe for a change so revolutionary. But Leo was always sanguine.—Ed.

overmatched by his. The following essay, which appeared at the beginning of 1866, was the first proof of this fatal predominance, which has in many ways cost me so dear.)—Ed.

MY COUNTRYMEN

About a year ago the *Saturday Review* published an article which gave me, as its articles often do give me, much food for reflection. The article was about the unjust estimate which, says the *Saturday Review*, I form of my countrymen, and about the indecency of talking of 'British Philistines.' It appears that I assume the truth of the transcendental system of philosophy,[1] and then lecture my wiser countrymen because they will not join me in recognising as eternal truths a set of platitudes which may be proved to be false. 'Now there is in England a school of philosophy which thoroughly understands, and, on theoretical grounds, deliberately rejects, the philosophical theory which Mr. Arnold accuses the English nation of neglecting ; and the practical efforts of the English people, especially their practical efforts in the way of criticism, are for the most part strictly in accordance with the principles of that philosophy.'

I do not quite know what to say about the transcendental system of philosophy, for I am a

[1] Philosophy has always been bringing me into trouble.—Ed.

mere dabbler in these great matters, and to grasp and hold a system of philosophy is a feat much beyond my strength ; but I certainly did talk about British Philistines, and to call people Philistines when they are doing just what the wisest men in the country have settled to be quite right, does seem unreasonable, not to say indecent. Being really the most teachable man alive, I could not help making, after I had read the article in the *Saturday Review*, a serious return, as the French say, upon myself ; and I resolved never to call my countrymen Philistines again till I had thought more about it, and could be quite sure I was not committing an indecency.

I was very much fortified in this good resolution by something else which happened about the same time. Every one knows that the heart of the English nation is its middle class ; there had been a good deal of talk, a year ago, about the education of this class, and I, among others, had imagined it was not good, and that the middle class suffered by its not being better. But Mr. Bazley,[1] the member for Manchester, who is a kind of representative of this class, made a speech last year at Manchester, the middle-class metropolis, which shook me a good deal. 'During the last few months,' said Mr. Bazley, 'there had been a cry that middle-class education ought to receive more attention.

[1] Now Sir Thomas Bazley, Bart.—Ed.

He confessed himself very much surprised by the clamour that was raised. He did not think that class need excite the sympathy either of the legislature or the public.' Much to the same effect spoke Mr. Miall, another middle-class leader, in the *Nonconformist*: 'Middle-class education seems to be the favourite topic of the hour, and we must confess to a feeling of shame at the nonsense which is being uttered on the subject. It might be thought from what is said, that this section of the community, which has done everything else so well,—which has astonished the world by its energy, enterprise, and self-reliance, which is continually striking out new paths of industry and subduing the forces of nature,—cannot, from some mysterious reason, get their children properly educated.' Still more strong were the words of the *Daily News* (I love to range all the evidence in black and white before me, though it tends to my own discomfiture) about the blunder some of us were making: 'All the world knows that the great middle class of this country supplies the mind, the will, and the power for all the great and good things that have to be done, and it is not likely that that class should surrender its powers and privileges in the one case of the training of its own children. How the idea of such a scheme can have occurred to anybody, how it can have been imagined that parents and schoolmasters in the most independent, and active, and enlightened class of English society,[1] how it can have been supposed that the class which has done all the great things that have been done in all departments, will beg the Government to send inspectors through its schools, when it can itself command whatever advantages exist, might seem unintelligible but for two or three considerations.' These considerations do not much matter just now; but it is clear how perfectly Mr. Bazley's stand was a stand such as it becomes a representative man like Mr. Bazley to make, and how well the *Daily Telegraph* might say of the speech: 'It was at once grand, genial, national, and distinct'; and the *Morning Star* of the speaker: 'He talked to his constituents as Manchester people like to be talked to, in the language of clear, manly intelligence, which penetrates through sophisms, ignores commonplaces, and gives to conventional illusions their true value. His speech was thoroughly instinct with that earnest good sense which characterises Manchester, and which, indeed, may be fairly set down as the general characteristic of England and Englishmen everywhere.'

Of course if Philistinism is characteristic of the British nation just now, it must in a special

[1] How very fine and striking is this language! Eloquent as is the homage which our newspapers still pay in the same quarter, it seems as if, in 1866, their eulogy had a ring and fulness which it has since in some measure lost.—Ed.

way be characteristic of the representative part of the British nation, the part by which the British nation is what it is, and does all its best things, the middle class. And the newspapers, who have so many more means than I of knowing the truth, and who have that trenchant authoritative style for communicating it which makes so great an impression, say that the British middle class is characterised, not by Philistinism, but by enlightenment; by a passion for penetrating through sophisms, ignoring commonplaces, and giving to conventional illusions their true value. Evidently it is nonsense, as the *Daily News* says, to think that this great middle class which supplies the mind, the will, and the power for all the great and good things that have to be done, should want its schools, the nurseries of its admirable intelligence, meddled with. It may easily be imagined that all this, coming on the top of the *Saturday Review's* rebuke of me for indecency, was enough to set me meditating; and after a long and painful self-examination, I saw that I had been making a great mistake. Instead of confining myself to what alone I had any business with,—the slow and obscure work of trying to understand things, to see them as they are,—I had been meddling with practice, proposing this and that, saying how it might be if we established this or that. So I was suffering deservedly in being taunted with hawking about my nostrums of State schools for a class much too wise to want them, and of an Academy for people who have an inimitable style already. To be sure, I had said that schools ought to be things of local, not State, institution and management, and that we ought not to have an Academy ; but that makes no difference. I saw what danger I had been running by thus intruding into a sphere where I have no business, and I resolved to offend in this way no more.

This I say as a sincere penitent ; but I do not see that there is any harm in my still trying to know and understand things, if I keep humbly to that, and do not meddle with greater matters, which are out of my reach. So, having once got into my head this notion of British Philistinism and of the want of clear and large intelligence in our middle class, I do not consider myself bound at once to put away and crush such a notion, as people are told to do with their religious doubts ; nor, when the *Saturday Review* tells me that no nation in the world is so logical as the English nation, and the *Morning Star*, that our grand national characteristic is a clear intelligence which penetrates through sophisms, ignores commonplaces, and gives to conventional illusions their true value, do I feel myself compelled to receive these propositions with absolute submission as articles of faith, transcending reason ; indeed, this would be transcendentalism, which the *Saturday Review* condemns. Canvass them, then, as mere matters of speculation, I may; and having lately had occasion to travel on the Continent for many months, during which I was thrown in company with a great variety of people, I remembered what Burns says of the profitableness of trying to see ourselves as others see us, and I kept on the watch for anything to confirm or contradict my old notion, in which, without absolutely giving it up, I had begun certainly to be much shaken and staggered.

I must say that the foreign opinion about us is not at all like that of the *Saturday Review* and the *Morning Star*. I know how madly the foreigners envy us, and that this must warp their judgment; I know, too, that this test of foreign opinion can never be decisive; I only take it for what it is worth, and as a contribution to our study of the matter in question. But I do really think that the admirers of our great middle class, which has, as its friends and enemies both agree, risen into such preponderating importance of late years, and now returns the House of Commons, dictates the policy of Ministers, makes the newspapers speak with its voice, and in short governs the country,—I do think, I say, the admirers of this great class would be astounded if they could hear how cavalierly a foreigner treats this country of their making and managing. 'It is not so much that we dislike England,' a Prussian official,[1] with

[1] Not Arminius.—Ed.

the graceful tact of his nation, said to me the other day, 'as that we think little of her.' The *Cologne Gazette*, perhaps the chief newspaper of Germany, published in the summer a series of letters, much esteemed, I believe, by military men, on the armies of the leading Continental powers. The writer was a German officer, but not a Prussian. Speaking of the false military system followed by the Emperor Nicholas, whose great aim was to turn his soldiers into perfectly drilled machines, and contrasting this with the free play left to the individual soldier in the French system : 'In consequence of their purely mechanical training,' says this writer, 'the Russians, in spite of their splendid courage, were in the Crimean war constantly beaten by the French, nay, decidedly beaten *even by the English and the Turks*.'[1] Hardly a German newspaper can discuss territorial changes in Europe but it will add, after its remarks on the probable policy of France in this or that event : 'England will probably make a fuss, but what England thinks is of no importance.' I believe the German newspapers must keep a phrase of that kind stereotyped, they use it so often. France is our very good friend just now, but at bottom our 'clear intelligence penetrating through sophisms,' and so on, is not held in much more esteem there than in Germany.

1 'Ja, selbst von den Engländern und Türkern entschieden geschlagen.'

One of the gravest and most moderate of French newspapers,—a newspaper, too, our very good friend, like France herself, into the bargain,—broke out lately, when some jealousy of the proposed Cholera Commission in the East was shown on this side the water, in terms which, though less rough than the 'great fool' of the *Saturday Review*, were still far from flattering. 'Let us speak to these English the only language they can comprehend. England lives for her trade; Cholera interrupts trade; therefore it is for England's interest to join in precautions against Cholera.'[1]

Compliments of this sort are displeasing to remember, displeasing to repeat; but their abundance strikes the attention; and then the happy unconsciousness of those at whom they are aimed, their state of imperturbable self-satisfaction, strikes the attention too, and makes an inquisitive mind quite eager to see its way clearly in this apparent game of cross purposes. For never, surely, was there such a game of cross purposes played. It came to its height when Lord Palmerston died the other day. Lord Palmerston was England; 'the best type of our age and country,' the *Times* well called him; he was 'a great representative man, emphatically the English Minister'; the inter-

[1] Poor France! As Mr. Bottles says, neither her favourable nor her unfavourable criticisms are of much consequence just now.—Ed.

preter of the wishes of that great middle class of this country which supplies the mind, the will, and the power requisite for all the great and good things that have to be done, and therefore 'acknowledged by a whole people as their best impersonation.' Monsieur Thiers says of Pitt, that though he used and abused the strength of England, she was the second country in the world at the time of his death, and the first eight years afterwards. That was after Waterloo and the triumphs of Wellington. And that era of primacy and triumphs, Lord Palmerston, say the English newspapers, has carried on to this hour. 'What Wellington was as a soldier, that was Palmerston as a statesman.' When I read these words in some foreign city or other, I could not help rubbing my eyes and asking myself if I was dreaming. Why, taking Lord Palmerston's career from 1830 (when he first became Foreign Secretary) to his death, there cannot be a shadow of doubt, for any one with eyes and ears in his head, that he found England the first Power in the world's estimation, and that he leaves her the third, after France[1] and the United States. I am no politician; I mean no disparagement at all to Lord Palmerston, to whose talents and qualities I hope I can do justice; and indeed it is not Lord Palmerston's policy, or any minister's policy, that is in question here, it is the policy

[1] Heu incredibiles humanarum rerum mutationes!—Ed.

of all of us, it is the policy of England; for in a government such as ours is at present, it is only, as we are so often reminded, by interpreting public opinion, by being 'the best type of his age and country,' that a minister governs; and Lord Palmerston's greatness lay precisely in our all 'acknowledging him as our best impersonation.' Well, then, to this our logic, our practical efforts in the way of criticism, our clear manly intelligence penetrating through sophisms and ignoring commonplaces, and above all, our redoubtable phalanx possessing these advantages in the highest degree, our great middle class, which makes Parliament, and which supplies the mind, the will, and the power requisite for all the great and good things that have to be done, have brought us; to the third place in the world's estimation, instead of the first. He who disbelieves it, let him go round to every embassy in Europe and ask if it is not true.

The foreigners, indeed, are in no doubt as to the real authors of the policy of modern England; they know that ours is no longer a policy of Pitts and aristocracies,[1] disposing of every movement of the hoodwinked nation to whom they dictate it; they know that our policy is now dictated by the strong middle part of England,—England happy, as Mr. Lowe, quoting Aristotle, says, in having her middle

[1] Arminius; he says it over again in his last letter but one.—Ed.

part strong and her extremes weak; and that, though we are administered by one of our weak extremes, the aristocracy, these managers administer us, as a weak extreme naturally must, with a nervous attention to the wishes of the strong middle part, whose agents they are. It was not the aristocracy which made the Crimean war; it was the strong middle part—the constituencies. It was the strong middle part which showered abuse and threats on Germany for mishandling Denmark; and when Germany gruffly answered, *Come and stop us*, slapped its pockets, and vowed that it had never had the slightest notion of pushing matters as far as this. It was the strong middle part which, by the voice of its favourite newspapers, kept threatening Germany, after she had snapped her fingers at us, with a future chastisement from France, just as a smarting schoolboy threatens his bully with a drubbing to come from some big boy in the background. It was the strong middle part, speaking through the same newspapers, which was full of coldness, slights, and sermons for the American Federals during their late struggle; and as soon as they had succeeded, discovered that it had always wished them well, and that nothing was so much to be desired as that the United States, and we, should be the fastest friends possible. Some people will say that the aristocracy was an equal offender in this respect: very likely: but the behaviour of the strong middle part makes more impression than the behaviour of a weak extreme; and the more so, because from the middle class, their fellows in numberless ways, the Americans expected sympathy, while from the aristocracy they expected none. And, in general, the faults with which foreigners reproach us in the matters named,—rash engagement, intemperate threatening, undignified retreat, ill-timed cordiality,—are not the faults of an aristocracy, by nature in such concerns prudent, reticent, dignified, sensitive on the point of honour; they are rather the faults of a rich middle class,—testy, absolute, ill-acquainted with foreign matters, a little ignoble, very dull to perceive when it is making itself ridiculous.

I know the answer one gets at home when one says that England is not very highly considered just now on the Continent. There is first of all the envy to account for it,—that of course; and then our clear intelligence is making a radical change in our way of dealing with the Continent; the old, bad, aristocratical policy of incessantly intermeddling with the affairs of the Continent,—this it is getting rid of; it is leaving the miserable foreigners to themselves, to their wars, despotisms, bureaucracy, and hatred of free, prosperous England. A few inconveniences may arise before the transition from our old policy to our new is fairly accomplished, and we quite leave off the habit of meddling where our own interests are not at stake. We may be exposed to a little mortification in the passage, but our clear intelligence will discern any occasion where our interests are really at stake. Then we shall come forward and prove ourselves as strong as ever ; and the foreigners, in spite of their envy, know it. But what strikes me so much in all which these foreigners say is, that it is just this clear intelligence of ours that they appear at the present moment to hold cheap. Englishmen are often heard complaining of the little gratitude foreign nations show them for their sympathy, their good-will. The reason is, that the foreigners think that an Englishman's good-will to a foreign cause, or dislike to it, is never grounded in a perception of its real merits and bearings, but in some chance circumstance. They say the Englishman never, in these cases, really comprehends the situation, and so they can never feel him to be in living sympathy with them. I have got into much trouble for calling my countrymen Philistines, and all through these remarks I am determined never to use that word ; but I wonder if there can be anything offensive in calling one's countryman a young man from the country. I hope not ; and if not, I should say, for the benefit of those who have seen Mr. John Parry's amusing entertainment, that England and Englishmen, holding forth on some great crisis in a foreign country,—Poland, say, or

Italy,—are apt to have on foreigners very much the effect of the young man from the country who talks to the nursemaid after she has upset the perambulator. There is a terrible crisis, and the discourse of the young man from the country, excellent in itself, is felt not to touch the crisis vitally. Nevertheless, on he goes; the perambulator lies a wreck, the child screams, the nursemaid wrings her hands, the old gentleman storms, the policeman gesticulates, the crowd thickens; still, that astonishing young man talks on, serenely unconscious that he is not at the centre of the situation.

Happening to be much thrown with certain foreigners, who criticised England in this sort of way, I used often to think what a short and ready way one of our hard-hitting English newspapers would take with these scorners, if they fell into its hands. But being myself a mere seeker for truth, with nothing trenchant or authoritative about me, I could do no more than look shocked and begin to ask questions. 'What!' I said, 'you hold the England of to-day cheap, and declare that we do not comprehend the situation; yet you rate the England of 1815 so high, and call our fathers and grandfathers the foremost people in Europe. Did they comprehend the situation better than we?' 'Yes,' replied my foreign friends, 'the situation as they had it, a great deal better. Their time was a time for energy, and they succeeded in it, perfectly. Our time is a time for intelligence, and you are not succeeding in it at all.'

Though I could not hear without a shudder this insult to the earnest good sense which, as the *Morning Star* says, may be fairly set down as the general characteristic of England and Englishmen everywhere, yet I pricked up my ears when my companions talked of energy, and England's success in a time for energy, because I have always had a notion myself that energy,—energy with honesty,—is England's great force ; a greater force to her, even, than her talent for penetrating through sophisms and ignoring commonplaces ; so I begged my acquaintances to explain a little more fully to me what they meant. 'Nothing can be clearer,' they answered. 'Your *Times* was telling you the other day, with the enlightenment it so often shows at present, that instead of being proud of Waterloo and the great war which was closed by it, it really seemed as if you ought rather to feel embarrassed at the recollection of them, since the policy for which they were fought is grown obsolete ; the world has taken a turn which was not Lord Castlereagh's, and to look back on the great Tory war is to look back upon an endless account of blood and treasure wasted. Now, that is not so at all. What France had in her head, from the Convention,—faithful to the principles of the sovereignty of the people, which will not permit them to acknowledge anywhere the institutions militating against it, to Napoleon, with his "immense projects for assuring to France the empire of the world,"—what she had in her head, along with many better and sounder notions destined to happier fortune, was *supremacy*. She had always a vision of a sort of federation of the States of Europe under the primacy of France. Now to this the world, whose progress no doubt lies in the direction of more concert and common purpose among nations, but these nations free, self-impelled, and living each its own life, was not moving. Whoever knocks to pieces a scheme of this sort does the world a service. In antiquity, Roman empire had a scheme of this sort, and much more. The barbarians knocked it to pieces;—honour to the barbarians. In the Middle Ages Frederick the Second had a scheme of this sort. The Papacy knocked it to pieces;—honour to the Papacy. In our own century, France had a scheme of this sort. Your fathers knocked it to pieces; —honour to your fathers. They were just the people to do it. They had a vigorous lower class, a vigorous middle class, and a vigorous aristocracy. The lower class worked and fought, the middle class found the money, and the aristocracy wielded the whole. This aristocracy was high-spirited, reticent, firm, despising frothy declamation. It had all the qualities useful for its task and time; Lord Grenville's words, as early as 1793: "England will never consent that France shall arrogate the power of annulling at her pleasure, and under the pretence of a pretended natural right, the political system of Europe,"—these few words, with their lofty strength, contain, as one may say, the prophecy of future success; you hear the very voice of an aristocracy standing on sure ground, and with the stars in its favour. Well, you succeeded, and in 1815, after Waterloo, you were the first power in Europe. "These people have a secret," we all said; "they have discerned the way the world was going, and therefore they have prevailed; while, on the other hand, the 'stars in their courses fought against Sisera.'" We held you in the greatest respect; we tried to copy your constitutional government; we read your writers. "After the peace," says George Sand, "the literature of Great Britain crossed the straits, and came to reign amongst us." It reigned in Byron and Scott, voices of the great aristocratical spirit which had just won the victory: Scott expressing its robust, genial conservatism, holding by a thousand roots to the past; Byron its defiant force and indomitable pride.

'We believed in you for a good while; but gradually it began to dawn upon us that the era for which you had had the secret was over, and that a new era, for which you had not the secret, was beginning. The work of the old era was to prevent the formation of a second

Roman empire, and to maintain a store of free, rich, various national lives for the future to work with and bring to harmony. This was a work of force, of energy: it was a work for an aristocratical power, since, as you yourself are always saying, aristocracies, poor in ideas, are rich in energy. You were a great aristocratical power, and did it. But then came an era with another work, a work of which it is the great glory of the French Revolution (pardon us for saying so, we know it makes some of your countrymen angry to hear it) passionately to have embraced the idea: the work of making human life, hampered by a past which it has outgrown, natural and rational. This is a work of intelligence, and in intelligence an aristocratic power, as you know, does not so much shine. Accordingly, since the world has been steadily moving this way, you seem to have lost your secret, and we are gradually ceasing to believe in you. You will say, perhaps, that England is no longer an aristocratical power, but a middle-class power, wielded by an industrial middle class, as the England of your fathers was wielded by a territorial aristocracy. This may be so; and indeed, as the style, carriage, and policy of England have of late years been by no means those of an aristocratical power, it probably is so. But whatever class dictates it, your course, allow us to say, has not of late years been intelligent; has not, at any rate, been successful. And depend upon it, a nation who has the secret of her era, who discerns which way the world is going, is successful, keeps rising. Can you yourselves, with all your powers of self-satisfaction, suppose that the Crimean war raised you, or that your Indian mutiny raised you, or that your attitude in the Italian war raised you, as your performances at the beginning of the century raised you? Surely you cannot. You held your own, if you will; you showed tenacity; you saved yourselves from disaster; but you did not raise yourselves, did not advance one jot. Can you, on the other hand, suppose that your attitude in the Danish business, in the American business, has not lowered you? You are losing the instinct which tells people how the world is going; you are beginning to make mistakes; you are falling out of the front rank. The era of aristocracies is over; nations must now stand or fall by the intelligence of their middle class and their people. The people with you is still an embryo; no one can yet quite say what it will come to. You lean, therefore, with your whole weight upon the intelligence of your middle class. And intelligence, in the true sense of the word, your middle class has absolutely none.'

I was aghast. I thought of this great class, every morning and evening extolled for its clear, manly intelligence by a hundred vigorous and influential writers; and though the fine enthusiasm of these writers had always seemed to me to be carrying them a little too far, and I had even been guilty of the indecency of now and then calling my countrymen Philistines, these foreign critics struck me as passing all bounds, and quite out-Heroding Herod. Fortunately I had just received from England a copy of Mr. Lowe's powerful and much-admired speech against Reform. I took it out of my pocket. 'Now,' said I to my envious, carping foreigners, 'just listen to me. You say that the early years of this century were a time for energy, and we did well in them; you say that the last thirty or forty years have been a time for intelligence, and we have done ill in them. Mr. Lowe shall answer you. Here is his reading of our last thirty or forty years' history, as made by our middle-class Parliament, as he calls it; by a Parliament, therefore, filled by the mind and will of this great class whose rule you disparage. Mr. Lowe says: "The seven Houses of Commons that have sate since the Reform Bill have performed exploits unrivalled, not merely in the six centuries during which Parliament has existed, but in the whole history of representative assemblies." He says: "Look at the noble work, the heroic work which the House of Commons has performed within these thirty-five years. It has gone through and revised every institution of the country;

it has scanned our trade, our colonies, our laws, and our municipal institutions; everything that was complained of, everything that had grown distasteful, has been touched with success and moderation by the amending hand. And to such a point have these amendments been carried, that when gentlemen come to argue this question, and do all in their power to get up a practical grievance, they fail in suggesting even one." There is what Mr. Lowe says. You see we have nothing left to desire, absolutely nothing. As Mr. Lowe himself goes on: "With all this continued peace, contentment, happiness, and prosperity,—England in its present state of development and civilisation,—the mighty fabric of English prosperity,—what can we want more?" Evidently nothing! therefore to propose "for England to make a step in the direction of democracy is the strangest and wildest proposition ever broached by man." People talk of America. "In America the working classes are the masters; does anybody doubt that?" And compare, Mr. Lowe means, England, as the middle class is making her, with America, as the working classes are making her. How entirely must the comparison turn to the advantage of the English middle class! Then, finally, as to the figure we cut in the eyes of the world, our grandeur and our future, here is a crowning sentence, worthy of Lord Macaulay himself, whose style Mr.

Lowe enthusiastically admires: "*The destiny of England is in the great heart of England!*"'

Mr. Bright had not then made his famous speech about the misdeeds of the Tories, but, if he had, I should certainly have added that our middle class, by these unrivalled exploits of theirs, had not only raised their country to an unprecedented height of greatness, but had also saved our foolish and obstructive aristocracy from being emptied into the Thames.

As it was, however, what I had urged, or rather what I had borrowed from Mr. Lowe, seemed to me exceedingly forcible, and I looked anxiously for its effect on my hearers. They did not appear so much disconcerted as I had hoped. 'Undoubtedly,' they said, 'the coming of your middle class to power was a natural, salutary event, to be blessed, not anathematised. Aristocracies cannot deal with a time for intelligence; their sense is for facts, not ideas. The world of ideas is the possible, the future; the world of aristocracies is the established, the past, which has made their fortune, and which they hope to prolong. No doubt, too, your middle class found a great deal of commercial and social business waiting to be done, which your aristocratic governments had left undone, and had no talents for doing. Their talents were for other times and tasks; for curbing the power of the Crown when other classes were too inconsiderable to do it; for managing (if one compares them with other aristocracies) their affairs and their dependants with vigour, prudence, and moderation, during the feudal and patriarchal stage of society; for wielding the force of their country against foreign powers with energy, firmness, and dignity. But then came the modern spirit, the modern time; the notion, as we say, of making human life more natural and rational,—or, as your philosophers say, of getting the greatest happiness for the greatest number. Have you succeeded, are you succeeding, in this hour of the many, as your aristocracy succeeded in the hour of the few? You say you are: you point to "the noble work, the heroic work which the House of Commons has performed within these last thirty-five years; everything that was complained of, everything that had grown distasteful, has been touched with success and moderation by the amending hand." Allow us to set clap-trap on one side; we are not at one of your public meetings. What is the modern problem? to make human life, the life of society, all through, more natural and rational; to have the greatest possible number of one's nation happy. Here is the standard by which we are to try ourselves and one another now, as national grandeur, in the old regal and aristocratical conception of it, was the standard formerly. Every nation must have wished to be in England in 1815, tried by the old standard: must we all wish to be

England, in 1865, tried by the new standard? Your aristocracy, you say, is as splendid, as fortunate, as enviable as ever: very likely; but all the world cannot be aristocracy. What do you make of the mass of your society, of its vast middle and lower portion? Are we to envy you your common people; is our common people to wish to change places with yours; are we to say that you, more than we, have the modern secret here? Without insisting too much on the stories of misery and degradation which are perpetually reaching us, we will say that no one can mix with a great crowd in your country, no one can walk with his eyes and ears open through the poor quarters of your large towns, and not feel that your common people, as it meets one's eyes, is at present more raw, to say the very least, less enviable-looking, further removed from civilised and humane life, than the common people almost anywhere. Well, then, you are not a success, according to the modern standard, with your common people. Are you a success with your middle class? They have the power now; what have they made of themselves? what sort of a life is theirs? A life more natural, more rational, fuller of happiness, more enviable, therefore, than the life of the middle classes on the Continent? Yes, you will say, because the English middle class is the most industrious and the richest. But it is just here that you go a great deal too fast, and so deceive yourselves. What brings about, or rather tends to bring about, a natural, rational life, satisfying the modern spirit? This: the growth of a love of industry, trade, and wealth; the growth of a love of the things of the mind; and the growth of a love of beautiful things. There are body, intelligence, and soul all taken care of. Of these three factors of modern life, your middle class has no notion of any but one, the first. Their love of industry, trade, and wealth, is certainly prodigious; and their example has done us a great deal of good; we, too, are beginning to get this love, and we wanted it. But what notion have they of anything else? Do but look at them, look at their lives. Some of us know your middle class very well; a great deal better than your own upper class in general knows them. Your middle class is educated, to begin with, in the worst schools of your country, and our middle class is educated in the best of ours. What becomes of them after that? The fineness and capacity of a man's spirit is shown by his enjoyments; your middle class has an enjoyment in its business, we admit, and gets on well in business, and makes money; but beyond that? Drugged with business, your middle class seems to have its sense blunted for any stimulus besides, except religion; it has a religion, narrow, unintelligent, repulsive. All sincere religion does something for the spirit, raises a man out of the bondage of his merely bestial part, and saves him ; but the religion of your middle class is the very lowest form of intelligential life which one can imagine as saving. What other enjoyments have they? The newspapers, a sort of eating and drinking which are not to our taste, a literature of books almost entirely religious or semi-religious, books utterly unreadable by an educated class anywhere, but which your middle class consumes, they say, by the hundred thousand ; and in their evenings, for a great treat, a lecture on teetotalism or nunneries. Can any life be imagined more hideous, more dismal, more unenviable? Compare it with the life of our middle class as you have seen it on the Rhine this summer, or at Lausanne, or Zurich. The world of enjoyment, so liberalising and civilising, belongs to the middle classes there, as well as the world of business ; the whole world is theirs, they possess life ; in England the highest class seems to have the monopoly of the world of enjoyment, the middle class enjoys itself, as your Shakspeare would say, in hugger-mugger, and possesses life only by reading in the newspapers, which it does devoutly, the doings of great people. Well, then, we do not at all want to be as your middle class ; we want to learn from it to do business and to get rich, and this we are learning a great deal faster than you think ; but we do not, like your middle class, fix our consummation here: we have a notion of a whole world besides, not dreamed of in your middle class's philosophy; so they, too, like your common people, seem to us no success. They may be the masters of the modern time with you, but they are not solving its problem. They cannot see the way the world is going, and the future does not belong to them. Talk of the present state of development and civilisation of England, meaning England as they represent it to us! Why, the capital, pressing danger of England is the barbarism of her middle class; the civilisation of her middle class is England's capital, pressing want.'

'Well, but,' said I, still catching at Mr. Lowe's powerful help, 'the Parliament of this class has performed exploits unrivalled not merely in the six centuries during which Parliament has existed, but in the whole history of representative assemblies. The exploits are there; all the reforms we have made in the last five-and-thirty years.'

'Let us distinguish,' replied the envious foreigners, 'let us distinguish. We named three powers,—did we not?—which go to spread that rational humane life which is the aim of modern society: the love of wealth, the love of intelligence, the love of beauty. Your middle class, we agreed, has the first; its commercial legislation, accordingly, has been very good, and in advance of that of foreign countries. Not that free-trade was really brought about by your middle class: it was brought about, as important reforms always are, by two or three great men. However, let your middle class, which had the sense to accept free trade, have the credit of it. But this only brings us a certain way. The legislation of your middle class in all that goes to give human life more intelligence and beauty, is no better than was to be expected from its own want of both. It is nothing to say that its legislation in these respects is an improvement upon what you had before; that is not the question; you are holding up its achievements as absolutely admirable, as unrivalled, as a model to us. You may have done,—for you,—much for religious toleration, social improvement, public instruction, municipal reform, law reform; but the French Revolution and its consequences have done, upon the Continent, a great deal more. Such a spectacle as your Irish Church Establishment[1] you cannot find in France or Germany. Your Irish land-question you hardly dare to face[2]—Stein settled as threatening a land-question in Prussia. Of the schools for your middle class we have already spoken; while these schools are what they are, while the schools for your poor are maintained in the expensive, unjust, irrational way they are,

[1] It is gone, thanks to Anti-State-Church-ism!—Ed.

[2] We have faced it!—Ed.

England is full of endowments and foundations, capable by themselves, if properly applied, of putting your public education on a much better footing. In France and Germany all similar funds are thus employed, having been brought under public responsible management; in England they are left to private irresponsible management, and are, in nine cases out of ten, wasted. You talk of municipal reform; and cities and the manner of life in them have, for the modern business of promoting a more rational and humane life in the great body of the community, incalculable importance. Do you suppose we should tolerate in France, Germany, Switzerland, Italy, your London corporation and London vestries, and London as they make it? In your provincial towns you do better; but even there, do the municipalities show a tenth part either of the intelligence or the care for the ends, as we have laid them down, of modern society, that our municipalities show? Your middle class man thinks it the highest pitch of development and civilisation when his letters are carried twelve times a day from Islington to Camberwell, and from Camberwell to Islington, and if railway-trains run to and fro between them every quarter of an hour. He thinks it is nothing that the trains only carry him from an illiberal, dismal life at Islington to an illiberal, dismal life at Camberwell; and the letters only tell him that such is the life there. A Swiss burgher takes heaven knows how many hours to go up from Berne to Geneva, and his trains are very few; this is an extreme on the other side; but compare the life the Swiss burgher finds or leaves at Berne or Geneva with the life of the middle class in your English towns. Or else you think to cover everything by saying: "We are free! we are free! Our newspapers can say what they like!" Freedom, like Industry, is a very good horse to ride;—but to ride somewhere. You seem to think that you have only got to get on the back of your horse Freedom, or your horse Industry, and to ride away as hard as you can, to be sure of coming to the right destination. If your newspapers can say what they like, you think you are sure of being well advised. That comes of your inaptitude for ideas, and aptitude for clap-trap; you can never see the two sides of a question; never perceive that every human state of things, even a good one, has its inconveniences. We can see the conveniences of your state well enough; and the inconveniences of ours, of newspapers not free, and prefects over-busy; and there are plenty of us who proclaim them. You eagerly repeat after us all we say that redounds to your honour and glory; but you never follow our example yourselves. You are full of acuteness to perceive the ill influence of our prefects on us; but if any one says to you, in your turn: "The

English system of a great landed aristocracy[1] keeps your lower class a lower class for ever, and materialises and vulgarises your whole middle class,"—you stare vacantly at the speaker, you cannot even take in his ideas; you can only blurt forth, in reply, some clap-trap or other about a "system of such tried and tested efficiency as no other country was ever happy enough to possess since the world was a world."'

I have observed in my travels, that most young gentlemen of our highest class go through Europe, from Calais to Constantinople, with one sentence on their lips, and one idea in their minds, which suffices, apparently, to explain all that they see to them: *Foreigners don't wash.* No doubt, thought I to myself, my friends have fallen in with some distinguished young Britons of this sort, and had their feelings wounded by them; hence their rancour against our aristocracy. And as to our middle class, foreigners have no notion how much this class, with us, contains; how many shades and gradations in it there are, and how little what is said of one part of it will apply to another. Something of this sort I could not help urging aloud. 'You

[1] What a contrast between this Jacobinism and the noble sentiments of Barrow: 'Men will never be heartily loyal and submissive to authority till they become really good; nor will they ever be very good, till they see their leaders such.' I remember once quoting this passage to Arminius at the time when we were all full of the Mordaunt trial. 'Yes,' remarked Arminius, in his thoughtful manner, 'that is what makes your Lord Coles so inexpressibly precious!' But was this an answer? I say, not.—Ed.

do not know,' I said, 'that there is broken off, as one may say, from the top of our middle class, a large fragment, which receive the best education the country can give, the same education as our aristocracy; which is perfectly intelligent and which enjoys life perfectly. These men do the main part of our intellectual work, write all our best newspapers; and cleverer people, I assure you, are nowhere to be found.'

'Clever enough,' was the answer, 'but they show not much intelligence, in the true sense of the word,—not much intelligence of the way the world is going. Whether it is that they must try to hit your current public opinion, which is not intelligent; whether it is that, having been, as you say, brought up with your aristocracy, they have been too much influenced by it, have taken, half insensibly, an aristocracy's material standard, and do not believe in ideas; certain it is that their intelligence has no ardour, no plan, leads them nowhere; it is ineffectual. Your intellect is at this moment, to an almost unexampled degree, without influence on the intellect of Europe.'

While this was being said, I noticed an Italian,[1] who was one of our party, fumbling with his pocket-book, from whence he presently produced a number of gray newspaper slips, which I could see were English. 'Now just listen to me for a moment,' he cried, 'and I

[1] Little Pompeo Pococurante. Almost all the rest is Arminius.

will show you what makes us say, on the Continent, that you English have no sense for logic, for ideas, and that your praise and blame, having no substantial foundation, are worth very little. You remember the famous French pamphlet before our war began in 1859: *Napoleon the Third and Italy*. The pamphlet appealed, in the French way, to reason and first principles; the upshot of it was this: "The treaties which bind governments would be invariable only if the world was immovable. A power which should intrench itself behind treaties in order to resist modifications demanded by general feeling would have doubtless on her side an acquired right, but she would have against her moral right and universal conscience." You English, on the other hand, took your stand on things as they were: "If treaties are made," said your *Times*, "they must be respected. Tear one, and all are waste paper." Very well; this is a policy, at any rate, an aristocratical policy; much may be said for it. The *Times* was full of contempt for the French pamphlet, an essay, as it called it, "conveying the dreams of an agitator expressed in the language of an academician." It said: "No one accustomed to the pithy comments with which liberty notices passing history, can read such a production without complacency that he does not live in the country which produces it. To see the heavy apparatus of an essay brought out to solve a question on which men have corresponded and talked and speculated in the funds, and acted in the most practical manner possible for a month past, is as strange as if we beheld some spectral review," and so on. Still very well ; there is the strong practical man despising theories and reveries. "The sentiment of race is just now threatening to be exceedingly troublesome. It is to a considerable extent in our days a literary revival." That is all to the same effect. Then came a hitch in our affairs, and fortune seemed as if she was going to give, as she often does give, the anti-theorists a triumph. "The Italian plot," cried the *Times*, "has failed. The Emperor and his familiars knew not the moral strength which is still left in the enlightened communities of Europe. To the unanimous and indignant reprobation of English opinion is due the failure of the imperial plots. While silence and fear reign everywhere abroad, the eyes and ears of the Continent are turned continually to these Islands. English opinion has been erected into a kind of Areopagus." Our business went forward again, and your English opinion grew very stern indeed. "Sardinia," said the *Times*, "is told very plainly that she has deserted the course by which alone she could hope either to be happy or great, and abandoned herself to the guidance of fatal delusions, which are luring her on to destruction. By cultivating the arts of peace she would have been solving, in the only possible way, the difficult problem of Italian independence. She has been taught by France to look instead to the acquisition of fresh territory by war and conquest. She has now been told with perfect truth by the warning voice of the British Parliament that she has not a moment to lose in retracing her steps, if indeed her penitence be not too late." Well, to make a long story short, we did not retrace our steps; we went on, as you know; we succeeded; and now let us make a jump from the spring to the autumn. Here is your unanimous English opinion, here is your Areopagus, here is your *Times*, in October: "It is very irregular (Sardinia's course), it is contrary to all diplomatic forms. Francis the Second can show a thousand texts of international law against it. Yes; but there are extremities beyond all law, and there are laws which existed before even society was formed. There are laws which are implanted in our nature, and which form part of the human mind," and so on. Why, here you have entirely boxed the compass and come round from the aristocratical programme to the programme of the French pamphlet, "the dreams of an agitator in the language of an academician"! And you approved not only our present but our past, and kindly took off your ban of reprobation issued in February. "How great a change has been effected by the wisely courageous policy of Sardinia! The firmness and boldness which have raised Italy from degradation form the enduring character of a ten years' policy. King Victor Emmanuel and his sagacious counsellor have achieved success by remembering that fortune favours the bold." There you may see why the mind of France influences the Continent so much and the mind of England so little. France has intelligence enough to perceive the ideas that are moving, or are likely to move, the world ; she believes in them, sticks to them, and shapes her course to suit them. You neither perceive them nor believe in them, but you play with them like counters, taking them up and laying them down at random, and following really some turn of your imagination, some gust of liking or disliking. When I heard some of your countrymen complaining of Italy and her ingratitude for English sympathy, I made, to explain it, the collection of those extracts and of a good many more. They are all at your service ; I have some here from the *Saturday Review*, which you will find exactly follow suit with those from the *Times*.' 'No, thank you,' I answered. 'The *Times* is enough. My relations with the *Saturday Review* are rather tight-stretched, as you say here, already ; make me a party to none of your quarrels with them.'

After this my original tormentor[1] once more took up his parable. 'You see now what I meant,' he said, 'by saying that you did better in the old time, in the day of aristocracies. An

[1] Arminius, of course.

aristocracy has no ideas, but it has a policy,—to resist change. In this policy it believes, it sticks to it; when it is beaten in it, it holds its tongue. This is respectable, at any rate. But your great middle class, as you call it, your present governing power, having no policy, except that of doing a roaring trade, does not know what to be at in great affairs,—blows hot and cold by turns, makes itself ridiculous, in short. It was a good aristocratical policy to have helped Austria in the Italian war; it was a good aristocratical policy to have helped the South in the American war. The days of aristocratical policy are over for you; with your new middle-class public opinion you cut, in Italy, the figure our friend here has just shown you; in America you scold right and left, you get up a monster-memorial to deprecate the further effusion of blood; you lament over the abridgment of civil liberty by people engaged in a struggle for life and death, and meaning to win: and when they turn a deaf ear to you and win, you say, "Oh, now let us be one great united Anglo-Saxon family and astonish the world"! This is just of a piece with your threatening Germany with the Emperor of the French. Do you not see that all these blunders dispose the Americans, who are very shrewd, and who have been succeeding as steadily as you have been failing, to answer: "We have got the lead, no thanks to you, and we mean to astonish the world without you"? Unless you change, unless your middle class grows more intelligent, you will tell upon the world less and less, and end by being a second Holland. We do not hold you cheap for saying you will wash your hands of all concerns but your own, that you do not care a rush for influence in Europe; though this sentence of your Lord Bolingbroke is true: "The opinion of mankind, which is fame after death, is superior strength and power in life." We hold you cheap because you show so few signs, except in the one department of industry, of understanding your time and its tendencies, and of exhibiting a modern life which shall be a signal success. And the reaction is the stronger, because, after 1815, we believed in you as nowadays we are coming to believe in America. You had won the last game, and we thought you had your hand full of trumps, and were going to win the next. Now the game has begun to be played, and we have an inkling of what your cards are; we shrewdly suspect you have scarcely any trumps at all.'

I am no arguer, as is well known, 'and every puny whipster gets my sword.'[1] So, instead of making bad worse by a lame answer, I held my tongue, consoling myself with the thought that these foreigners get from us, at any rate, plenty of Rolands for any stray Oliver they may have

[1] And this is why it was peculiarly unlucky for me to be thrown so much with Arminius, who loved arguing.—ED.

the luck to give us. I have since meditated a good deal on what was then said, but I cannot profess to be yet quite clear about it. However, all due deductions made for envy, exaggeration, and injustice, enough stuck by me of these remarks on our logic, criticism, and love of intelligence, to determine me to go on trying (taking care, of course, to steer clear of indecency) to keep my mind fixed on these, instead of singing hosannahs to our actual state of development and civilisation. The old recipe, to think a little more and bustle a little less, seemed to me still the best recipe to follow. So I take comfort when I find the *Guardian* reproaching me with having no influence ; for I know what influence means,—a party, practical proposals, action ; and I say to myself : 'Even suppose I could get some followers, and assemble them, brimming with affectionate enthusiasm, in a committee-room at some inn ; what on earth should I say to them ? what resolutions could I propose ? I could only propose the old Socratic commonplace, *Know thyself ;* and how black they would all look at that !' No ; to inquire, perhaps too curiously, what that present state of English development and civilisation is, which according to Mr. Lowe is so perfect that to give votes to the working class is stark madness ; and, on the other hand, to be less sanguine about the divine and saving effect of a vote on its possessor than my friends in the committee-room at the 'Spotted Dog,'—that is my inevitable portion. To bring things under the light of one's intelligence, to see how they look there, to accustom oneself simply to regard the Marylebone Vestry, or the Educational Home, or the Irish Church Establishment, or our railway management, or our Divorce Court, or our gin-palaces open on Sunday and the Crystal Palace shut, as absurdities,—that is, I am sure, invaluable exercise for us just at present. Let all persist in it who can, and steadily set their desires on introducing, with time, a little more soul and spirit into the too, too solid flesh of English society.

I have a friend who is very sanguine, in spite of the dismal croakings of these foreigners, about the turn things are even now taking amongst us. 'Mean and ignoble as our middle class looks,' he says, 'it has this capital virtue, it has seriousness. With frivolity, cultured or uncultured, you can do nothing; but with seriousness there is always hope. Then, too, the present bent of the world towards amusing itself, so perilous to the highest class, is curative and good for our middle class. A piano in a Quaker's drawing-room is a step for him to more humane life; nay, perhaps, even the penny gaff of the poor East Londoner is a step for him to more humane life; it is,—what example shall we choose? it is *Strathmore*, let us say,—it is the one-pound-eleven-and-sixpenny gaff of the young gentlemen of the clubs and the young ladies of Belgravia, that is for them but a step in the primrose path to the everlasting bonfire. Besides, say what you like of the idealessness of aristocracies, the vulgarity of our middle class, the immaturity of our lower, and the poor chance which a happy type of modern life has between them, consider this: Of all that makes life liberal and humane,—of light, of ideas, of culture,—every man in every class of society who has a dash of genius in him is the born friend. By his bringing up, by his habits, by his interest, he may be their enemy; by the primitive, unalterable complexion of his nature, he is their friend. Therefore, the movement of the modern spirit will be more and more felt among us, it will spread, it will prevail. Nay,' this enthusiast often continues, getting excited as he goes on, 'the *Times* itself, which so stirs some people's indignation,—what is the *Times* but a gigantic Sancho Panza, to borrow a phrase of your friend Heine;—a gigantic Sancho Panza, following by an attraction he cannot resist that poor, mad, scorned, suffering, sublime enthusiast, the modern spirit; following it, indeed, with constant grumbling, expostulation, and opposition, with airs of protection, of compassionate superiority, with an incessant byplay of nods, shrugs, and winks addressed to the spectators; following it, in short, with all the incurable recalcitrancy of a lower nature, but still following it?' When my friend talks thus, I always shake my head, and say that this sounds very like the transcendentalism which has already brought me into so many scrapes.

I have another friend again (and I am grown so cowed by all the rebuke my original speculations have drawn upon me that I find myself more and more filling the part of a mere listener), who calls himself Anglo-Saxon rather than English,[1] and this is what he says: 'We are a small country,' he says, 'and our middle class has, as you say, not much gift for anything but making money. Our freedom and wealth have given us a great start, our capital will give us for a long time an advantage; but as other countries grow better governed and richer, we must necessarily sink to the position to which our size, and our want of any eminent gift for telling upon the world spiritually, doom us. But look at America; it is the same race; whether we are first or they, Anglo-Saxonism triumphs. You used to say that they had all the Philistinism of the English middle class from which they spring, and a great many faults of their own besides. But you noticed too, that, blindly as they seemed following in general the star of their god Buncombe, they showed, at the same time, a feeling for ideas, a vivacity and play of mind, which our middle

[1] *Not* the talented author of *Greater Britain*, though the reader might be inclined to suppose so.—Ed.

class has not, and which comes to the Americans, probably, from their democratic life, with its ardent hope, its forward stride, its gaze fixed on the future. Well, since these great events have lately come to purge and form them, how is this intelligence of theirs developing itself? Now they are manifesting a quick sense to see how the world is really going, and a sure faith, indispensable to all nations that are to be great, that greatness is only to be reached by going that way and no other? And then, if you talk of culture, look at the culture their middle, and even their working class is getting, as compared with the culture ours are getting. The trash which circulates by the hundred thousand among our middle class has no readers in America; our rubbish is for home consumption; all our best books, books which are read here only by the small educated class, are in America the books of the great reading public. So over there they will advance spiritually as well as materially; and if our race at last flowers to modern life there, and not here, does it so much matter?' So says my friend, who is, as I premised, a devotee of Anglo-Saxonism; I, who share his pious frenzy but imperfectly, do not feel quite satisfied with these plans of vicarious greatness, and have a longing for this old and great country of ours to be always great in herself, not only in her progeny. So I keep looking at her, and thinking of her; and as often as I consider how history is a series of waves, coming gradually to a head and then breaking, and that, as the successive waves come up, one nation is seen at the top of this wave, and then another of the next, I ask myself, counting all the waves which have come up with England at the top of them: When the great wave which is now mounting has come up, will she be at the top of it? *Illa nihil, nec me quaerentem vana moratur!*—

Yes, we arraign her; but she,
The weary Titan, with deaf
Ears, and labour-dimm'd eyes,
Regarding neither to right
Nor left, goes passively by,
Staggering on to her goal;
Bearing, on shoulders immense,
Atlantéan, the load,
Wellnigh not to be borne,
Of the too vast orb of her fate.

(A Frenchman signing himself 'Horace,'—not one of our own set, but a person full of intellect, —wrote to the Editor of the *Pall Mall Gazette* a sort of electioneering letter from Paris in answer to the foregoing essay, saying what blessings our liberty and publicity were, and how miserable the French middle class was without them. I cannot do better than conclude with the answer I made to him, from which it will appear, I hope, how courteous was always my moderation when I was left to myself, and had not Arminius at my elbow to make me say what he chose. I should premise that 'My Countrymen' had been received with such a storm of obloquy, that for several months after its appearance I was in hiding;—not, indeed, leaving Grub Street, but changing my lodgings there repeatedly.)—Ed.

A COURTEOUS EXPLANATION

SIR, GRUB STREET, *March* 19, 1866.

ALTHOUGH I certainly am rather pained to find myself, after my long and arduous labours for the deliverance from Philistinism of this nation in general, and the civilisation and embellishment of our great middle class in particular, an object of aversion and mistrust to my countrymen, when I expected nothing from them but gratitude and love, still I have learnt to try and wrap myself on these occasions in my own virtue, knowing very well that the benefactors of mankind are seldom popular, and that your public favourite is generally some Barabbas. Meanwhile, for posterity's sake, I keep out of harm's way as much as I can; but as I sit shivering in my garret, listening nervously to the voices of indignant Philistines asking the way to Grub Street, a friend brings me the *Pall Mall Gazette* with 'Horace's' two letters. Perhaps it would be my best way to keep perfectly still, and not to give any sign of life to my enemies; but such is my inveterate weakness (dear enough it has cost me, this weakness !) for the amiable nation to which 'Horace' belongs, that I cannot find it in my heart to leave his letters without a word of acknowledgment. I write with a bit of coal on the lining of my hat, and in much perturbation of mind besides ; so 'Horace' will kindly excuse faults in my style, which indeed, as he has observed, even when I am at my best, is far from correct. But what is one to do ? So few people know what it is to be born artless.

It is very kind of 'Horace,' and just like his generous nation, to come forward when he sees I am in trouble, to confirm what he thinks I said ; only I did not say it, but the foreigners. 'Horace' says that with us mediocrity does make itself heard more loudly and more frequently than the thoughtful part of the nation, through the press and even in Parliament ; he says that he is inclined to think the middle classes in Germany and Switzerland enjoy life more than the same classes in England ; he says he is quite of opinion that the conduct of England in the affair of the Duchies lowered her considerably in the eyes of Europe, nor did she gain honour by the Crimean war, or by her attitude in Italian affairs. He adds, indeed, that it is probable some fifty years hence certain episodes of the Indian mutiny, and the heroism and charity displayed during the cotton famine, will be accepted as a set-off for many shortcomings ; and I am sure I devoutly hope they may ; but my foreign friends were only talking of the present.

It was the life of the middle class in Switzerland and Germany that my foreign friends said was more enjoyable than the life of the corresponding class in England, and 'Horace' declares my foreign friends were right. But he goes on to draw a frightful picture of the middle class in his own country, France. This is what I so admire in these continental writers, and it is just what my foreign friends claimed for them : 'We foreigners can see our own deficiencies well enough, and are not backward in proclaiming them ; you English can see and say nothing but what redounds to your own honour and glory.' It makes me blush to think how I winced under what the foreigners said of England, how I longed to be able to answer it, how I rejoiced at hearing from the English press that there was nothing at all in it, when I see the noble frankness with which these foreigners judge themselves. How 'Horace' does give it to his poor countrymen when he thinks they deserve it ! So did Monsieur de Tocqueville, so does Monsieur Renan. I lay up the example for my own edification, and I commend it to the editor of the *Morning Star* for his.

I have seen very little of the French middle class which 'Horace' describes, and I dare say what he says of them is all true. But what makes me look at France and the French with such inexhaustible curiosity and indulgence is this,—their faults are not ours, so we are not likely to catch them ; their merits are not ours, so we are not likely to become idle and self-sufficient from studying them. It is not that I so envy 'Horace' his Paris as it is ;—I no longer dance, nor look well when dressed up as the angel Gabriel, so what should I now do in Paris ?—but I find such interest and instruction in considering a city so near London, and yet so unlike it ! It is not that I so envy 'Horace' his café-haunting, dominoes-playing *bourgeois ;* but when I go through Saint Pancras, I like to compare our vestry-haunting, resolution-passing *bourgeois* with the Frenchman, and to say to myself : 'This, then, is what comes of not frequenting cafés nor playing dominoes ! My countrymen here have got no cafés, and have never learnt dominoes, and see the mischief Satan has found for their idle hands to do !' Still, I do not wish them to be the café-haunting, dominoes-playing Frenchmen, but rather some third thing, neither the Frenchmen nor their present selves.

And this brings me to the one little point of difference (for there is just one) between 'Horace' and me. Everything, as he himself says, depends on a man's point of view. Now, his point of view is French, mine English. He and his friends have, he says, one absorbing desire,—to diffuse in France the knowledge and love of true political liberty. For this purpose they are obliged to point to other countries, and England is, says 'Horace,' their 'great stand-by.' Now, those who speak evil of the English constituencies, of our great middle class, etc. etc., discredit, 'Horace' says, English parliamentary government and the power of the press, and tend to damage the great stalking-horse behind which he and his friends are moving to the attack of the French Emperor, and so spoil their game for them.

'Horace' and his friends are evidently Orleanists, and I have always observed that the Orleanists are rather sly. They can put their tongue in their cheek as well as anybody at the expense of my dear country, but she is to be an angel of light as long as it serves their turn. So the *Morning Star* and I are to go on crying, 'We are free! we are free! Our newspapers can say what they like,' whether this cry does us good or no, because true political liberty is the one thing needful for 'Horace' and the French. The *Morning Star*, I must say, does its duty nobly, and 'Horace' ought to be very grateful to it; but because I, thinking only of England, venture to go on a little farther, and to inquire what we do with ourselves when we are free to do just what we like, I give umbrage to 'Horace'; he says I destroy his stalking-horse, and he accuses me of railing at parliamentary government and the power of the press. In short, he and his friends have lost their tails, and want to get them back again ; and unless I talk of nothing but tails, and keep always saying that whoever has a tail is perfect, and whoever has not a tail is not worth twopence, 'Horace' is vexed with me.

To prevent all such misunderstanding for the future, let me say, in the fullest, frankest, most unreserved manner, that I admit the French have lost their tails, and that I pity them for it. I rejoice that the English have kept theirs. I think our 'true political liberty' a beautiful, bushy object, and whoever says I do not think so slanders me. But I do not see the slightest danger of our losing it. Well, then comes the question, whether, to oblige 'Horace' and his friends, I am to talk of nothing but this beautiful tail of ours, and our good fortune in having it. I should not mind doing this if our human economy took in nothing but tails, if we were all tail ; but our economy takes in other things as well,—hearts, for instance, and heads. In hearts we are (except when we find ourselves in India or Jamaica) very well off ; but in heads there is always room for improvement. Now, I think it was after witnessing a great constitutional stand by the Saint Pancras Board of Guardians, —no, it was after reading the second or third of the *Daily Telegraph's* funeral orations on Lord Palmerston,—that it struck me there was a danger of our trading too extensively upon our tails, and, in fact, running to tail altogether. I determined to try and preach up the improvement and decoration of our heads. Our highest class, besides having of course true political liberty,—that regulation tail which every Briton of us is blessed with,—is altogether so beautiful and splendid [1] that for my part I hardly presume to inquire what it has or has not in the way of heads. So I turn to my own class, the middle class, which, not being so beautiful and splendid, does not dazzle my eyes so much. And for this class I want to work out a deliverance from the horrid dilemma in which 'Horace' and others try to fix us ;—liberty and Philistinism, or else culture and slavery.

After this candid explanation on our one point of difference (for the rest of his letters I heartily thank him), I trust that 'Horace' will not in future think it his duty, whenever he finds me preaching to my countrymen that with all our political liberty we are still, in many respects, unprofitable servants,—I trust, I say, that whenever he sees this, he will not now think it his duty to administer to me a sharp pinch and exclaim : 'False one, what are you about? what have you done with your tail? begin brandishing it in our tyrant's face again directly!' Let him and the French rather themselves get back their lost tails from their tyrant, who is generally supposed, too, to have

[1] And above all, as Mr. Carlyle says, *polite*.—Ed.

had, when he talked of 'crowning the edifice,' this appendage in view.

I do hope, Sir, that the sentiments expressed in this letter may be the means of procuring for your excellent newspaper that free circulation in the French capital which is at present, I am told, denied you; and as my bit of coal is worn to a stump, I sign myself, your humble servant,

MATTHEW ARNOLD.

To the EDITOR *of the* PALL MALL GAZETTE.

(In May of this year (1866) Arminius arrived in London; an event which I sometimes fancy future ages will parallel with the arrival of Augustine at Canterbury. In July, six weeks later, began what, in talking to Arminius, I loved to call, half-playfully, half-seriously, 'the preaching of *Geist*.' In November 1870, four short years afterwards, he lay buried under the Bougival poplar-tree! Shadows, indeed, as Mr. Sala says, we are, and shadows we pursue.

Farewell, Arminius!—Thou good soul, thou great intellect, farewell!)—ED.

END OF VOL. VI

Printed by R. & R. CLARK, LIMITED, *Edinburgh*.